Capricorn

DECEMBER 22–JANUARY 20

QUANTITY SALES

Most Dell books are available at special quantity discounts when purchased in bulk by corporations, organizations, or groups. Special imprints, messages and excerpts can be produced to meet your needs. For more information, write to: Dell Publishing, 666 Fifth Avenue, New York, NY 10103. Attention: Director, Diversified Sales.

Please specify how you intend to use the books (e.g., promotion, resale, etc.).

INDIVIDUAL SALES

Are there any Dell books you want but cannot find in your local stores? If so, you can order them directly from us. You can get any Dell book currently in print. For a complete up-to-date listing of our books and information on how to order, write to: Dell Readers Service, Box DR, 666 Fifth Avenue, New York, NY 10103.

Dell Horoscope

PRESENTS

1992

DAY-BY-DAY

Capricorn

DECEMBER 22–JANUARY 20

A DELL BOOK

Published by
Dell Publishing
a division of
Bantam Doubleday Dell Publishing Group, Inc.
666 Fifth Avenue
New York, New York 10103

How to Find Your Moon's Sign and Degree—charts by Grant Lewi from *Astrology for the Millions*.

ISBN: 0-440-20974-9

Printed in the United States of America

Published simultaneously in Canada

August 1991

10 9 8 7 6 5 4 3 2 1

OPM

Editor's Note

For the third year in a row, the editors of *Dell Horoscope Magazine* present a series of twelve astrological books—one for each sign of the zodiac. With the resources of the world's most popular astrology magazine at our disposal, we bring you a capsule of the history of astrology; your personal and professional astrological indicators; sign descriptions; financial, health and career advice; hobbies and pastimes inherent in your personal sign; advice for parents; relationship guidance; unique stellar combinations; how to determine where each planet was at the time of your birth and its astrological meaning; and fifteen months of daily predictions from three of *Horoscope*'s most experienced and skilled forecasters—all of which can help you to achieve personal fulfillment and greater self-understanding, assist you in decision-making for your important life choices, and aid you in your quest to find greater peace of mind in your place on this planet and within the boundaries you share with your closest associations.

I'd like to extend a special thanks to Edward Kajkowski and Jack Pettey for their assistance in this project; to Julia

Lupton Skalka for the many valuable and insightful articles she wrote exclusively for this series; to Daniel Heydon for his pop-culture piece; and to Lloyd Cope, Doris Kaye, and Evy Tishelman for their top-notch daily forecasts.

RONNIE GRISHMAN
Editor

Contents

Capricorn

DECEMBER 22–JANUARY 20

Astrology Through the Centuries

No one knows exactly when the notion of divining by the stars caught hold of the human mind. In every part of the world, in every culture and clime, the Sun, Moon, planets, and stars have played some part in the mythological scheme of human society. It is inevitable that this should be so, for what is more breathtaking than the sunrise? What is more awesome than the countless beads of starlight? It is no wonder that primitive people revered them.

Although societies have generally delegated some significance to astrology, not all of them have ascribed an astrological meaning to the planets and the signs of the zodiac. The earliest records we have of a belief in astrology were unearthed in Mesopotamia. The stellar art began developing into its "modern" form around 4000 B.C., when the first temples were built along the banks of the Euphrates River in honor of the Sumerian star gods. These ingenious people were adept in many branches of divinatory practices, including a technique of interpreting the patterns of oil poured into a bowl of water, observing the flight of birds, and studying the entrails of sacrificed animals. They were the first to devise a primitive astroscopy that involved the observation of the Sun, Moon, and planets, without, however, taking note of their relative positions in the zodiac.

The Sumerians were later to develop the twelve-house system of horoscopy in combination with the twelve signs of the zodiac, which were then identified with the constellations of the ecliptic. Dating from about 2870 B.C., during the reign of Sargon of Agade, documents have been found involving predictions based upon the positions of the Sun, Moon, and the five known planets, also including such phenomena as comets and meteors. At this time astrology had already begun to acquire a distinctively modern flavor.

In 3000 B.C. the house system was already described in the same fashion as that used in contemporary astrology: first house—self-assertiveness; second—poverty/riches, finances; third—brothers, sisters, communications; fourth—parents, home life; fifth—children, creativity; sixth—illness/health, work; seventh—wife/husband, marriage; eighth—death, sex; ninth—religion, education; tenth—dignities, career; eleventh—friendship, hopes; and twelfth—enmity, restrictions, subconsciousness.

With the spread of Sumerian culture, astrology became of central importance to early civilized humankind. From the Mesopotamian mythogenetic zone, astrology, the religion and science of the priestly cult, spread into Egypt, Persia, and India. From there it eventually crossed into Europe and to the East, encountering the primitive civilizations of China and Japan, and finally into Central and South America. Astrology had so great an influence on the beginning of technological humankind that the finest, most beautiful, and long-lived architectural works of the ancient world were none other than temples to the planetary deities, to the wanderers, places of worship that were also used as observatories. The priests ruled their people with absolute authority and were felt to be in touch with the very source of nature itself (in their eyes) and able to predict exactly what would befall their people.

There was no direct communication between the Sumerians and the builders of Stonehenge in England, but that marvelous work of primitive architecture was, in fact, a megalithic computer, begun sometime around 2500 B.C. The gigantic stones of this pre-Druidic temple are situated so that the rising and setting of the solstitial Sun and Moon, plus solar and lunar eclipses throughout the year, could be seen between two of the strategically placed colossal standing stones.

Astrology entered India at least as early as 3000 B.C., and even now the stellar science plays an all-important role in the lives of most Hindus. The main difference between Oriental and Occidental horoscopy today is that, in the East, an actual sidereal zodiac is the rule, observing the positions of the planets in relation to the constellations. In the West, however, the position of the Sun on the first day of spring is taken to be the first degree of Aries; because of the precession of the equinoxes, the Western "Aries" is now almost into the constellation Aquarius, marking the beginning of a new eon or "great year."

Soon after astrology was introduced in India from Sumerian sources, it was carried by way of trade routes into China, where it was received, as usual, with reverence. The Chinese themselves elaborated to some extent on the Indian form of astrology, combining it with the indigenous Taoist religion and the philosophy of the *I Ching*. Correlating the five elements, the cardinal points and the zenith, the five known planets, colors of the spectrum, emotional dispositions, and so forth, the Chinese evolved a highly complex system of divination that resembles the Hebrew Kabbalah in many ways. In association with native religion, astrology was successful as an aid in the ruling of the Chinese Empire for thousands of years.

The Chinese signs of the zodiac were not placed on the ecliptic, as are the signs of Indian and Western astrology, but on the equator. Each of the twelve signs ruled a two-hour period of the day, one of the months of the year, and one entire year during a twelve-year cycle. Therefore, it can be said that one was born in the Year of the Rat or the Year of the Monkey, and these animals would convey a particular astrological significance. The Chinese names for the signs of the zodiac are as follows: Dog, Boar, Rat, Ox, Tiger, Hare, Dragon, Snake, Horse, Goat, Monkey, and Cock.

In the seventh century before the Christian era, King Ashurbanipal of Assyria built a great library in the city of Nineveh and furnished it with thousands of astrological cuneiform tablets, some dating from around 4000 B.C. In the year 612 B.C. Nineveh was conquered by the Chaldeans and the library was destroyed. The assailants, however, were soon to become masters of stellar divination themselves, and the name Chaldean was later synonymous in the West with an adept of the occult arts.

Astrology entered the Hellenic world at least as early as the Alexandrian wars, when hosts of Greek warriors fought their way to the banks of the Indus River and came under the influence of Egypt, Persia, and Babylonia on the one hand, and of the mystical, introspective philosophies of India and the Far East on the other. Astrological works said to have been written by the pharaoh Nechepso and the priest Petosiris were translated into Greek around 150 B.C. and became the cornerstone of pre-Christian European astrology.

As the Roman Republic was gradually infiltrated by Asian religious and philosophical thought, its citizens turned to astrology as the central theme of this new consciousness. The star-minded prophets of Baal and Ishtar were evicted from Rome in 139 B.C. along with the Jews, but as the Eastern cults gained massive public support over the years, the Roman government could eventually do nothing but tolerate the existence of various astrological sects. During the time of the Roman general Pompey (106–48 B.C.), the senator Nigidius Figulus wrote a textbook on the science in Latin. More influential were the studies of Posidonius of Apamea, written at the end of the republic.

With the founding of the Roman Empire in 27 B.C. and the subsequent official adoption of Oriental cults, astrology was accepted by nearly everyone. The emperor Tiberius

turned from the worship of the elder gods in favor of the
new science, which everywhere manifested itself more as
a religion than as the pure mathesis (science) it is. It was
thought then, as it is sometimes believed today, that the
planets and signs (being representatives of theological and
exalted paganism that replaced the old, stale forms of
Roman religion) controlled events on earth. Astrology
gained such a hold on Rome that the nation's citizens did
nothing without consulting its oracles. According to one
report, the Romans would not even take a bath without the
assurance that it would be astrologically profitable.

The Alexandrian scholar Claudius Ptolemaeus, or Ptolemy, wrote the famous treatise on astrology entitled *Tetra-
biblos* during the second century A.D., probably drawing
on Egyptian and Babylonian sources. With the aid of such
eminent minds as this, astrology became ingrained in the
people's thinking to such an extent that virtually all philosophy and scientific thought in this period were dependent
on its precepts. *The Dream of Scipio* by Cicero, written
some two hundred years before Ptolemy's treatise, speaks
of the heavenly spheres in much the same way as the
medieval Kabbalists describe their system of *sephiroth,*
and it was this type of occultism that continued to inspire
the best minds in the West well past the fall of the Roman
Empire and served as a foundation for modern-day astrology.

When astrology was still quite new to Europe, many
Greek philosophers were doubtful of the accuracy of its
forecasts. Carneades, before the advent of the Roman
Empire, posed the question, "Are all the men that perish
together in a battle born at the same moment, because they
have the same fate?" Of course, there was also the argument concerning the destinies of twins. The Chaldeans
were able to answer all of the objections to their science,
noting the effect of the Sun on the seasons of the year, the
effect of the Moon on the ocean's tides, not to mention the
more complicated evidence revealed in natal horoscopy.
Nobody could refute this logic, and because their testi-

mony proved true year after year and their personality analysis quite exact, astrology conquered the West with little difficulty. The skeptics refused to accept it, rejecting it along with all other learning. The Stoics, who believed in the omnipotence of fate, accepted astrology wholeheartedly. By the end of the second century anyone who would dare contest the validity of sidereal divination would have been considered idiotic.

To the early Christians, though, excluding those wonderfully bizarre Gnostic sects, astrology was undeniably interwoven with the paganism they abhorred. Polemics against the science were launched, using the language of the Greek dialecticians who had argued against the art when it first entered the Hellenic sphere. The same arguments that had been proved false by the early stellar prophets were used, but in the frenzy of Christian conversion the astrologers were condemned along with the rest of European paganism. The library at Alexandria, containing many thousands of astrological textbooks, was burned to the ground; the ancient monuments were destroyed or turned into Christian churches. In the fourth century of the Christian era (the Piscean Age), Theodosius the Great outlawed all forms of paganism under penalty of death. A bloodbath, resembling the horrible autos-da-fé of the later Inquisition, ensued. Thousands of Roman citizens fled their native lands because of the terrible cruelty of their new "enlightened" rulers. Many went to India, where a cultural flowering occurred, signaling the beginning of the Indian golden age.

With the reign of Theodosius and the forbidding of the traditional European forms of religion as well as the Asian cults, the ghastly thousand-year journey of the Dark Ages began. It is at this point that the history of astrology in the West comes predominantly under the sphere of the Arabs. In Rome the papacy rejected astrology as a pagan (i.e., evil) practice. In Byzantium, however, it was recognized to some degree that astrology and Christianity were not incompatible, for many accepted Scriptures implied a be-

lief in stellar significance ("And God said, Let there be
lights in the firmament of the heaven to divide the day from
the night; and let them be for signs, and for seasons, and
for days, and years" [Genesis 1:14]. There are numerous
Kabbalistic/astrological references all through the Old and
New Testaments, primarily in the ultimate book, Revela-
tion.). St. Augustine had declared that astrology was a
fraud and that even if its predictions were accurate, they
were obviously made under the influence of evil spirits.

With the appearance of Islam and the sudden emer-
gence of the Arab empire in the seventh century A.D.,
astrology was saved from a state of ignominy. Damascus
became a center of occult learning. Al-Mansur established
a grand observatory in Baghdad. In the ninth century
Albumazar wrote *Introductorium in Astronomiam,* a textbook of astrological theory. By way of Spain, Arab scientific knowledge revived the faltering European educational
centers.

Throughout the Middle Ages in Europe there was a
raging controversy about whether astrology should be accepted as a science or as a "black art." By the thirteenth
century, following the example of St. Thomas Aquinas,
academicians generally accepted that the stars were the
cause of all that took place on earth. The University of
Bologna established a chair of astrology in the year 1125.
Dante found astrology to be a source of inspiration in the
writing of *The Divine Comedy* in the fourteenth century—
for example, when the poet hero visits the angels of the
planetary spheres.

By the fifteenth century even the papacy was using
astrology to make important decisions. Pope Sixtus IV was
himself an astrologer of repute, and Julius II recognized
the need for astrological counsel. Johann Müller drew up
horoscopes for the pope, established the first European
observatory in Nuremberg, and published a thirty-year
ephemeris on his own printing press. Copernicus (1473–
1543), renowned for his discovery that the Earth is not the
center of the solar system, was an astrologer. It is peculiar

that modern anathemas against astrology use his discovery as a tool for contradicting astrological theory, but the founder of modern astronomy himself proclaimed that stellar divination was not in the least affected by his then-controversial deductions.

Michel de Notredame (Nostradamus) was one of the foremost astrologers of his time and the author of a book called *Centuries,* a collection of prophecies that remains popular to this day. In 1556 he was hired to compute the horoscopes of the royal children of the French court. Queen Catherine de' Medici honored him all his life after she discovered that his interpretations concerning the fate of her children were correct.

The Danish astrologer Tycho Brahe, the Englishman Francis Bacon, and the Italian Tommaso Campanella all helped to keep astrology alive through the sixteenth and seventeenth centuries. The Elizabethan court astrologer John Dee (1527–1608) was also a professional alchemist and magician. It was he who believed he had conversed with angels, leading him to discover a system of "Enochian" keys, or calls, that could unlock the worlds of the five elements and the thirty aethyrs. After experimentation with these magical methods, he was forced to retract what he had declared concerning their sanctity, for the content of the visions they produced clearly ran counter to the Christian code of ethics.

It remained for Aleister Crowley in the twentieth century to take up the thread of Dee's magical (or psychological) research by invoking the thirty aethyrs in the desert of North Africa. Crowley left behind a record of spiritual achievement unparalleled in the rationalistic West, entitled *The Vision and the Voice*. Within these aethyrs, or psychic substrata, exist various combinations of astrological powers, though it is difficult to say whether they are objective astral phenomena or subjective dreamlike experiences.

In the seventeenth century Johannes Kepler and William Lilly were representative of their age's astrological thought. The former, a mathematician, had definite doubts about the accuracy of astrological delineation as he knew it, but expressed a belief that an authentic science of the stars could be developed if serious-minded men put it to the test. The latter, Lilly, was a prodigious writer and a leading horoscope maker in England. He predicted the Great Fire of London in 1666.

In more recent years, Alan Leo and Dane Rudhyar both have tried to bring their chosen profession into line with current scientific trends, giving it a new, more intellectual framework. During World War II Karl Ernst Krafft was employed by the Nazis to translate the teachings of Nostradamus, which, it was felt, could be used profitably as propaganda. On the British side, Louis de Wohl was convinced that the Germans were using astrology in their effort to win and that the British should use the same means. The government agreed, and de Wohl became the official astrological mouthpiece of the Allies.

While the West has been growing ever more divorced from its mystical beginnings, the East (namely, India and its neighboring countries) has retained its age-old belief in astrology and, in many instances, the primitive magic associated with it. In the non-Communist countries of the Far East, astrological practices have remained virtually unchanged. The Buddhist priests of Sri Lanka perform a ceremony with the intention of invoking planetary forces in the curing of disease, fever, and poverty; Chandra (the Moon), Buddha (Mercury), Shukra (Venus), Kuja (Mars), Guru (Jupiter), Shani (Saturn), Rahu (North Node), and Ketu (South Node) all represent spiritual powers which, when adverse, produce diseases and misfortune analogous to the Westerner's analysis of each planet's negative effects.

In present-day Europe and America astrology is once again gaining a place in the universities, and surprisingly enough, psychology is investigating its uses in therapy. Sigmund Freud, ever loath to lend any credence to astrology, stated shortly before his death that he did hold a masked interest in the occult. Carl Jung, the most influential psychologist since Freud, used horoscopes to aid him in diagnosing the causes of his patients' illnesses. His studies have done much to validate astrology's claim to be a science, not a parlor game for the superstitious.

The theories of sidereal effects have become more sophisticated with the passing of the centuries. Radiation, cosmobiological impulses, subatomic conscious forces (a euphemism for "gods") have all been put forth as explanations of astrological accuracy. Perhaps the most convincing argument presented by modern science is that of Carl Jung. He propounded a theory that divinatory arts such as astrology, the tarot, and the *I Ching* are examples of a universal principle that he called "acausal synchronicity." The significance of this hypothesis is that it states, in effect, that there are no influences whatsoever acting upon the daily life of humanity originating in the position of the planets, but rather that the planets portray a pattern of events synchronized to the life of the individual or group of individuals (such as a nation). This seems much more suitable than the theory of cosmic radiation, for no matter how much radiation exists in the earth's atmosphere, it cannot account for all the aspects of human life that astrology can accurately predict.

Acausal synchronicity does, to some extent, account for psychological analysis by the way of the natal chart, but many predictions would be impossible according to this theory. It may account for changes within the individual organism, but it is difficult to explain how planetary vibrations can cause events to happen to an individual, events that could be accurately predicted by ordinary horoscopy. To recognize the fact that every aspect of the universe acts in conformity with the remainder of the universe is only to extend the concept of ecology one step further. One can find significance in every aspect of the physical world. Astrology happens to be the most logical, mathematically determined divinatory science we have developed thus far. The fact is that the stars do not have a *causal* effect on the Earth, but a connection between the

planets and individuals that is rooted in astrological meaning does much to alleviate it from the age-old objections to
its validity.

As for the spiritualistic theory of cosmic effects, there
is no evidence to support it which cannot be explained by
more practical hypotheses. This does not mean that it is
necessarily false, but it lowers the probability of its being
true. The theory of acausal synchronicity presents a
cleaner, more efficient astrological theory and explains
how the planets can actually describe every detail of human experience without being the direct cause. They are
an abstraction of our daily activities. If the spiritualistic
theory were, in fact, true, then the *causal* arts of magic
(i.e., the omnipotence of the magician in controlling his
universe through controlling spiritual noumena) must be
granted. Here one begins to fall into the trough of uncer-
tain, difficult, and pretentious metaphysics—difficult to
prove and impossible to integrate with the truths of physical existence. It may be that astrology and magic are
examples of psychic causality. If so, everything we know
is *wrong!* Not only that, but natural laws are thrown topsy-
turvy, *psychological facts are disgraced as mere fables,*
and we become the victim of a rampaging solipsism. In the
years to come, we may see science turn its attention to
problems such as these, and the outcome may be very
surprising.

A History of Popular Culture
from the 70s to the 90s

The idea of a hit TV series based on the adventures of a coroner would have been ludicrous in 1950; but with Uranus's stay in Scorpio—the sign of death—from 1974–1981, *Quincy,* starring Jack Klugman, made a strong impact on the public's consciousness. While Uranus was in Scorpio, horror films came into their own. Anyone with a planet in Libra, the sign of gentleness and peace, would have been put off by the blood and gore that dominated film, theatre, fiction, and TV during that period. Such films as *The Shining, Friday the 13th, Carrie, Jaws, Coma,* and *Halloween* placed a premium on horror and violence. Even Count Dracula made a reappearance on the Broadway stage, to appease the appetite of audiences who wanted yet more blood. The public's fascination with death and the criminal consciousness was satisfied by Norman Mailer's *The Executioner's Song,* a true account of the life and death of murderer Gary Gilmore, while the search for excitement became an invitation to murder in the film *Looking for Mr. Goodbar.*

Since Scorpio is an occult sign, the use of psychic powers for the purposes of evil also became a dominant motif in the culture of the mid-seventies. Witness the popularity of the novels of Stephen King (such as *The Fire Starter, Cujo*) and the appearance of the devil in such films as *The Omen* and *The Devil Within Her*. Andy Warhol's 3-D film *Frankenstein* featured necrophilia, dismemberment, and disembowelment, along with entrails that seemed to ooze right off the screen. The title of William Golding's 1979 novel, *The Darkness Visible,* would serve as an apt title for the whole period when Uranus was in Scorpio.

Since Neptune was in Sagittarius—the sign of religion—during the same years that Uranus tenanted Scorpio, good and evil coexisted in the 1970s. Indeed, with Neptune at the first degree of Sagittarius in 1970, an ad in the *New York Times* announced the opening of *Jesus Christ Superstar*. This was soon followed by Jesus Freaks, Guru Maharaji, *Godspell,* and a genuine religious revival throughout the country. In the years of Neptune's stay in Sagittarius (1970–1984), the sale of religious books steadily escalated. For example, according to *Publishers Weekly,* in 1975, when the total sales of all publishers rose 7.9 percent over the previous year, general religious book sales soared an amazing 23.6 percent. Perhaps people ran to clutch their Bibles, since 1975 was the year of the film *The Exorcist*.

With Neptune in Sagittarius, people got into transcendental meditation; and *Jonathan Livingston Seagull* (1970), with its combination of Sagittarian optimism and Neptunian mysticism, became one of the best-selling titles of all time. Since Sagittarius is the sign of long journeys, it is not surprising that with Neptune—the planet of the mysterious and the unknown—in the sign of travel, science fiction also reached new heights of popularity. George Lucas, with his trilogy of films beginning with *Star Wars* and ending with *The Return of the Jedi,* created a new space (Sagittarius) mythology (Neptune). Religion and space travel become intertwined in Von Daniken's *Chariots of the Gods* (1970), a book that suggests that God might have been an ancient astronaut.

The eminent scientist Crick in 1981 suggested in his

Life Itself that the genetic code might have been tele-graphed to Earth via extraterrestial intelligence. Though mankind did not contact beings from out of space while Neptune and Uranus visited Sagittarius (1970–87) the pop-ularity of the film *E.T.* remains a testament to mankind's need for "close encounters of the third kind."

While parents may or may not have been enthralled with James Michener's book *Space* (1982), their children certainly could be found at the local video arcade, enrap-tured with the video-game craze begun in 1979 with *Space Invaders*. According to *Time,* in its January 18, 1982, cover story on the video craze, many a ten year old became addicted to games like *Asteroids* and *Defender*—and here we see the link between Neptune and addictive behavior. These kids were really flipped out (Neptune) on space (Sagittarius)!

A more unfortunate—indeed, tragic, manifestation of Neptune's obverse side as the planet of addiction in Sagit-tarius—the sign of religion—were the stories of kids being brainwashed by religious cults. The tragedy of Jonestown, with its mass suicide in 1981, reminded the world that Neptune can deceive as well as inspire. Neptune as the planet of deception in Sagittarius—the sign of publishing— also made its presence felt, with the fake Hitler diaries and Clifford Irving's fake biography of Howard Hughes.

In 1981, Uranus joined Neptune in Sagittarius and until 1984 both these planets exercised their influence in this sign. At this point we should note the differences between Uranus and Neptune as they affect the sign Sagittarius, and culture in general. Neptune's trip through a sign is often a journey from idealism to disillusionment, as can be seen from the transition from *Jesus Christ Superstar* to Jonestown. This process was only quickened with Uran-us's entrance into Sagittarius. Uranus, the planet of rebel-lion, in the sign of religion and middle-class morality, led to a series of plays satirizing Catholic education. *Mass Appeal, Sister Mary Ignatius Explains It All for You,* and *Catholic School Girls* were well-directed satires exposing weak spots in the armor of the conventional. Let us not forget "The Church Lady" from TV's *Saturday Night Live*—Dana Carvey's 1987 parody of the moral majority.

In this same period, though, we had the best-selling novels of a Catholic priest, Father Andrew Greeley. Books such as *The Cardinal Sins* and *Thy Brother's Wife* dealt with such taboo topics as illegitimacy and financial corruption in the Church. A priest who writes sex scenes and makes the best-seller list goes against our Barry Fitzgerald–Bing Crosby stereotyped image of a priest. Father Greeley is a true Uranian iconoclast!

Gay clergy and nuns (TV film *Shattered Vows*) and priests who break their vows (TV miniseries *The Thorn Birds*) became hot topics while Uranus was in Sagittarius. The real-life Cardinal Cody, of Chicago, was suspected of involvement with embezzled funds; the Vatican itself was rocked with financial scandal; and allegations that Pope John Paul may have been murdered were other issues of public concern then. In the final months of Uranus's transit through Sagittarius, the public learned of the marital troubles of Jim and Tammy Bakker; the shenanigans of "I have sinned" Jimmy Swaggert; and Oral Roberts's vision of God in which he supposedly was told he would be called home on March 31, 1987, unless believers came up with $4.5 million for his missionary work.

This is the 1990s, and we're now looking back at the 80s as a decade of greed and corruption. But let us not forget how the decade of the rich and famous began. With the Establishment at its lowest ebb ever in the 60s, there seemed to be no one to look up to—even Hemingway and his stoic masculine hero was in the doghouse then.

But Neptune's entrance into Capricorn in 1984 brought a rebirth of the hero. Rambo (*First Blood: Part II,* 1984) and Rocky (*Rocky IV,* 1984), with their musclebound masculinity, came into their own in this period as symbols of patriotism, but it was Ronald Reagan who actually took the bullets in the chest and rose from his assassination attempt to become a larger-than-life figure. I mean, how many colon operations can you have and still be able to ride a horse!

Capricorn is a conservative sign, and it goes without saying that Neptune as the ideal conservative is Ronald Reagan, whose second administration began with the entrance of Neptune in Capricorn in 1984. Never mind the fact that the Iran-Contra scandal cast doubts on his credibility, he still was a vibrant president whose example gave dignity to the fact that it was all right to be seventy, still working, and still enjoying life. Seeing Reagan's face on TV at regular intervals did more for the spirit of the elderly in the eighties than the combination of Metamucil and Medicare.

But Reagan wasn't the only hero to emerge in the 80s. Lee Iacocca, whose reputation began to soar in the late 70s with his successful rescue of Chrysler Corporation after its near bout with bankruptcy, published his autobiography, *Iacocca,* in 1984, the year Neptune entered Capricorn. His book established record sales in the publishing industry and solidified his reputation as the ideal (Neptune) corporate leader (Capricorn). For the first time since J. P. Morgan, America had a businessman as a genuine hero. Think of Neptune as "the ideal" and Capricorn as "businessman," and in Iacocca we have the example par excellence of this combination of astrological influences.

In contrast to Lee Iacocca, we have the example of Roger Smith, chairman of the board of General Motors, who became the object of a satirical attack in the film *Roger and Me* (1989) by Michael Moore. In this documentary, Moore keeps trying to meet with Roger, to force him to address the problems that have occurred in Flint, Michigan, in the aftermath of layoffs there. It's not my purpose here to take sides with the filmmaker or his subject matter, only to point out that a corporation and its leading executive, a theme that was exalted in 1984—when Neptune entered Capricorn—became the subject of ridicule five years later, as idealism moved toward disillusionment.

If we look at the *New York Times* Best Seller List the

day Neptune entered Capricorn, in January of 1984, the number-one book was *In Search of Excellence,* which the *New York Times*'s summarized as "lessons to be learned from well-run American corporations." Of course, the journey from idealism to disillusionment in this five-year period was helped along by the industrial accident at Bhopal, India, the Exxon oil spill, and corporate raiders, who were portrayed, as in the film *Wall Street* (1987), as executives who bought corporations for the purpose of gaining personal windfalls by selling off the conglomerate's holdings. A record for corporate takeovers was set in 1984, and perhaps 1990 set a record in books exposing the machinations that went along with those takeovers. From the 1984 *In Search of Excellence* to the 1990 *Barbarians at the Gate* (a book about the Nabisco takeover), the picture is summed up pretty accurately.

Capricorn is the sign of the city and also the sign of government. If we add these two words together we come up with the word "mayor." With Neptune as the planet of the ideal in the sign of the city in 1984, it is not surprising that *Mayor,* the autobiography of New York City's Mayor Ed Koch, reached number one on the *New York Times* Best Seller List a few short months after Neptune entered Capricorn. Fresh from his late seventies triumph as the head of city government at a time when New York was threatened with bankruptcy, Koch, like Iacocca, proved himself able to weather the crisis. Though this book in some ways is self-serving, Mayor Koch emerges as the typical New Yorker, and if not the ideal writer, at least the ideal New Yorker—certainly, no one ever questioned his dedication to the job. So charismatic was Koch that this book was soon made into an off-Broadway musical!

But there is a price to pay if you become a Neptune-in-Capricorn symbol of the ideal, for Koch failed in his efforts to win a fourth term as mayor of what Tom Wolfe, in his celebrated *Bonfire of the Vanities,* calls "the city of ambition." Though Koch himself emerged unscathed, the corruption that surrounded his third administration, and his relationship with blacks, worked against his bid for reelection. By 1990, however, Koch and his administration were old news, for the public was caught up in the soap-opera-like scandal of Marion Barry, mayor of Washington, D.C.

We know that crack (Neptune) entered the cities (Capricorn) in 1984 with Neptune's entrance into Capricorn, but we didn't know until 1990 that crack entered the mayor of D.C.'s pipe until the videotape of the FBI sting (or set-up) of Marion Barry was shown on national TV. Again, we have an example here of the Neptunian journey from the ideal to disillusionment—remember, Mayor Barry began his career as a promising civil rights leader.

If the year 1984 keeps coming up in this chapter, it's because that's the year Neptune entered Capricorn and significant themes were set in motion then that will continue until Neptune leaves Capricorn in 1998. Perhaps not since Thackeray's *Vanity Fair* has the Capricorn city been portrayed in its many aspects, as it was in Tom Wolfe's best seller *The Bonfire of the Vanities,* which was begun in serial form as a novel for *Rolling Stone* in 1984 and was released as a film in 1990.

At the tail end of 1983, Wolfe's book *The Right Stuff* was produced as a Hollywood film, dramatizing the accomplishments of not only astronauts but test pilot Chuck Yeager as well. Yeager, too, was a hero in the public's eye in 1984, for his autobiography, the story of the first man to fly faster than sound, joined Iacocca's and Koch's on the *New York Times* Best Seller List. Yeager's example became the inspiration for a short-lived TV series about a test pilot, *Call to Glory.*

Bruce Springsteen almost single-handedly reintroduced patriotism into America with his *Born in the U.S.A.* album, which was released in that pivotal year of 1984. The American dream gained new life with Springsteen's *Born in the U.S.A.* and led to the popularity of the slogan "Made in the U.S.A." And to think that Springsteen turned down $15 million to become a spokesman for Chrysler Corporation. But still, the release of this album was a publicist's dream come true, as this record came out just when Reagan was lowering taxes and the country was entering a new period of economic prosperity.

Of all the celebrated Neptune-in-Capricorn figures from 1984, one hasn't been mentioned yet. Bill Cosby, who was perfectly cast as the ideal (Neptune) father (Capricorn) in *The Cosby Show,* which premiered in the fall of 1984 and was the top show on TV for the next four years. It was inevitable that Cosby, too, was due for a fall, and his 1990 film *Ghost Dad* opened to very bad reviews. However, let us not forget that Cosby joined Iacocca, Yeager, Tom Wolfe, and Koch as a *New York Times* number-one best-selling author with *Fatherhood* (1986), which eclipsed the record that Iacocca had just set for the number of best-selling hardcovers to be sold in a single year.

Of all the Capricorn themes introduced in this period, the link between fatherhood and Capricorn seems to be quintessential in an understanding of Neptune's transit of Capricorn. Any beginning student of astrology can tell you that these keywords are commonly associated with Neptune: idealism, deception, compassion, ghost, communism, confusion, and drugs. Let us now combine these keywords with Capricorn as the father and see what we come up with.

Neptune, the planet of deception, in the sign of the father equals Germaine Greer's book *Daddy, We Hardly Knew Thee* (1989), in which she relates that after many years of searching, she learned that her father's last name was false, and that he lied about himself and his background. Neptune as the planet of communism in the sign of the father equals *Loyalties* (1989), the Carl Bernstein (coauthor of the Watergate book *All the President's Men*) book about his parents, who were communists. Neptune, the planet of compassion, in the sign of the father equals the 1989 study by McGill University psychologist Richard Koestner and Carol Franz of Harvard University, which concludes that compassion is a quality that is developed depending on the father's presence during child-rearing. (See *USA Today,* March 30, 1990.)

As reported by the *New York Times* (March 17, 1990), specialists in drug addiction say crack (Neptune) interferes with the parental instinct (Capricorn and Cancer). Neptune as thief in the sign of the father equals the film *Family Business* (1989) in which Dad is a crook and a con man who urges his son to get involved in a crooked scheme. Neptune as spy in the sign of the father equals the Walkers, a father and son spy team who were arrested in 1985 for selling government secrets to the U.S.S.R. Again, a similar motif shows up in the 1985 film *Target,* in which the father, a former CIA agent, with the help of his son rescues his kidnapped wife. Neptune as ghost in the sign of the father, of course, is Bill Cosby in the 1990 film *Ghost Dad.*

We learn more of fathers' relationships with their children in such books and films as *Indiana Jones and the Last Crusade* (1989), featuring Sean Connery and Harrison Ford as father and son. The country-music hit *My Father and Me* and the rock hit *The Living Years,* a top-selling single in 1989, also deal with the relationship between father and son.

In the best seller *Father, Son & Co.* (1990), by Thomas J. Watson, Jr., and Peter Petre, Capricorn becomes both the father and the corporation. In this autobiography, which tells of the father-son relationship between Thomas Watson, Sr., and Thomas Watson, Jr., who succeeded each other as head of IBM. *Brynner on Brynner,* a biography of Yul Brynner by his son, and *Khrushchev on Khrushchev* (1990) are two more books written in this period exploring father-son relationships. With Neptune as confusion in the sign of the father we get the 1989 hit *Dad,* with Jack Lemmon playing a dad on the verge of withdrawing from reality until his son reenters his life. Cosby is not our only example of the ideal dad coping with the trials of parenthood. Witness Steve Martin's humorous and touching portrait of the dad who tries his best but still comes up short in the film *Parenthood* (1989).

Though themes like the abovementioned will continue until Neptune leaves Capricorn in 1998, we should note a trend that is occurring in both art and life concerning the corporation, the father, and politics since Uranus's entrance into Capricorn in 1988. If we take our cue from when Uranus entered Sagittarius and the flurry of satires on religious subjects that occurred then, we can expect that dads, businessmen, mayors, and others will be satirized now that Uranus is in Capricorn.

Early examples of Uranus-in-Capricorn satires are TV's irreverent *The Simpsons* (1990), which presents dad as a bunglehead, a far cry from the poised Cliff Huxtable of the *Cosby Show*. Of course, we should also mention here the Bundys, and their somewhat crude patriarch, Al Bundy, from TV's *Married . . . with Children* (1990), another sitcom in which the typical American family becomes extremely untypical.

First Hubby (1990), by Ray Blount, Jr., is a funny and fictional view of the White House as seen by the husband of the first female President. The story is set in 1993. Marilyn Quayle is hiding out in Libya after her unsuccessful attempt to poison President Bush, and Mikhail Gorbachev has been deposed and is living in the USA with Susan Sarandon.

Roger and Me is just the beginning of a series of muckraking films and novels that will expose abuses related to Capricorn themes. *A Shock to the System* (1990), starring Michael Caine, is a black comedy in which the celebrated British star plays a man who takes it into his own hands to rectify the abuses of the corporate system. No doubt there will be more films, TV shows, plays, and novels with this theme while Uranus remains in Capricorn until 1995.

Personality Traits:
Sun in Capricorn

Basic Nature. Born with Sun in Capricorn your nature is tied to structure and form. Like it or not, the evolution of your thoughts, behavior, and talents needs to grow out of a structured foundation, even if you eventually reject the traditions on which it was based. That does not mean that you lack appreciation or affinity for intellectual or spiritual orientations, but these influences are not likely to develop in an ephemeral environment. No matter what emotional, intellectual, or religious path you take, it is firmly directed by personal ambition and goals as well as definite rules and regulations. Your identification with tradition and family is strong as is your sense of responsibility concerning them. You have a very physical nature, and no matter how formal or correct your public personality, privately, you are a sensuous, pleasure-seeking individual. Part of the celestial heritage of Capricorns involves the aging process. Capricorn children often prefer the company of adults and older children. They can physically appear much older than their years, an appearance helped by a maturity of attitude and behavior. Then, in middle age and beyond, unless conditions of ill health interfere, they retain a youthful appearance that belies their actual years.

Strengths and Weaknesses. Setting definite goals and patiently waiting, working hard, accepting responsibility, and doing whatever else is required to attain that goal no matter how long it takes are what sets you apart and brings the success you have earned. However, the admirable strength of your ambition can turn into moral weakness if you become its victim by adopting a philosophy that the end justifies the means. There are great polarities in your nature that can be a confusing mixture of strength and weakness. A strong competitive spirit, for example, can bring you great success and worthy accomplishments. However, the aggressiveness with which you compete can be the result of nagging personal insecurities that you take pains to hide. Your ability to get along with authority figures is also admirable and justified in many people whose accomplishment are worthy of such esteem. However you may be guilty of loyalties to unworthy people simply because of their highly rated positions or influence. You have a very pragmatic, though self-serving nature, there being few instances where your motives are purely altruistic. Pragmatism can be the source of your ingenious solutions to many problems that are of great benefit to others as well as yourself.

Career and Money. Many jobs are suited to different factors of your Capricorn disposition. Jobs, for example, with definite methods, routines, and limits. Operating or working in a business offers a structured, pragmatic environment in which you can successfully compete. Other areas include financial planning, property management, real estate sales and development. Administration and management, appropriate to your identification with responsibility and authority, includes business, finance, retail sales, management of clubs and organizations, administration of schools, and working for security organizations. Not often mentioned but having close association with Capricorn are the arts and entertainment. Natural affinity for these areas has produced many Capricorn composers, performers, and promoters. Work in government and religion, two well established, structured institutions, may be suited to your disposition.

Much of your attitude toward money may depend on the control you develop over physical desires. Though the potential is strong for talent in business and finance, it may not be well developed, especially if there has been no motivation to use it. Ambition and goal orientation can be your best assets in learning to handle money, assets that are also the source of powerful motivation to acquire wealth and the status and authority that accompanies such a life style.

Hobbies and Pastimes. When it comes to sports you may have as much success being the manager of a sports team as you have as a player. You have a competitive streak that makes you a serious opponent in any athletic endeavor. Some of your choices are likely to include running, jogging, boxing, soccer, martial arts, tennis, or racquet ball. Hunting, shooting, or collecting weapons are also Capricorn pastimes. Your basic affinity for the physical world can mean a deep love and appreciation for nature itself, this making it a delight to spend leisure time out of doors gardening, hiking, camping, rock collecting, mountain climbing, or bird watching. Your love for art or music is apt to be satisfied in the pleasure of developing whatever skills you have in these areas. Electric train sets have great appeal for Capricorn children, and as adults, many of them retain not only the fondness for trains in general but toy train sets as well, collecting and adding pieces to it through the years. Coins, stamps, and toy soldiers are among the favorite items Capricorns collect. Respect for tradition and society may urge you to volunteer your time and talents to local civic organizations and charitable agencies.

Sun Signs Around the Zodiac

Aries

 Aries is called the sign of the pioneer. That's because Aries individuals like to start new ventures, and they enjoy being first in everything. Most Aries people are bold and daring, willing to try almost anything, at least once.

The active natures of the Aries-born make them outstanding workers and sports enthusiasts. Most of them have so much natural energy, in fact, it can cause problems if they haven't learned to channel it into constructive activities. If they don't have enough to occupy them physically, they can become moody or temperamental. They are quite clever and possess mechanical skills. Because of this and their tremendous energy, they make wonderful engineers, builders, and manufacturers.

Aries individuals regard practically every experience as some kind of adventure or challenge. Their enthusiasm is boundless, but it makes it difficult for them to set limits, which can cause them to overestimate their own abilities.

Though others may have a hard time keeping up, it is their fast-paced style and optimistic attitude that makes Aries people successful.

The passionate and idealistic side of those born in Aries makes them courageous soldiers, enthusiastic lovers, and outstanding artists in many fields. Their immediate, hasty response to everything can sometimes get them into situations or relationships they soon regret, but it is also responsible for their being able to enjoy a wide variety of experiences and people as they go through life. They can fit more into one lifetime than it would take others two or three lifetimes to accomplish.

Taurus

 Taurus is the sign associated with stubbornness, and most Taurus individuals are indeed hard to get around once they make up their minds. However, their stubborn nature is also responsible for more admirable behavior, such as being able to stick to projects or relationships they believe in—a trait few people can muster, but many admire. This trait is often what makes Taurus individuals successful.

There is a deep-seated need in Taurus people for personal security. For some it means accumulation of wealth in order to gain economic security. If this need gets out of hand, they turn into misers. For others, it can mean emotional security. It makes them especially warm and loving toward family members and friends. However, if they are unsure of the affection of others, they can become jealous and possessive.

Disappointment is difficult for Taurus individuals to handle. They want to be able to trust others or rely on situations that won't change. They go a long way before they finally give up on failed relationships or enterprises that don't work out. They have great strength and stamina, but they need time to feel sure of what they are doing and will not readily accept unexpected or sudden changes.

Most Taurus-born are addicted to personal comfort and physical pleasures. They love being comfortably dressed and comfortably situated. They are very appreciative of the finer things in life, including food, music, art, rich materials, and beautiful surroundings. They know how to live well.

Gemini

 It isn't hard to catch the interest of Gemini individuals, since they are interested in practically everything. Their curiosity is endless, and they enjoy nothing better than to collect information that ranges from trivial facts and gossip to serious scholarly research.

Natural communicators, most Gemini-born are extremely talkative. Some, however, are content to use other methods to communicate, such as writing or teaching. As talkative and ready to share information as they are, they can be surprisingly secretive about themselves. A natural instinct for knowing what others are thinking makes them often say what others want to hear instead of voicing their own opinions or discussing their own affairs. Most Geminis love secrets and mysteries. Many of them happily will engage in intrigue and gossip, while others limit themselves to solving puzzles and reading (or writing) mysteries.

Because they usually have such a wide variety of interests accompanied by a number of different skills that enable them to do many things, Gemini individuals seem to be everywhere at once. In order to truly master certain studies or skills, they must learn to limit what they take on. Channeling their efforts to specific areas enables them to become remarkably efficient as well as proficient.

Those born in Gemini have remarkable ability to adapt to different situations and different people. The result is that they often are highly adept at imitation and mimicry. Their ability to imitate many different emotional responses is what gives them the appearance of having many different personalities.

Cancer

 There is no doubt about the emotional vulnerability of those born in the sign of Cancer. These sensitive individuals take everything personally. They wear their hearts on their sleeves and are not in the least adept at hiding deep disappointment when their affections are not returned. They must guard against the excessive moodiness that can result from lack of emotional control. These individuals are greatly attached to home and family, or at least the concept of home and family.

Cancer individuals hate to throw anything away. They collect masses of outmoded and unused items, until someone else comes along to tidy things up. They have well-developed intuitions when dealing with others or sizing up situations. They are often shrewd with money and many of the world's great fortunes have been made by Cancerian individuals—fortunes that, in many cases, are passed from one generation to the next through family trusts.

Cancerians have a well-known capacity for nurturing. Their concern for the welfare of others is quickly exhibited toward anyone who demonstrates economic, emotional, or spiritual deprivation. However, nurturing to them means food, and even though they are not all excellent, or even interested cooks, they often use food as an emotional pacifier.

The sensitive nature of Cancerians is a source of creativity, which makes many of them very artistic. Even those who may not possess outstanding talent can still use their moderate skills and great appreciation of the arts in some form of participation as a valuable emotional outlet.

Leo

An infectious and inspiring enthusiasm enlivens the personalities of those born in the sign of Leo. They have enormous capacity for enjoyment. For them, life is meant to be lived to the fullest and each experience is looked upon as an adventure. They want to bring joy to others as well as to themselves, and it is this spirit that makes so many of them such natural hosts and wonderful entertainers— and on the serious side, philanthropists and humanitarians.

For all their enthusiasm and good nature, Leos can be surprisingly stubborn and opinionated. This is because they have sensitive egos, which they invariably trip over when it comes to being right about things. They are very passionate and idealistic, which leads many of them to philosophy, religion, and the arts. Though this is a very creative sign, not all Leos possess artistic talent. However, it's a rare Leo that does not have appreciation for entertainment and the arts.

As a rule, Leos are risk-takers, sports enthusiasts, animal lovers, and are attracted to the grandeur and beauty of nature. Though their passions can translate into many physical activities, many of them can also become so addicted to the good life they become lazy or all too willing to take the easy way out of things.

Those born in Leo love attention and flattery. With the flash and dash of legendary heroes, they are happy to help others, and this, in combination with their naturally generous spirit, earns them many friends and admirers.

Virgo

Those born in the sign of Virgo seek perfection and have a well-developed need to improve situations as well as people. This is why so many of them end up in service-

oriented jobs or careers. Their perfection-seeking personalities can sometimes cause them to be overly critical of
those around them, especially when they criticize others
for something of which they themselves are guilty. Though
Virgo is the sign associated with neatness and organization, many Virgos can be very sloppy and disorganized.
This does not mean, however, that they don't have a high
level of appreciation for these qualities in others.

Virgo individuals are very information and communication oriented. They may have shy personalities when it
comes to personal matters, but when they are involved
with other matters they turn into super salesmen, effective
negotiators, and passionate givers of advice. They have a
remarkable ability to adapt to different circumstances and
people, and have an instinct for making themselves useful.
Virgos love to pick up all sorts of information, especially
through travel, whether it means getting around in their
own communities or throughout the world. They make
excellent traveling salesmen, travel agents, and archaeolo-
gists.

Though many Virgos tend to have modest, even self-
effacing outer personalities, this does not mean they are
shrinking violets in the bedroom or are as inhibited in their
personal tastes as they may seem. Underneath their concern with practical matters they also harbor a great appreciation for physical pleasures and comforts, as well as
beauty and luxuries.

Libra

Libra is the sign of relationships and interaction with others, and indeed, most Libras have people-oriented personalities.
They enjoy working with and studying various aspects of human relations, efforts that are often
directed to law, counseling, and reading and writing biographical and other types of personal information. Libras

have a special fondness for books and illustrated periodicals. They have a strong cooperative spirit and work so well with others that, in many cases, it is detrimental for them to be loners or in some way cut off from the stimulation they get from being with other people. Partnership is an essential part of their nature and having compatible marriage or business partners is extremely important.

The gymnasium isn't the favorite hang-out for Libras. Though they can work hard and become interested in certain sports, they demonstrate a streak of laziness when it comes to routine exercise. Few will walk when they can ride. For them, exercising the brain has far more appeal than exercising the body.

Love of beauty and harmony describes the inner nature of Libras. Apt to be artistically talented themselves, they have affinity for music and art. They are disposed toward exhibiting good manners and tactful dispositions, and are immediately attracted to these qualities in others. They abhor violence and go out of their way to avoid atmospheres of disharmony and fractious personalities. However, Libra is also the sign of strategy. When forced to do battle, either physically or verbally, they plan their moves with cunning and unsuspected daring.

Scorpio

An intense nature is to be expected in those born in the sign of Scorpio. Even those who possess outwardly friendly, even easygoing personalities can summon up an intensity and concentration of which few others are capable. They are emotionally oriented, though not necessarily emotionally vulnerable. What this means is that their desires and passions are strong, but as a rule, few of them display their feelings altogether openly. There is always a secretive side to Scorpios, part of which is necessary to them, since it hides their vulnerability.

Scorpios love to manipulate and control, though this doesn't have to be on a grand scale. In fact, for some of them it may only be a matter of gaining control over various aspects of their own nature. For others it can lead to the desire to control their relationships; others seek to acquire powerful positions in business or society. As a rule, most Scorpios want their source of control to be hidden or behind the scenes. Sometimes their need to control coupled with their passionate natures gets out of hand and turns into jealousy, possessiveness, and the obsessive need for revenge.

Because of their essentially emotional nature, there is also the potential of much creativity, which makes many Scorpios artistically talented. They also have deeply inquiring dispositions. They enjoy knowing how things work and function (including people) and they want to get to the bottom of things. This is why so many of them are excellent investigators and researchers.

Sagittarius

 Personal independence is the hallmark of those born in the sign of Sagittarius. These individuals dislike confinement in any form. They want to feel free, even though in reality this may not be the case. In school, Sagittarian youngsters have a hard time settling down when their lessons get too repetitive and the classroom environment begins to seem like a prison. However, there is also a deep love for truth and knowledge in the hearts of Sagittarius. When allowed to independently pursue their wide range of interests and freely indulge their natural curiosity, many of them become admirable scholars and enlightened educators.

With the exception of those whose upbringing or environment has forced them into unnatural miserliness, Sagittarians have unlimited capacity for enjoying the good life and an addiction to the finer things that wealth and social status can provide. They are natural politicians with a gift of gab and a flair for exaggeration. They are also skilled imitators, which is why many of them are outstanding actors and impersonators.

Sagittarians are idealistic. Their passionate enthusiasm can truly be inspired as well as inspiring. They can be as effective in advertising and diplomacy as they are inspirational when pursuing religion, art, or philosophy. They are risk-takers, a trait that can produce river-boat gamblers as well as shrewd stock-market speculators and investment brokers. Their generosity of spirit attracts many friends and admirers, though at times their tendency for hyperbole and self-aggrandizement can drive more timid personalities away.

Capricorn

 Capricorns are ambitious, goal-oriented people, whether they like it or not, and whether they admit it or not. No goals and no structure produces unhappy Capricorns. They need to think they are moving ahead, no matter how imperceptible to others their progress might be. They can be extremely patient when they are fixed on a certain direction, and will do whatever is necessary to get there. However, they can be very impatient when they think they are doing something for nothing or that others are taking advantage of them.

Those born in Capricorn have a lively sense of humor, but will not tolerate being teased. Their egos are fragile, though many go to great pains to hide vulnerability behind a facade of competitiveness and strength. They accept responsibility and indeed often invite it, especially when they can see it is accompanied by a position of authority.

The sense of family and tradition is pronounced in the Capricorn nature, and they lovingly care for parents as well as their own offspring. Even in cases where there may not be much love behind it, they still take responsibility for the care of family members.

There is a healthy appetite for physical pleasures in even the most outwardly reserved Capricorns. Their basic material orientation to life includes a well-developed physical nature, when they allow it to emerge. Affinity for the physical world gives them deep appreciation of nature and they should always give themselves the opportunity to spend time out of doors.

Aquarius

 The nature of Aquarians is unpredictable. In this case unpredictable doesn't mean unstable, and indeed, most of them are very traditional, leading solid lives of work and commitment. However, there is within their nature the inherent capacity to rebel against whatever is imposed rather than what they freely choose. It can mean rejection of traditional values if those values have been forced on them. For others, it means rejection of material goals and assets in the spirit of humanitarianism, which disguises some deeper rejection associated with wealth or status.

Aquarians love history, music, sports, and most of all, the society of others, though in some cases an eccentric nature may result in a more solitary existence. For reasons that may not be understood even by themselves, Aquarians often find themselves out of synch with popular trends in society. They are either too far back or too far forward in their behavior or lifestyles.

One of the most wonderful traits in the nature of Aquarians is an egalitarianism. Unless negative factors in their individual personalities or backgrounds spoil it, they are among the most unprejudiced people in the world. They have sincere interest in and concern for others no matter what their race, creed, or culture happens to be.

They can also be refreshingly unimpressed by those with wealth and power.

There is a stubborn side to Aquarians, and trying to get them to change their opinions is impossible, unless they can independently find a reason to change their minds.

Pisces

 The nature of those born in Pisces is one of great contrast, but a contrast not always observable. For the most part they demonstrate highly sensitive, many times shy personalities. They are easily intimidated and their self-confidence continually needs to be bolstered and reinforced. However, what is not so obvious is that they possess the inner strength and instincts of survivors. Like trees that bend with the wind so as not to be blown away by the force of it, Pisceans adapt so readily to changing circumstances and different people they outlast many stronger, heartier people.

The chameleonlike nature of those born in Pisces makes them among the most fascinating personalities to be around. They can imitate the traits and characteristics of others so well that they sometimes lose track of their own personalities. This skill coupled with their strong emotional orientation and vivid imaginations is all quite remarkable and the reason why Pisceans are among the world's best actors, storytellers, writers, and artists. Pisces is associated with the feet and many are attracted to dancing.

Pisceans seek perfection in the universe and when they don't find it, they can become disillusioned and even bitter. Some attempt to soften personal disappointment or vulnerability through the use of addictive substances. Even those who do not abuse or rely on artificial stimulants are apt to possess sensitivity to them. Their emotional sensitivity can lead to deep spirituality. Their compassion and intelligence also makes them excellent judges, counselors, and enlightened educators.

Stellar Tips for Parents

Fire, Earth, Air, or Water Element. While an element has a common mold, each sign falling under it has individual characteristics. The fire signs are Aries (March 21–April 20), Leo (July 24–August 23), and Sagittarius (November 23–December 21); the earth signs are Taurus (April 21–May 21); Virgo (August 24–September 23), and Capricorn (December 22–January 20); the air signs are Gemini (May 22–June 21), Libra (September 24–October 23), and Aquarius (January 21–February 19); the water signs are Cancer (June 22–July 23), Scorpio (October 24–November 22), and Pisces (February 20–March 20). Here is the way to place children in their own particular environment.

Capricorn Parents with Fire Children. Fire-sign children are endowed with an abundance of energy that allows them to accomplish many things. However, it also makes them resentful of restrictions and structured environments such as school. If not kept constantly busy, they grow restless and bored. You'll need to instill respect for authority and the need for discipline, but be careful not to crush the eager spirit of these youngsters. Fire-sign children are not apt to be attracted to mundane things in life. So you'll have to find imaginative ways to teach them to be organized. Make chores and schoolwork into a game so as to arouse the spirit of competition—a far better approach than merely demanding these matters be promptly taken care of with boring repetitiveness. Overeagerness and a sense of exaggerated ability can prompt fire-sign children to volunteer opinions and services readily. To avoid trouble, make sure these youngsters understand how essential it is to be fully prepared before getting involved or assuming responsibility.

Capricorn Parents with Earth Children. Earth-sign children have the easiest temperaments for a Capricorn parent to understand. Since you share many characteristics with them, you have a chance to observe traits in them that are also part of your own nature. A strong sense of reality and practicality are desirable traits, but in earth-sign children they can be carried to the point that spontaneity, joy, and emotional responsiveness are suppressed. Living life and enjoying the fullness of its pleasures are things you should teach them to aspire to. These children may develop a tendency to be overcritical of others, an attitude that leads to difficulties in personal relationships. The goal-oriented earth-sign children pushing relentlessly to get things done must be taught that no one is indispensable and that the end does not justify the means. It is critical that these children also be made aware of the dangers of trying to "buy" things that should never be bought—such as the love and devotion of another human being.

Capricorn Parents with Air Children. A Capricorn parent will find his/her biggest asset in dealing with air-sign children is an ability to give reasons (assuming they are mature enough to understand it). Offering explanations is more likely to elicit cooperation than adopting the arbitrary parental authority role. Establish verbal communication with air-sign children as soon as they are born. They will readily respond to the sound of your voice, and a powerful bond will be forged in the process. As they get older, reading books and relating stories should be a daily event. Air-sign children will thrive best in an environment that is structured but not strict, busy but not chaotic. For these mentally oriented children—bent on talking and theorizing their way through life—two valuable lessons to learn are that what people do is often more important than what they say, and what works in theory doesn't always work in reality. As a practical Capricorn parent, find simple ways to demonstrate this.

Capricorn Parents with Water Children. Capricorn parents have a tendency to worry. While a normal show of parental concern is necessary, too much worry on your part can frighten sensitive water-sign children. They need plenty of encouragement and will benefit a great deal from your Capricorn strength. Definite guidelines for correct attitude and behavior should be established early so they will understand clearly what is expected of them. Be firm, but allow some flexibility so as not to instill feelings of failure or guilt. Their emotional approach to life is quite different from your practical viewpoint. Recognize this, and do not mistake sensitivity for weakness. If their emotional environment is not supportive, water-sign children may fail to develop properly or will lose the motivation to succeed. Provide a family atmosphere that encourages creative talent while inspiring its practical application.

Your Birthday's Planetary Ruler

Planetary Rulerships. The system of planetary rulership of the days was evolved by the Egyptians, under Greek influence. The system spread over the entire then-known world and resulted in the days of the week being named after the planetary rulers. The planetary ruler of the day you were born exerts a powerful influence on your life. You can determine the planetary ruler on your birth day using the tables on pages 42–43. Find the year in question on Table 1. On the same line, to the right, note the key number under the month you were born. Add the key number to your date of birth (i.e., the day of the month); find the total in Table 2. On that line, to the left, will be found the day of the week you were born.

Born on Sunday/the Sun. You're daring, with a strong sense of romance and adventure. You're well liked by others and are social. Though confident, you have an inner need to live up to the best of your potentials. You give a lot to life and expect a lot in return. Arrogance could lead to problems.

Born on Monday/the Moon. You know how to get along with others but can be moody and self-centered. At times you hurt people without realizing it. You love home but may feel confined by domesticity. Nervous tension may interfere with your fulfilling your potentials, though these are great, especially in art.

Born on Tuesday/Mars. You have strong desires and are a fighter. Undoubtedly you will do your own thing, come what may. Individuality brings you success, but you need more tact and consideration for others. Your energy often keeps the midnight oils burning, for you keep going longer than most.

Born on Wednesday/Mercury. You have many irons in the fire but may only skim the surface. You're too often quick to abandon a project if success isn't immediate. Restlessness can interfere with study, which you need to be successful. Be less judgmental. Your versatility leads to achievement in such areas as medicine, writing, science, and theater.

Born on Thursday/Jupiter. You'd make a good fighter for a cause. You're quite independent in your outlook on life and have your own definition of honor. A love of ideas can make you overlook the human factor. Luck is with you, but don't overplay your hand. Though personable, you appear detached.

Born on Friday/Venus. You like life's finer things and spend freely on what you want. Though anxious to please others, you're not always considerate of their feelings. An artistic or professional career can lead you to popularity with the masses. Your sex appeal will bring you many admirers.

Born on Saturday/Saturn. You're ambitious, but do better on your own among strangers than in the family milieu. You must like your work for you to succeed. You can easily rise to the heights, though you may resent authority. You need to learn when to be passive and when to be aggressive in timing, in order to fulfill your potentials. Patience is your ally.

TABLE 1

Year	Year	Year	Year	Jan.	Feb.	Mar.	Apr.	May	June	July	Aug.	Sept.	Oct.	Nov.	Dec.
	1918	1946	1974	2	5	5	1	3	6	1	4	0	2	5	0
	1919	1947	1975	3	6	6	2	4	0	2	5	1	3	6	1
	*1920	*1948	*1976	4	0	1	4	6	2	4	0	3	5	1	3
	1921	1949	1977	6	2	2	5	0	3	5	1	4	6	2	4
	1922	1950	1978	0	3	3	6	1	4	6	2	5	0	3	5
	1923	1951	1979	1	4	4	0	2	5	0	3	6	1	4	6
	*1924	*1952	*1980	2	5	6	2	4	0	2	5	1	3	6	1
	1925	1953	1981	4	0	0	3	5	1	3	6	2	4	0	2
	1926	1954	1982	5	1	1	4	6	2	4	0	3	5	1	3
	1927	1955	1983	6	2	2	5	0	3	5	1	4	6	2	4
	*1928	*1956	*1984	0	3	4	0	2	5	0	3	6	1	4	6
1901	1929	1957	1985	2	5	5	1	3	6	1	4	0	2	5	0
1902	1930	1958	1986	3	6	6	2	4	0	2	5	1	3	6	1
1903	1931	1959	1987	4	0	0	3	5	1	3	6	2	4	0	2
*1904	*1932	*1960	*1988	5	1	2	5	0	3	5	1	4	6	2	4
1905	1933	1961	1989	0	3	3	6	1	4	6	2	5	0	3	5
1906	1934	1962	1990	1	4	4	0	2	5	0	3	6	1	4	6
1907	1935	1963	1991	2	5	5	1	3	6	1	4	0	2	5	0
*1908	*1936	*1964	*1992	3	6	0	3	5	1	3	6	2	4	0	2
1909	1937	1965	1993	5	1	1	4	6	2	4	0	3	5	1	3
1910	1938	1966	1994	6	2	2	5	0	3	5	1	4	6	2	4
1911	1939	1967	1995	0	3	3	6	1	4	6	2	5	0	3	5
*1912	*1940	*1968	*1996	1	4	5	1	3	6	1	4	0	2	5	0
1913	1941	1969	1997	3	6	6	2	4	0	2	5	1	3	6	1
1914	1942	1970	1998	4	0	0	3	5	1	3	6	2	4	0	2
1915	1943	1971	1999	5	1	1	4	6	2	4	0	3	5	1	3
*1916	*1944	*1972	*2000	6	2	3	6	1	4	6	2	5	0	3	5
1917	1945	1973	2001	1	4	4	0	2	5	0	3	6	1	4	6

*Leap Year.

TABLE 2

Sunday	1	8	15	22	29	36
Monday	2	9	16	23	30	37
Tuesday	3	10	17	24	31	
Wednesday	4	11	18	25	32	
Thursday	5	12	19	26	33	
Friday	6	13	20	27	34	
Saturday	7	14	21	28	35	

Your Moon Sign: Getting in Touch with Your Emotions

Moon. The Sun and the Moon are the most important parts of your horoscope. The Sun represents your active role in life. It indicates how much and what kind of an impact you want to make. This is represented by the strength of your willpower and ego. The Moon, however, represents your passive role. It describes how you react to the impact life has on you; that is, how you respond to the various people and situations you experience. The Moon represents your creative and artistic talents, imagination, desires, and the way in which you function on a daily basis. In your horoscope the Moon is also associated with home and family life, your mother, and other strong female influences.

Moon in Aries. Moon in Aries suggests that your emotional make-up is based on an energetic, enthusiastic response to almost everything. If other factors in your personality or background have not acted to discourage the development of your eager approach to life, you'll want to enjoy and experience anything and anyone that excites your interest. Your feelings and reactions are immediately turned into some sort of action. Of course, somewhere along the line you'll have to develop the maturity to be discriminating about your involvements, since too much passion or haste can cause trouble. Your attraction to others, for example, is spontaneous and enthusiastic. However, those to whom you are attracted may need more time to develop similar feelings, and your impatience or aggressiveness can prove too overwhelming or be viewed as ill-timed or even ill-mannered. You may have an unfortunate tendency to lose respect for those who may not appear strong. Aries is the sign of combat and the warrior, so it isn't surprising if you tend to rush into battle, verbal as well as physical, at the drop of a hat. Anger lies as close to the surface as all the other passions in your emotional make-up. On the positive side of your quick temper lies a willingness to forget frustration and anger. Aggressive enthusiasm can mean outstanding success when it comes to achieving academic and business goals or pursuing other worthwhile ambitions. Courage in following ideals, generosity, and the ability you can develop to inspire and provide leadership to others are admirable advantages associated with your Aries Moon. Your mother and other important females in your life are apt to be energetic and possess domineering or combative natures. You prefer a home and lifestyle that are active and emotionally stimulating.

Moon in Taurus. Moon in Taurus indicates that your emotional orientation is based on a deep need for personal security. That's why you require tangible proof of the affection others have for you. Your reaction to any experience or relationship is a conscious or subconscious evaluation of the personal advantages likely to be gained or the personal needs likely to be gratified. Even though your reactions toward someone or some situation may initially be positive, in most cases you'll only really become committed after you have had time to let your feelings develop. If other factors in your background or personality cause you to become disappointed or lose confidence, you may have the tendency to put more emphasis on material possessions, feeling that such things will make up for whatever flaws or lack of status there may be in other areas of your life. Moon in Taurus indicates sociability. Whether or not you are outgoing and gregarious, you'll enjoy social gatherings as well as various aspects of society itself. Your fashions or lifestyle may, for example, become trend setters. You'll enjoy being the arbiter of social manners and customs, or social commentator, even if it is only among members of your own family or circle of friends. Because you have such a deep sense of self-preservation, you will find it difficult to deal with those who betray your trust or break their promises. Appreciation for music or art may be accompanied by artistic talent. Your mother or strong females in your life are likely to be sources of material and practical help. Natural attraction to beauty and luxury urges you to seek a home and lifestyle of wealth and privilege, though this by no means has to be your only guiding force.

Moon in Gemini. Moon in Gemini is a strong indication that you are very talkative, and your emotional reactions to people and situations are based on intellectual curiosity and adaptability. This Moon position sharpens the sensory perceptions, which means you can be prone to nervousness and related complaints, but also increases the potential for possessing impressive musical or mechanical skills. The adaptability of your emotional make-up is remarkable. It allows you to easily identify with what others think and feel. However, it may not be so easy for others really to get to know you, at least not as easy as your talkative nature may indicate. For one thing, you are more apt to say what you instinctively know others want to hear rather than state the truth or your own feelings. You can be secretive when it comes to revealing your feelings. You can demonstrate an outwardly bright and cheerful personality even though you may harbor inner feelings of loneliness or sorrow. What is worse, your emotional flexibility makes it that much harder for even you to pinpoint your real feelings. You have a fast and ready wit, and an emotional understanding of people and their motivations that helps you succeed in achieving many goals. Since Gemini is a dual-natured sign, female influences can be represented equally well by individuals of either sex. In other words, your mother may also play the role of father or your father can also play the role of mother. Other female influences in your life are also apt to be represented in the same way. Home and lifestyle consist of many hobbies or projects, substantial collections of books and magazines, much travel and running around within the community, and more than one home at a time.

Moon in Cancer. Moon in Cancer leaves little doubt that you possess an extremely sensitive emotional nature. Unless other factors in your background and personality discourage their development, you have remarkable intuition and psychic energy. A strong identification with home and family, even in the most rugged of bachelors, is exhibited by an identifiable streak of interest in some aspect of the domestic environment and a responsible attitude toward parents and other family members. The normally passive role of the Moon becomes intensified when in Cancer, which means you passively put up with the most grueling of relationships for an interminable time until ultimately something comes along to initiate a break. Cancer Moon also suggests that you are very reflective of your environment, which means you are highly influenced by those with whom you spend the most time. Of course, other strengths or weaknesses in your individual personality and make-up determine the extent to which you reflect the opinions, ideas, and feelings of others, rather than your own. The sensitivity of Cancer indicates high potential for creative talent and appreciation for music and art. There is marked tendency for worry, which in turn, can be the source of great mental stress. You need to feel you belong somewhere even if you aren't always there, and that you belong to someone even if you aren't always together.

Your mother is apt to play a prominent role in your life, and you may physically resemble her or her side of the family. If she is missing, either through death or for other reasons, you will constantly search for someone to fill this role in one capacity or another. Your home is your castle and your life-style is built around your family or those you regard as family.

Moon in Leo. Moon in Leo indicates that your emotional reactions and desires are energetic and enthusiastic. The spontaneous eagerness with which you respond to new situations or relationships is very sincere, but can sometimes be ill-timed or misplaced. If serious flaws begin to surface, or you experience a change of heart, you abandon your original enthusiasm, which in turn, can be interpreted by others as your lack of sincerity in the first place. Many of your emotional responses are dictated by a conscious or unconscious ego involvement. This provides strong incentive to achieve important goals in life, but too much ego can damage relationships. For example, desire to dominate or manipulate relationships or indulge in temper tantrums when others disappoint you or refuse to comply with your requests are two of the unfortunate possibilities. However, Leo Moon is also indicative of a lively imagination, theatrical talent, intense idealism or spirituality, and great generosity. Art, design, and architecture attract you, and even if you do not use such interests or talents in work, you may develop them through a hobby or other leisure-time activity. Social activities and financial interests are two areas that also arouse your positive response and participation. You are able successfully to mix business with pleasure, enjoy entertaining and being entertained, and may be a wonderful fund-raiser or promoter. Stubborn pride makes it difficult to admit when you are wrong and inspires a need always to have the last word. On the other hand, it is also what engenders admirable loyalty to friends and high principles. Female influences in your life are apt to be flamboyant, prideful, and inspiring. Your home and life-style are energetic, social, and contemporary, and aspire to grandness at whatever level they are maintained.

Moon in Virgo. Moon in Virgo indicates that your emotional responses are very quick, but the quickness is based on keenly developed senses and intellectual curiosity rather than spontaneous and passionate enthusiasm. It does not mean you lack eagerness or passion; but for those reactions you need more time, since you are apt to be somewhat shy when it comes to highly personal matters. On the other hand, if the object of attention or situation at hand involves not you personally but a person, product, or principle in which you strongly believe, you can be a remarkably effective spokesperson. Contradictory traits have to find comfortable arrangement within your emotional make-up. You are, for example, communication oriented, but may be quite shy. At heart an information gatherer, you may not necessarily enjoy a scholarly pursuit of knowledge. You possess common sense and practicality, but not in all things, since there is also a tendency to indulge in fantasy and idealism. A relentless perfectionist in some things, you pay attention to the slightest of detail, but you can also be appallingly lax and disorganized in other areas. The key to successfully blending these opposite traits lies in the fact that your emotional nature is quite flexible, and you can adapt to different people and situations as the need arises. Strong female influences may not necessarily be represented by strong women. The type of nurturing, encouragement, or other influences associated with a mother or strong female can be represented equally well in your life by individuals of either sex. Home and lifestyle are not easily defined, since much change is probable. However, travel, community activities, books, magazines and a myriad of projects and interests are likely to be strongly envidenced in how and where you live.

Moon in Libra. Moon in Libra indicates that your emotional reactions are based on an intellectual orientation.

The people or situations you experience in life are objectively viewed by your brain and then your emotions take over. Under ordinary circumstances, if the person or situation at hand arouses your interest, you will respond with appropriate eagerness or action, but if the experience fails to arouse your interest or promise to gratify some other desire, your responses are minimal. You have fondness for music and are attracted to beautiful things and beautiful people. You are apt to particularly enjoy looking attractive yourself, especially when it comes to dressing well. You are fascinated by people, their interactions, and relationships. Your favorite reading material consists of biographies or short descriptions of the exploits and societal activities of others. Though you may or may not possess an outwardly gregarious personality, you possess the ability to relate well to others, at least on a one-to-one basis. Since Libra is the sign of equality, you try to respond with equal measure to the affection you receive. In turn, however, you want equal measure in what you give and are reluctant to pursue or stay in relationships where there is unequal emotional response and commitment. Family and home are very important and you have an affectionate, caring, and romantic nature. However, the intellectual orientation of your emotional responses can appear to be less than passionate to those who approach things from a different angle. Your mother and other strong females who influence your life are likely to be attractive, possess artistic or literary tastes, and are very flattering in their attentions to you. You aspire to a home and lifestyle that reflect beauty, elegance, and above all, harmonious dispositions.

Moon in Scorpio. Scorpio Moon indicates emotional depth and intensity, but your potential to be guarded and circumspect makes it difficult to predict how much and under what circumstances you reveal feelings, desires, and reactions. When you are up, you are really up, and when you are down, there is no one gloomier. The creative force is strong, and your sexual energy may be very potent. However, it is also apt to be represented, and perhaps sublimated, by remarkable artistic ability and other creative talents. Power and control, prominent though not always obvious elements in your emotional make-up, elicit strong interest and reactions as you observe them in individuals and society. Identifying with nature, understanding human motivation, and the use of resources are all part of your emotional orientation. When you focus your energies, you can be a formidable presence. Once involved in a struggle of wills or ability, if other factors in your background and personality have not contributed a measure of softness, you ignore those without sufficient challenge and will not be a willing or gracious loser to those who overtake you. For all the intensity that is possible with Moon in Scorpio there is also love of entertainment, children, risk-taking ventures, much humor, and the ability to enjoy life. You are apt to be a first-class cook, gardener, or hobbyist. Your mother and other females in your life are apt to be either manipulative themselves or possess a helplessness or naïveté that gives you control. Living on or near water is the most emotionally satisfying environment. Your home and lifestyle may reflect your desires in design, location, and interest in nature, but there is the possibility that what is seen may not reveal much about the real you.

Moon in Sagittarius. Moon in Sagittarius indicates your emotional responses and reactions are open and honest, which for the most part makes you refreshingly uncomplicated. However, others will not always appreciate your being so candid about your feelings or opinions. Unless other factors in your personality and background have discouraged their development, you have a merry wit and prodigious appetite for the pleasures and luxuries in life. With you, idealism and passion are interchangeable. Reactions are spontaneous, and you want to turn those feelings into physical action, which at times is ill-advised or ill-timed. Too much haste in relationships may not give others time to develop similar feelings, or haste involves you in undesirable situations that could have been avoided if you had responded in a slower manner and gained additional understanding. Moon in Sagittarius bestows love of knowledge, though it does not automatically indicate the pursuit of higher education and other scholarly activities. It does suggest that you can become well versed through self-education, and your interests are varied. Whether or not you are outwardly gregarious, you are a natural communicator. Love of travel, salesmanship, spirituality, and fondness for politics, art, and entertainment are all part of your emotional make-up. Friends may be easier to acquire than lovers. Your mother and other important females are apt to be scholarly, sports or travel oriented, and of strongly independent natures. Your mother may be of a different race, religion, or culture than your father, or more than one language may be spoken at home. Your home and lifestyle will reflect interest or association with travel, education, art, or communication. Your home is apt to be contemporary and located in a foreign land or in the neighborhood of a university, church, museum, or other cultural institutions.

Moon in Capricorn. Capricorn Moon indicates that your reactions are quick, but responses are cautious and purposeful. The influence of Capricorn implies restriction, ambition, and structure. Emotions, which by their nature are passive, reflective, and fragile, have a potentially difficult development when the Moon is in Capricorn. Identification with home, family, and tradition is strong, though your responses generated by love are interchangeable with responses generated by a sense of responsibility. No matter how passionate your actions, delightful your humor, and romantic you can be, underneath it all there are formality and inhibitions connected with the expression of your feelings. While you are very responsive to others who need your help, you find it hard to confide your own fears or problems to others. Tendency for overworry may cause mental depression. Worry may actually be lack of self-confidence that you take great pains to hide. Fear of rejection makes you very uncomfortable with vague relationships or situations. You must know where you stand at all times. These seemingly negative traits have some very positive side effects. For one thing, you can relate extremely well to children. For another, you are very goal-oriented, very competitive and ambitious to succeed. Your mother and other females are apt to be strong-willed and possess great ambition for themselves as well as you. Whatever the case, your emotional reactions to these ladies are likely to be inhibited or restricted, either by choice or circumstance. You may tend in looks or preference to favor your father's side of the family. Since extremes in emotional outlook can dominate your home and lifestyle, you may go overboard in a too formal or austere approach on the one hand, or by way of overcompensation, go too far in your expressions of informality.

Moon in Aquarius. Moon in Aquarius indicates unpredictable changes in your emotions. You may espouse certain feelings for a very long time, and then quite unexpectedly develop the opposite response. An essential social orientation inspires your enthusiastic reactions, especially to people and people-related situations. Your emotional make-up is directed outward rather than being intensely personal. At times this approach can seem unemotional or less than passionate, since focusing on one individual may not, after a certain length of time, elicit the level of enthusiasm you experience dealing with groups of people. Independence is another hallmark. You resent being told how you feel or should feel. You want to form your own opinions and reactions, and resist being swayed by the judgments of others. If other factors in your personality or background do not discourage its development, your emotions are remarkably egalitarian, and under most circumstances, you react with poise and minimal bias. You are not easily surprised, frightened, or repelled by the strange behavior or appearance of others. Not quick to judge one person by another, or one experience by previous encounters, your response to new relationships and experiences is highly influenced by circumstances that exist at that moment. You continue to respond to these same situations and people largely according to their individual behavior or factors that relate only to them. It is in this way that your emotional orientation goes from being directed to society in general to a more individually directed response. There may be nontraditional relationships with your mother and other females, these ladies being as much a friend to you as anything else. Your home and lifestyle are unpredictable, given the nontraditional and independent nature of Aquarius, though lack of ostentatiousness or obvious wealth is one likely description.

Moon in Pisces. Moon in Pisces indicates that you are extremely sensitive. Your responses and reactions are primarily directed by the emotional environment and your emotional state. Such sensitivity is likely to be accompanied by artistic ability, though you may need to work as hard to develop self-confidence as you do in developing the creative talents you possess. Highly developed imagination and a penchant for fantasy and idealism color your responses and motivate your desires and actions. This, of course, can lead to outstanding achievements or disappointment and disillusionment. Much depends on the kind of strength and support you receive from other factors in your personality and background. Your compassionate, caring nature makes it easy for others to take advantage of you. However, your extremely flexible nature instinctively understands and adapts to different people and situations so well that you are the one who may gain the upper hand. Love for art, music, or dance are strong potentials with Moon in Pisces. You are apt to have theatrical or promotional ability, talent for mathematics and abstract theory, or you may become a master of disguise. You imbue relationships with highly idealized and romantic elements, as well as mystery and intrigue. Sensitive though your emotional orientation may be, you do not lack courage, and a risk-taking adventurous spirit can put you in real peril from time to time. Though sorrow or disappointment can be connected with your mother and other females, it is just as likely they are ladies of highly spiritual and sensitive natures, a description that also applies to your relationships with them. Living on or near water is the most emotionally soothing environment for you. Home and life-style are other areas heavily influenced by your idealized notions, sensitivity, imagination, and illusion.

Your Moon Sign Nature

How to Find Your Moon's Sign and Degree

This is the simplest and briefest table that has been devised for getting the Moon's place on any date over a great many years, and if you follow carefully the directions below, you will have a part of your individual horoscope that heretofore has been available only to those who knew how to use an Ephemeris, or who were able to have an individual chart drawn up for them. If you follow the simple directions, you get not only the sign occupied by the Moon, but also the actual degree, correct within 1½°, for any hour of any date between 1880 and 2000 inclusive.

HOW TO FIND YOUR MOON'S PLACE

1. Note your birth year in the tables (pages 60–83).

2. Run down the left-hand column and see if your date is there.

3. IF YOUR DATE IS IN THE LEFT-HAND COLUMN, run over this line till you come to the column under your birth year. Here you will find a number. This is your BASE NUMBER. Write it down, and go directly to the part of the directions below, under the heading "What to Do with Your Base Number."

4. IF YOUR BIRTH DATE IS NOT IN THE LEFT-HAND COLUMN, get a pencil and paper. Your birth date falls between two numbers in the left-hand column. Look at the date closest *after* your birth date, run over this line to your birth year. Write down the number you find there, and label it "TOP NUMBER." Having done this, write directly beneath it on your piece of paper the number printed just above it in the table. Label this "BOTTOM NUMBER." Subtract the bottom number from the top number. If the top number is smaller, add 360 to it and then subtract. The result is your DIFFERENCE.

5. Go back to the left-hand column and find the date next *before* your birth date. Determine the number of days between this date and your birth date by subtracting. Write this down and label it "INTERVENING DAYS."

6. In the Table of Difference below, note which group your DIFFERENCE (found through Step 4) falls in.

Difference	Daily Motion
80–87	12°
88–94	13°
95–101	14°
102–106	15°

Note: If you were born in Leap Year *and* use the difference between February 26 and March 5, use the special table following:

Difference	Daily Motion
94–99	12°
100–108	13°
109–115	14°
116–122	15°

Write down the DAILY MOTION corresponding to your place in the proper Table of Difference above.

7. Multiply this daily motion by the number labeled "INTERVENING DAYS" (found through Step 5).

8. Add the result of Step 7 to your BOTTOM NUMBER (under 4). The result of this is your BASE NUMBER. If it is more than 360, subtract 360 from it and call the result your BASE NUMBER. Now turn to the table of Base Numbers on page 59.

WHAT TO DO WITH YOUR BASE NUMBER

LOCATE YOUR BASE NUMBER in the table on page 59. At the top of the column you will find the SIGN your MOON WAS IN. At the left you will find the DEGREE (°) your Moon occupied at: 7 A.M. of your birth date if you were born under eastern standard time, 6 A.M. of your birth date if you were born under central standard time, 5 A.M. of your birth date if you were born under mountain standard time, 4 A.M. of your birth date if you were born under Pacific standard time.

IF YOU DON'T KNOW THE HOUR OF YOUR BIRTH, accept this as your Moon's sign and degree.

IF YOU DO KNOW THE HOUR OF YOUR BIRTH, get the exact degree as follows:

If you were born *after* 7 A.M., EST (6 A.M. CST, etc.), determine the number of hours after this time of birth. Divide this by two. *Add* this to your BASE NUMBER, and the result in the table will show the exact degree and sign of the Moon on the year, month, date, and hour of your birth.

If you were born *before* 7 A.M., EST, (6 A.M., CST, etc.), determine the number of hours before that time that you were born. Divide this by two. *Subtract* this from your base number, and the result in the table will be the exact degree and sign of the Moon on the year, month, date, and hour of your birth.

TABLE OF BASE NUMBERS

	♈	♉	♊	♋	♌	♍	♎	♏	♐	♑	♒	♓
0°	0	30	60	90	120	150	180	210	240	270	300	330
1°	1	31	61	91	121	151	181	211	241	271	301	331
2°	2	32	62	92	122	152	182	212	242	272	302	332
3°	3	33	63	93	123	153	183	213	243	273	303	333
4°	4	34	64	94	124	154	184	214	244	274	304	334
5°	5	35	65	95	125	155	185	215	245	275	305	335
6°	6	36	66	96	126	156	186	216	246	276	306	336
7°	7	37	67	97	127	157	187	217	247	277	307	337
8°	8	38	68	98	128	158	188	218	248	278	308	338
9°	9	39	69	99	129	159	189	219	249	279	309	339
10°	10	40	70	100	130	160	190	220	250	280	310	340
11°	11	41	71	101	131	161	191	221	251	281	311	341
12°	12	42	72	102	132	162	192	222	252	282	312	342
13°	13	43	73	103	133	163	193	223	253	283	313	343
14°	14	44	74	104	134	164	194	224	254	284	314	344
15°	15	45	75	105	135	165	195	225	255	285	315	345
16°	16	46	76	106	136	166	196	226	256	286	316	346
17°	17	47	77	107	137	167	197	227	257	287	317	347
18°	18	48	78	108	138	168	198	228	258	288	318	348
19°	19	49	79	109	139	169	199	229	259	289	319	349
20°	20	50	80	110	140	170	200	230	260	290	320	350
21°	21	51	81	111	141	171	201	231	261	291	321	351
22°	22	52	82	112	142	172	202	232	262	292	322	352
23°	23	53	83	113	143	173	203	233	263	293	323	353
24°	24	54	84	114	144	174	204	234	264	294	324	354
25°	25	55	85	115	145	175	205	235	265	295	325	355
26°	26	56	86	116	146	176	206	236	266	296	326	356
27°	27	57	87	117	147	177	207	237	267	297	327	357
28°	28	58	88	118	148	178	208	238	268	298	328	358
29°	29	59	89	119	149	179	209	239	269	299	329	359

♈ Aries
♉ Taurus
♊ Gemini

♋ Cancer
♌ Leo
♍ Virgo

♎ Libra
♏ Scorpio
♐ Sagittarius

♑ Capricorn
♒ Aquarius
♓ Pisces

MOON SIGN TABLES

	1880	1881	1882	1883	1884	1885	1886	1887	1888	1889
Jan. 1	144	294	67	190	315	105	238	359	127	276
8	240	32	152	278	52	202	323	89	224	12
15	341	116	239	18	151	286	49	190	321	96
22	67	202	342	113	236	13	153	284	46	185
29	154	302	77	198	325	113	248	8	136	285
Feb. 5	250	41	161	286	63	211	331	97	235	20
12	349	124	248	29	159	295	58	200	329	104
19	75	212	351	122	244	24	161	293	59	196
26	163	311	86	207	334	122	257	16	144	294
Mar. 5	275	49	170	294	88	218	340	105	260	28
12	10	133	257	38	180	303	69	209	350	112
19	94	222	359	132	264	34	169	302	74	205
26	185	320	95	215	356	133	265	25	166	305
Apr. 2	286	57	179	303	98	226	349	114	270	36
9	18	141	267	47	189	311	79	217	359	120
16	102	232	7	141	272	43	178	311	83	214
23	194	331	103	224	4	143	273	34	175	315
30	297	65	187	312	108	235	357	124	279	45
May 7	28	149	278	54	198	319	89	225	8	128
14	111	241	17	149	281	52	108	319	92	223
21	202	342	111	233	13	154	281	43	184	325
28	306	73	195	323	117	243	5	155	288	54
June 4	37	157	288	63	207	327	99	234	17	137
11	119	250	27	158	291	60	199	327	101	231
18	211	352	119	241	22	164	289	52	194	335
25	315	82	203	333	126	252	13	145	296	63

MOON SIGN TABLES

July 2	46	165	297	72	216	336	108	244	26	146
9	129	258	37	165	299	69	209	335	110	240
16	220	2	127	250	32	173	298	59	204	343
23	323	91	211	344	134	261	21	155	304	72
30	54	174	306	82	224	345	117	254	34	156
Aug. 6	138	267	48	174	309	78	219	343	119	250
13	231	11	136	258	43	181	307	68	215	352
20	331	100	220	354	142	270	30	165	313	50
27	63	184	314	93	232	355	125	265	42	165
Sept. 3	147	276	58	182	317	88	228	352	127	260
10	242	19	145	266	54	190	316	76	226	359
17	340	109	229	3	152	278	40	173	323	88
24	70	193	323	103	239	4	134	275	50	174
Oct. 1	155	286	67	191	325	99	237	1	135	271
8	252	27	154	274	64	198	324	85	236	8
15	350	117	238	11	161	286	49	181	332	96
22	78	202	332	113	248	12	144	284	58	182
29	163	297	75	200	333	110	245	10	143	282
Nov. 5	262	36	163	263	74	207	332	94	245	18
12	359	124	248	19	171	294	59	190	342	104
19	87	210	342	122	257	20	154	292	67	190
26	171	308	83	208	341	120	253	18	152	292
Dec. 3	271	45	171	293	82	216	340	104	253	27
10	10	132	257	28	181	302	67	199	351	112
17	95	218	353	130	265	28	165	300	76	198
24	179	318	91	217	351	130	262	26	162	301
31	279	55	179	302	89	226	348	113	261	37

MOON SIGN TABLES

		1890	1891	1892	1893	1894	1895	1896	1897	1898	1899
Jan.	1	49	170	298	87	220	340	109	258	30	149
	8	132	259	37	183	303	69	209	352	114	240
	15	221	2	131	266	32	174	301	76	203	335
	22	323	94	215	357	135	265	25	169	305	76
	29	58	178	307	96	229	348	117	268	39	157
Feb.	5	141	267	47	190	312	78	219	359	122	249
	12	230	12	140	274	42	162	310	84	214	353
	19	332	103	223	7	143	274	34	179	314	84
	26	67	187	315	106	236	357	125	278	46	168
Mar.	5	150	276	72	198	321	87	243	8	130	259
	12	241	20	161	282	52	190	331	92	225	1
	19	340	113	244	17	152	283	55	188	323	93
	26	75	196	337	117	244	6	148	289	54	177
Apr.	2	159	285	81	206	329	97	252	17	138	269
	9	251	28	170	290	63	198	340	100	235	9
	16	350	121	253	25	162	291	64	196	333	101
	23	83	204	346	127	252	15	157	299	62	185
	30	167	295	89	215	337	108	261	25	146	280
May	7	261	36	179	299	73	207	349	109	244	19
	14	0	129	262	33	172	299	73	204	344	108
	21	91	213	355	137	261	23	167	308	71	193
	28	174	307	98	224	345	119	269	34	155	291
June	4	271	46	188	308	81	217	357	119	253	29
	11	11	137	272	42	182	307	82	213	354	117
	18	99	221	6	146	269	31	178	316	80	201
	25	183	317	106	233	353	129	277	43	164	300

MOON SIGN TABLES

July 2	278	56	195	317	89	227	5	128	261	39
9	21	145	281	51	192	315	91	223	3	125
16	108	229	17	154	278	39	189	324	89	209
23	192	327	115	241	2	138	286	51	173	309
30	287	66	203	327	99	237	13	138	269	49
Aug. 6	31	153	289	62	201	324	99	234	11	134
13	117	237	28	162	287	48	200	332	97	219
20	201	336	124	250	12	147	296	59	183	317
27	295	76	211	336	108	247	21	146	279	58
Sept. 3	39	162	297	72	209	333	107	245	19	143
10	125	246	38	171	296	57	209	341	105	228
17	211	344	134	257	22	155	305	67	193	326
24	305	86	220	345	118	256	29	155	290	67
Oct. 1	47	171	305	83	217	341	116	256	27	151
8	134	256	47	179	304	67	218	350	113	238
15	220	352	144	265	31	164	315	75	202	335
22	315	94	228	352	128	264	39	162	301	75
29	55	179	314	94	225	350	125	266	36	160
Nov. 5	142	265	56	189	312	77	226	359	121	248
12	229	2	153	274	40	173	324	84	210	346
19	327	102	237	0	139	272	47	171	311	82
26	64	188	323	103	234	358	135	275	45	167
Dec. 3	149	275	63	198	320	86	235	9	129	257
10	237	12	162	282	47	184	332	93	218	356
17	338	110	246	9	149	280	56	179	321	91
24	72	196	333	112	243	5	145	282	54	175
31	158	284	72	208	328	95	244	18	138	265

MOON SIGN TABLES

	1900	1901	1902	1903	1904	1905	1906	1907	1908	1909
Jan. 1	280	55	188	308	76	227	358	119	246	39
8	21	149	272	37	179	320	82	208	350	129
15	112	234	2	141	270	43	174	311	81	213
22	195	327	101	234	353	138	273	44	164	309
29	288	66	196	317	83	238	6	128	255	50
Feb. 5	31	158	280	46	188	328	89	219	359	138
12	121	241	12	149	279	51	184	319	89	221
19	204	335	111	242	2	146	283	52	173	317
26	296	76	204	326	92	248	13	136	264	59
Mar. 5	40	166	288	57	211	334	98	229	21	147
12	130	249	22	157	300	59	194	328	110	230
19	213	344	121	250	24	154	293	59	195	325
26	305	86	212	334	116	258	22	144	288	69
Apr. 2	49	175	296	68	219	345	106	240	29	156
9	138	258	31	157	309	69	202	338	118	239
16	222	352	132	258	33	163	304	68	204	334
23	315	96	220	342	127	267	31	152	299	77
30	57	184	304	78	227	354	114	250	38	164
May 7	177	268	40	177	316	78	210	348	126	249
14	231	1	142	266	42	172	313	76	212	344
21	325	104	229	350	138	275	40	160	310	85
28	65	193	313	87	236	3	124	259	47	172
June 4	155	277	48	187	324	88	219	358	134	259
11	239	11	151	275	50	182	322	85	220	355
18	336	112	238	359	149	283	48	169	320	93
25	74	201	322	96	245	11	133	267	57	180

MOON SIGN TABLES

July 2	163	286	57	197	333	97	228	8	142	267
9	248	21	160	283	58	193	330	94	228	6
16	347	121	247	7	159	291	57	178	330	102
23	84	209	332	105	255	19	143	276	66	188
30	171	295	66	206	341	105	239	17	151	275
Aug. 6	256	32	168	292	66	204	338	103	237	17
13	357	130	255	17	168	301	65	188	339	111
20	94	217	341	113	265	27	152	285	76	196
27	179	303	77	215	350	113	250	25	160	283
Sept. 3	264	43	176	301	75	215	346	111	246	27
10	6	229	263	27	176	310	73	198	347	121
17	103	225	350	123	274	35	161	294	85	206
24	188	311	88	223	358	122	261	33	169	292
Oct. 1	273	53	185	309	85	224	355	119	256	36
8	14	149	271	36	185	320	81	207	356	130
15	113	233	359	133	283	44	169	305	93	214
22	197	319	99	231	7	130	271	42	177	301
29	283	62	194	317	95	233	5	127	266	44
Nov. 5	22	158	279	45	193	329	89	216	5	139
12	121	242	6	144	291	53	177	316	101	223
19	206	328	109	239	15	140	281	50	185	311
26	293	70	203	325	105	241	14	135	276	52
Dec. 3	31	167	288	54	203	338	98	224	15	147
10	129	251	14	155	299	61	185	327	109	231
17	214	338	118	248	23	149	289	59	193	322
24	303	78	213	333	115	249	23	143	286	61
31	41	176	296	61	213	346	107	232	26	155

MOON SIGN TABLES

	1910	1911	1912	1913	1914	1915	1916	1917	1918	1919	1920
Jan. 1	168	289	57	211	337	100	228	23	147	270	39
8	252	20	162	299	61	192	332	110	231	5	143
15	346	122	251	23	158	293	61	193	329	103	231
22	84	214	334	119	256	23	145	290	68	193	316
29	175	298	65	221	345	108	237	32	155	278	49
Feb. 5	259	31	170	308	69	203	340	118	249	16	150
12	356	130	260	32	167	302	70	203	338	113	239
19	94	222	344	128	266	31	154	298	78	201	325
26	184	306	75	231	353	116	248	41	164	286	60
Mar. 5	267	42	192	317	77	214	2	127	248	26	172
12	5	140	280	41	176	311	89	212	346	123	259
19	105	230	5	136	276	39	176	308	87	209	346
26	192	314	100	239	2	124	273	49	173	294	85
Apr. 2	276	52	200	326	86	223	10	135	257	35	181
9	13	149	288	51	184	321	97	232	355	133	267
16	115	238	14	146	286	48	184	318	96	218	355
23	201	322	111	247	11	132	284	57	181	303	96
30	285	61	208	334	96	232	19	143	267	43	190
May 7	21	160	296	60	192	331	105	231	4	142	275
14	124	246	22	157	294	56	192	329	104	227	3
21	209	331	122	255	20	141	294	66	190	312	105
28	294	69	218	342	106	240	29	151	277	51	200
June 4	30	170	304	69	202	341	114	249	14	151	284
11	132	255	30	167	302	65	200	340	112	235	11
18	218	340	132	264	28	151	304	74	198	322	114
25	304	78	228	350	115	249	59	159	286	60	209

MOON SIGN TABLES

July											
2	40	179	312	78	212	349	122	248	25	159	293
9	140	264	38	178	310	74	209	350	120	244	21
16	226	349	141	273	36	161	312	84	206	332	123
23	314	87	237	358	125	258	48	168	295	70	218
30	51	187	321	86	223	357	131	256	36	167	302
Aug.											
6	148	272	48	188	319	82	219	359	129	252	31
13	234	359	149	282	44	170	320	93	214	342	131
20	323	96	246	6	133	268	57	177	303	81	226
27	62	195	330	94	234	5	140	265	46	175	310
Sept.											
3	157	281	57	198	328	90	229	8	138	260	41
10	242	9	158	292	52	180	329	102	222	351	140
17	331	107	255	15	141	279	65	186	312	91	234
24	73	204	339	103	244	13	149	274	56	184	319
Oct.											
1	166	289	68	206	337	98	239	17	148	268	51
8	250	18	167	301	61	189	338	111	231	359	150
15	339	118	263	24	149	290	73	195	320	102	242
22	83	212	347	113	254	22	157	284	65	193	326
29	176	296	78	214	346	106	250	25	157	276	61
Nov.											
5	259	27	177	309	70	197	348	119	240	7	161
12	347	129	270	33	158	300	81	203	329	112	250
19	91	221	355	123	262	31	164	295	73	202	334
26	185	305	88	223	355	115	259	34	165	285	70
Dec.											
3	268	34	187	317	79	205	359	127	249	16	171
10	356	138	279	41	168	310	89	211	340	120	259
17	99	230	3	134	270	40	172	305	81	211	343
24	194	313	97	232	4	124	267	44	173	294	78
31	277	42	198	325	87	214	9	135	257	25	181

MOON SIGN TABLES

	1921	1922	1923	1924	1925	1926	1927	1928	1929	1930
Jan. 1	194	317	80	211	5	127	250	23	176	297
8	280	41	177	313	90	211	349	123	260	22
15	4	141	275	41	175	312	86	211	346	123
22	101	239	3	127	272	51	172	297	83	221
29	203	325	88	222	13	135	258	34	184	306
Feb. 5	289	49	187	321	99	220	359	131	269	31
12	14	149	284	49	185	320	95	219	356	131
19	110	249	11	135	281	59	181	305	93	230
26	211	334	96	233	21	144	266	45	191	314
Mar. 5	297	58	197	343	107	230	8	153	276	41
12	23	157	294	69	194	328	105	238	6	139
19	119	258	19	157	292	68	189	327	104	238
26	219	343	104	258	29	153	275	70	199	323
Apr. 2	305	68	205	352	115	239	16	163	284	51
9	33	166	303	77	204	337	114	247	14	149
16	130	266	28	164	303	76	198	335	115	246
23	227	351	114	268	38	161	285	79	208	331
30	313	78	213	1	123	250	25	172	292	61
May 7	42	176	313	85	212	348	123	255	23	160
14	141	274	37	173	314	84	207	344	125	254
21	236	359	123	277	47	169	295	88	217	339
28	321	88	222	11	131	259	34	181	301	70
June 4	50	186	321	94	220	358	131	264	31	171
11	152	282	45	182	324	92	215	354	135	263
18	245	7	134	285	56	177	305	96	226	347
25	329	97	232	20	139	268	44	190	310	78

MOON SIGN TABLES

July 2	58	197	329	103	229	9	139	273	40	181
9	162	291	54	192	333	101	223	4	144	272
16	254	15	144	294	65	185	315	104	236	355
23	338	106	242	28	148	276	54	198	319	87
30	67	208	337	112	238	20	147	282	49	191
Aug. 6	171	299	62	202	341	110	231	15	152	281
13	264	24	153	302	74	194	324	114	244	4
20	347	114	253	36	157	284	65	206	328	95
27	76	218	345	120	248	29	156	290	59	200
Sept. 3	179	309	70	213	350	119	239	25	161	290
10	273	32	162	312	83	203	332	124	252	13
17	356	122	264	44	166	293	75	214	337	105
24	86	227	354	128	258	38	165	298	70	208
Oct. 1	188	318	78	223	358	128	248	35	169	298
8	281	41	170	322	91	212	340	134	260	23
15	5	132	274	52	175	303	85	222	345	115
22	97	235	8	136	269	46	174	306	81	216
29	196	327	87	233	7	137	257	44	179	307
Nov. 5	289	50	178	332	99	221	349	144	268	31
12	13	142	283	61	183	313	93	231	353	126
19	107	243	12	144	279	54	183	315	91	225
26	206	335	96	241	17	145	266	52	189	314
Dec. 3	297	59	187	343	106	230	359	154	276	39
10	21	152	291	70	190	324	101	239	1	137
17	117	252	21	153	289	63	191	324	99	234
24	216	343	105	249	28	152	275	59	199	322
31	305	67	197	352	115	237	9	162	285	47

MOON SIGN TABLES

	1931	1932	1933	1934	1935	1936	1937	1938	1939	1940
Jan. 1	61	196	346	107	231	8	156	277	41	181
8	162	294	70	193	333	104	240	5	145	275
15	257	20	158	294	68	190	329	105	239	0
22	342	108	255	32	152	278	67	202	323	88
29	68	207	353	116	239	19	164	286	50	191
Feb. 5	171	302	78	203	342	113	248	15	153	284
12	267	28	168	302	78	198	339	113	248	8
19	351	116	266	40	161	286	78	210	332	96
26	77	217	2	124	248	29	172	294	59	200
Mar. 5	179	324	86	213	350	135	256	24	161	306
12	276	48	177	311	87	218	348	123	257	29
19	1	137	277	48	170	308	89	218	340	119
26	87	241	10	132	258	53	180	302	70	223
Apr. 2	187	334	94	223	358	144	264	34	169	314
9	285	57	185	321	95	227	356	133	265	38
16	9	146	287	56	179	317	99	226	349	128
23	96	250	19	140	268	61	189	310	80	231
30	196	343	102	232	7	153	273	43	179	323
May 7	293	66	193	332	103	237	4	144	272	47
14	17	155	297	65	187	327	108	235	357	139
21	107	259	28	148	279	69	198	318	90	240
28	205	351	111	241	17	161	282	52	189	331
June 4	301	75	202	343	111	246	13	154	281	56
11	25	165	306	73	195	337	117	244	5	150
18	117	267	37	157	288	78	207	327	99	248
25	215	0	120	250	28	169	291	60	200	339

MOON SIGN TABLES

July 2	309	83	211	353	119	254	23	164	289	64
9	33	176	315	82	203	348	125	253	13	160
16	126	276	46	165	297	87	216	336	108	258
23	226	8	130	258	39	177	300	69	210	347
30	318	92	221	2	128	262	33	173	297	72
Aug. 6	41	187	323	91	211	359	133	261	22	171
13	135	285	54	175	306	97	224	346	117	269
20	237	16	139	267	49	185	309	78	220	355
27	326	100	232	10	136	270	44	181	307	80
Sept. 3	50	197	331	100	220	9	142	270	31	180
10	144	296	62	184	314	107	232	355	125	279
17	246	24	147	277	58	194	317	89	228	4
24	335	108	243	18	145	278	55	189	316	89
Oct. 1	59	206	341	108	229	17	152	278	40	188
8	152	306	70	193	323	117	240	4	135	288
15	255	32	155	287	66	203	325	100	236	13
22	344	117	253	27	154	287	65	198	324	98
29	68	215	351	116	239	26	162	286	50	196
Nov. 5	161	316	78	202	332	126	248	12	145	297
12	264	41	163	298	74	212	333	111	244	22
19	353	126	262	36	162	297	74	208	332	108
26	77	223	1	124	248	34	172	294	59	205
Dec. 3	171	325	87	210	343	135	257	20	156	305
10	271	50	171	309	82	220	342	121	253	30
17	1	135	271	46	170	306	81	217	340	118
24	87	231	11	132	257	43	181	302	66	215
31	182	333	95	218	354	143	266	28	167	313

MOON SIGN TABLES

	1941	1942	1943	1944	1945	1946	1947	1948	1949	1950
Jan. 1	326	88	212	353	135	258	23	165	305	70
8	50	176	316	86	220	348	126	256	29	163
15	141	276	50	169	312	87	220	340	123	261
22	239	12	133	259	52	182	303	69	224	354
29	334	96	221	2	143	256	33	174	314	78
Feb. 5	57	186	324	95	227	358	134	265	37	173
12	150	285	58	178	321	96	228	349	132	271
19	250	20	142	267	62	190	312	78	234	2
26	342	104	231	11	152	274	43	182	323	86
Mar. 5	65	196	332	116	236	8	142	286	46	182
12	158	295	67	199	329	107	236	10	140	282
19	261	28	150	290	72	198	320	102	243	10
26	351	112	242	34	162	282	53	204	332	94
Apr. 2	74	205	340	125	245	17	152	294	55	191
9	166	306	74	209	337	118	244	19	148	292
16	270	36	158	300	81	206	328	112	252	19
23	0	120	252	42	170	290	64	212	340	103
30	83	214	351	133	254	25	163	302	64	199
May 7	175	316	82	218	346	128	252	28	158	302
14	279	45	166	311	89	215	336	123	260	28
21	9	128	262	50	179	299	73	222	349	112
28	92	222	1	141	263	34	173	310	74	207
June 4	184	326	91	226	356	137	261	36	168	310
11	287	54	174	322	98	224	345	134	268	37
18	17	138	271	60	187	308	81	231	357	122
25	102	231	12	149	272	42	183	318	83	217

MOON SIGN TABLES

July 2	194	335	99	234	7	145	270	44	179	318
9	296	63	183	332	106	233	353	144	276	45
16	25	147	279	70	196	318	90	241	5	132
23	111	240	21	157	281	52	192	327	91	227
30	205	343	108	242	18	153	278	52	190	327
Aug. 6	304	72	192	342	115	241	3	153	287	53
13	33	156	288	80	203	327	99	251	13	141
20	119	250	30	165	289	63	201	336	99	238
27	216	351	117	251	29	162	287	61	200	335
Sept. 3	314	80	202	351	125	249	13	162	296	61
10	41	166	297	90	211	336	108	260	21	149
17	127	261	39	174	297	74	209	345	107	249
24	227	0	125	260	39	171	295	71	210	344
Oct. 1	323	68	211	359	135	257	23	170	306	69
8	49	174	306	99	220	344	119	269	30	157
15	135	272	47	183	305	85	217	353	116	259
22	236	9	134	269	47	180	303	81	217	353
29	334	95	221	7	144	265	31	179	315	78
Nov. 5	58	182	317	107	229	352	130	277	39	165
12	143	283	55	192	314	94	226	1	126	269
19	244	18	142	280	55	190	311	91	226	3
26	343	104	229	17	153	274	39	189	323	86
Dec. 3	67	190	328	114	237	0	140	285	47	174
10	153	292	64	200	324	103	235	9	136	277
17	252	28	149	289	64	199	319	100	234	12
24	352	112	237	27	162	282	47	199	332	95
31	76	198	338	123	246	9	150	293	57	180

MOON SIGN TABLES

	1951	1952	1953	1954	1955	1956	1957	1958	1959	1960
Jan. 1	193	335	115	237	5	146	285	47	178	317
8	296	66	198	331	106	237	8	143	277	47
15	29	150	293	70	199	320	104	241	9	131
22	113	239	35	161	283	51	207	351	93	222
29	204	344	123	245	16	154	284	54	188	325
Feb. 5	304	75	207	340	115	245	17	152	287	55
12	37	159	301	80	207	329	112	252	17	140
19	122	249	45	169	291	61	216	339	101	233
26	214	352	132	253	27	162	303	65	199	333
Mar. 5	313	96	216	349	125	265	27	180	297	75
12	45	180	309	90	215	351	121	248	25	161
19	130	273	53	178	299	86	224	548	109	258
26	225	14	141	261	37	185	311	72	308	255
Apr. 2	323	104	225	357	135	273	36	168	307	83
9	53	189	319	100	223	359	131	271	33	169
16	137	284	62	186	307	96	232	357	117	269
23	234	23	150	270	45	194	319	81	216	5
30	334	111	235	6	145	281	45	157	317	91
May 7	62	197	329	109	222	7	141	279	42	177
14	146	295	70	195	316	107	240	5	127	279
21	243	32	158	280	54	203	327	91	224	14
28	344	120	244	15	155	289	54	187	326	99
June 4	70	205	340	117	241	15	152	287	51	185
11	154	305	78	204	325	117	249	14	136	288
18	251	42	166	290	62	213	335	100	233	24
25	363	128	252	25	164	298	62	197	334	108

MOON SIGN TABLES

July 2	79	213	351	125	250	24	163	295	59	194
9	164	315	87	212	335	125	258	22	146	296
16	260	52	174	299	71	223	344	110	243	33
23	2	137	260	36	172	307	70	208	342	117
30	88	222	1	133	258	33	173	304	68	204
Aug. 6	173	323	97	220	345	134	268	29	156	305
13	269	61	182	307	81	232	352	118	253	42
20	10	145	269	47	180	316	79	219	350	126
27	97	231	11	142	266	43	182	313	75	214
Sept. 3	183	331	107	228	354	142	277	38	165	314
10	280	70	191	316	92	240	1	126	264	50
17	18	154	277	58	188	324	88	229	359	134
24	105	241	20	152	274	53	190	323	84	225
Oct. 1	192	340	116	236	3	152	286	46	174	323
8	290	78	200	324	105	248	10	134	275	58
15	26	162	286	68	197	332	98	238	8	142
22	112	252	26	161	270	63	190	332	92	235
29	201	350	125	245	11	162	295	35	182	334
Nov. 5	301	86	208	332	113	256	19	143	285	66
12	35	170	296	76	206	340	108	246	17	150
19	121	262	36	170	290	73	208	341	100	244
26	209	0	153	254	19	172	302	64	190	344
Dec. 3	312	94	217	341	123	264	27	153	293	74
10	45	178	307	84	216	348	119	254	26	158
17	129	271	45	179	299	81	217	349	109	252
24	217	11	140	263	27	183	310	73	198	355
31	321	103	225	352	132	273	34	164	302	

MOON SIGN TABLES

	1961	1962	1963	1964	1965	1966	1967	1968	1969	1970
Jan. 1	96	217	350	128	26	27	163	298	76	197
8	179	315	89	217	350	126	260	27	161	297
15	275	53	179	302	86	225	349	112	257	36
22	18	141	263	65	189	311	74	207	359	122
29	105	225	1	135	275	35	173	307	85	206
Feb. 5	189	323	98	225	0	134	270	35	171	305
12	284	64	187	310	95	234	357	121	267	45
19	26	149	272	46	197	320	81	218	7	130
26	113	234	11	144	283	45	182	314	93	156
Mar. 5	198	331	109	245	9	142	280	54	180	313
12	293	73	195	332	105	244	5	142	277	53
19	34	159	280	71	204	329	90	243	15	139
26	122	243	19	166	291	54	190	338	101	226
Apr. 2	208	340	119	253	19	151	290	63	189	323
9	304	82	204	340	114	252	14	150	288	61
16	42	167	289	81	213	337	99	252	23	147
23	130	253	28	176	299	64	198	347	109	235
30	216	349	128	261	26	161	298	71	197	333
May 7	315	90	212	348	127	260	23	158	299	70
14	51	176	298	91	222	345	109	261	31	155
21	137	263	36	185	307	74	207	357	117	245
28	225	359	136	270	35	172	306	81	205	344
June 4	325	98	222	355	137	268	31	168	309	78
11	60	184	308	99	231	353	119	270	42	163
18	146	272	45	195	315	82	217	6	126	253
25	233	10	144	279	43	183	315	89	214	355

MOON SIGN TABLES

July 2	336	106	230	6	147	276	40	178	318	87
9	70	191	318	108	241	1	129	278	51	171
16	154	281	54	204	324	91	227	14	134	261
23	241	21	153	288	52	193	323	98	223	335
30	345	115	239	16	156	286	47	188	327	97
Aug. 6	79	200	327	116	250	10	138	288	60	180
13	163	289	66	212	333	99	238	22	144	270
20	250	32	161	296	61	203	331	106	233	14
27	353	124	246	27	164	295	55	199	335	106
Sept. 3	88	208	336	126	259	19	147	297.	68	189
10	171	297	77	220	342	108	249	30	152	279
17	259	41	170	304	72	212	340	114	243	22
24	1	134	254	37	173	304	64	208	344	114
Oct. 1	97	217	345	136	267	28	155	308	76	198
8	181	306	88	228	351	117	259	38	161	289
15	270	50	179	312	82	220	349	122	254	31
22	10	143	262	47	182	313	72	217	353	123
29	105	226	352	146	275	37	163	318	84	207
Nov. 5	189	315	97	237	359	127	268	47	168	299
12	281	58	188	320	93	228	358	130	264	39
19	19	151	271	57	191	321	82	225	3	131
26	113	235	1	157	282	45	173	308	92	215
Dec. 3	197	326	105	245	7	138	276	55	176	310
10	291	66	197	329	102	237	7	139	273	47
17	30	159	280	63	202	329	91	234	13	139
24	121	243	11	166	291	53	183	337	101	223
31	205	336	113	254	14	148	284	64	185	319

MOON SIGN TABLES

	1971	1972	1973	1974	1975	1976	1977	1978	1979	1980
Jan. 1	335	108	246	7	147	279	56	179	318	90
8	71	198	332	107	243	6	144	278	54	176
15	158	283	69	207	328	93	240	18	139	263
22	244	20	169	292	54	192	339	102	224	4
29	344	117	255	17	156	288	64	189	327	99
Feb. 5	81	204	342	115	253	14	153	287	63	184
12	167	291	79	216	337	101	251	26	147	271
19	252	30	177	300	62	203	347	110	233	14
26	353	126	263	27	164	297	72	199	334	109
Mar. 5	91	224	351	124	262	34	162	296	72	204
12	176	312	60	224	346	122	262	34	156	293
19	261	55	184	309	72	226	356	118	244	37
26	1	149	270	37	172	320	80	208	343	130
Apr. 2	100	233	359	134	270	43	170	307	80	213
9	184	320	101	232	354	131	273	42	164	302
16	271	64	194	317	82	235	5	126	254	45
23	9	158	278	47	181	329	88	217	352	139
30	109	242	8	145	278	52	178	318	88	222
May 7	193	329	111	240	3	140	282	50	173	312
14	281	73	203	324	92	243	14	134	264	54
21	19	167	287	55	191	337	97	226	3	147
28	117	251	16	156	286	61	187	328	96	231
June 4	201	339	120	249	11	151	291	59	180	323
11	291	81	153	333	102	251	23	143	273	63
18	29	176	296	64	201	346	106	234	13	155
25	125	260	25	167	294	69	196	338	105	239

MOON-SIGN TABLES

July 2	209	350	129	257	19	162	299	68	188	334
9	300	90	222	341	111	261	32	152	282	72
16	40	184	305	72	212	354	115	243	23	163
23	133	268	5	176	307	78	206	347	104	248
30	217	0	137	267	27	172	308	77	197	344
Aug. 6	309	99	230	350	120	271	40	161	290	83
13	51	192	314	81	222	2	124	252	33	171
20	172	276	45	185	312	86	217	356	123	256
27	225	10	146	276	36	62	317	86	206	353
Sept. 3	317	109	238	0	128	281	48	170	299	93
10	61	200	322	90	232	10	132	262	43	180
17	151	284	56	193	321	94	228	4	132	264
24	234	20	125	284	45	191	326	94	215	2
Oct. 1	325	120	246	9	137	291	56	179	308	103
8	70	238	330	101	241	19	140	273	51	189
15	160	292	36	201	330	102	238	12	140	273
22	243	28	165	292	54	199	336	102	225	10
29	334	130	254	17	146	301	64	187	318	112
Nov. 5	79	217	338	112	249	27	148	284	59	197
12	169	301	76	210	339	111	247	21	148	282
19	253	36	175	300	63	207	347	110	234	18
26	344	139	262	25	156	310	73	195	329	120
Dec. 3	86	226	346	122	257	36	157	294	67	206
10	177	310	83	220	347	121	255	31	156	292
17	261	45	185	308	12	216	356	118	242	28
24	355	148	271	33	167	318	81	203	340	128
31	95	228	354	132	265	44	166	303	76	217

MOON SIGN TABLES

		1981	1982	1983	1984	1985	1986	1987	1988	1989	1990
Jan.	1	227	350	128	261	36	162	299	72	206	333
	8	315	88	225	346	126	260	36	156	297	71
	15	52	188	309	73	225	358	120	243	37	168
	22	149	273	35	176	319	82	206	347	130	252
	29	235	0	136	270	44	172	307	81	214	343
Feb.	5	324	98	234	355	134	269	44	165	305	82
	12	63	196	318	81	236	6	128	252	47	176
	19	157	281	45	184	328	90	217	355	139	260
	26	242	10	144	280	52	181	316	90	222	352
Mar.	5	332	108	243	15	142	280	52	186	313	93
	12	74	204	327	103	246	14	137	275	57	184
	19	166	289	55	207	337	98	227	18	148	268
	26	251	19	153	301	61	190	325	111	231	0
Apr.	2	340	119	251	24	150	291	60	195	321	103
	9	84	212	335	113	255	23	145	286	68	193
	16	176	296	65	216	346	106	237	26	157	276
	23	259	28	164	309	70	198	336	119	240	8
	30	348	129	259	33	159	301	68	203	331	113
May	7	93	221	343	124	263	32	152	296	74	202
	14	185	305	75	224	355	115	246	35	165	285
	21	268	36	174	317	79	206	347	127	249	17
	28	357	139	267	42	169	311	77	211	341	122
June	4	101	230	351	135	271	41	161	307	82	211
	11	194	313	83	234	4	124	254	45	173	295
	18	277	44	185	325	88	215	357	135	258	27
	25	8	149	275	50	180	319	86	219	352	130

MOON SIGN TABLES

July 2	109	239	359	145	280	50	169	317	91	220
9	202	323	92	244	12	133	262	55	181	304
16	286	53	195	333	96	225	7	144	266	37
23	18	157	285	58	191	328	95	227	3	138
30	118	248	8	154	289	58	178	326	101	168
Aug. 6	210	332	100	254	20	142	271	66	189	313
13	294	63	205	342	104	235	15	152	274	48
20	29	165	294	66	201	336	104	236	13	147
27	128	257	17	163	299	66	188	334	111	236
Sept. 3	218	341	109	264	28	151	281	75	198	321
10	302	74	213	351	112	246	23	161	282	59
17	39	174	302	75	181	345	112	245	22	156
24	138	267	27	171	309	74	197	342	121	244
Oct. 1	226	349	119	274	36	159	291	84	206	329
8	310	85	221	0	120	257	31	170	291	69
15	49	183	311	84	220	354	120	255	30	166
22	148	272	36	180	319	82	206	351	130	252
29	235	357	130	282	45	167	302	92	215	337
Nov. 5	319	95	229	8	129	267	40	178	300	78
12	57	193	318	94	228	4	128	265	38	175
19	158	280	44	189	329	90	184	1	139	261
26	244	5	141	290	54	175	313	100	224	345
Dec. 3	328	105	238	17	139	276	49	186	310	87
10	65	203	326	103	236	14	136	274	47	185
17	167	289	52	200	337	99	222	12	147	270
24	252	13	151	298	62	184	323	108	232	355
31	337	113	248	24	149	284	59	194	320	95

MOON SIGN TABLES

	1991	1992	1993	1994	1995	1996	1997	1998	1999	2000
Jan. 1	110	243	16	145	280	53	185	317	92	224
8	206	326	107	243	16	137	278	55	186	307
15	290	54	209	338	100	225	21	148	270	36
22	18	158	300	62	190	329	111	231	2	139
29	118	252	24	154	289	62	194	325	101	232
Feb. 5	214	335	115	254	24	146	286	66	194	316
12	298	63	219	346	108	235	30	156	278	47
19	28	166	309	70	200	336	120	239	12	147
26	127	261	332	163	299	71	203	334	111	240
Mar. 5	222	356	123	265	32	167	294	76	202	337
12	306	87	228	354	116	259	39	165	286	71
19	39	188	318	78	210	359	129	248	21	170
26	137	281	42	171	309	91	212	342	121	260
Apr. 2	230	5	132	275	40	175	304	86	210	345
9	314	98	236	4	124	270	47	174	294	82
16	48	197	327	87	219	8	137	257	30	180
23	148	289	51	179	320	98	221	350	132	268
30	239	13	142	284	49	183	315	94	219	353
May 7	322	108	244	13	132	280	55	182	303	92
14	57	197	335	96	227	18	145	267	38	190
21	158	297	60	188	330	106	230	0	141	277
28	247	21	153	292	58	191	326	102	228	1
June 4	331	118	253	21	141	290	64	191	312	101
11	65	217	343	105	235	28	153	276	47	200
18	168	305	68	198	339	115	238	10	150	285
25	256	29	164	300	67	199	336	111	237	10

MOON SIGN TABLES

July 2	340	128	262	29	151	299	193	199	321	110
9	73	227	351	114	244	38	161	285	56	210
16	177	314	76	209	348	124	246	21	158	294
23	265	38	175	309	75	208	346	119	245	19
30	349	136	272	37	160	307	83	207	331	118
Aug. 6	83	237	359	123	254	48	169	293	67	218
13	186	322	84	220	356	133	254	32	166	303
20	274	47	184	318	83	218	355	129	253	29
27	359	145	282	45	170	316	93	215	340	127
Sept. 3	93	246	8	131	265	56	178	301	78	226
10	194	331	92	231	4	141	263	43	174	311
17	282	57	193	327	92	228	4	138	261	39
24	8	153	292	53	178	325	103	223	348	137
Oct. 1	104	255	17	139	276	64	187	309	89	234
8	202	340	102	241	13	150	273	52	183	319
15	290	67	201	337	99	238	12	148	269	49
22	16	163	301	62	186	335	111	232	356	147
29	115	262	26	147	287	72	195	318	99	243
Nov. 5	211	348	111	249	22	158	283	60	193	327
12	298	76	210	347	107	247	21	157	278	58
19	24	173	309	71	194	346	119	240	4	158
26	125	270	34	157	297	80	204	328	108	251
Dec. 3	221	356	121	257	32	165	293	68	202	335
10	306	85	219	356	116	255	31	166	286	66
17	32	184	317	79	202	357	127	250	13	169
24	134	279	42	166	305	89	212	338	116	260
31	230	4	131	265	41	173	303	77	212	343

Your Unique Sun and Moon Combination: How Your Inner and Outer Beings Merge

Since the luminaries are the most important bodies in any chart, the positions of the Sun and Moon, and their relationship to each other, furnish an important key to the understanding of human nature. The following exploration of these factors reveals the manner in which the individuality (Sun) is expressed through the personality (Moon).

Sun in Capricorn—Moon in Aries: In the energetic sign Aries, the restless, emotional, and impulsive implications of the Moon are emphasized. Adventure and exploration will hold your interest. You are usually fascinated by anything new. The Sun in Capricorn and the Moon in Aries form a combination that indicates a great capacity for leadership. Aries implies an urge for action, for starting new enterprises. Capricorn notes a sense of responsibility as well as the urge for accomplishment. It also indicates the presence of obstacles to be overcome. Therefore, you will want to lead in the field of new accomplishments—action and leadership being the means used for your achievement. With this combination, you are seldom able to remain subservient to others for long, for you are motivated to act from your own initiative. Meeting obstacles or faced with disagreements with superiors, you may have the problem of controlling your temper. However, when you are placed in a position of authority, you are usually conscientious and responsible, although you may be rather exacting in requiring quick obedience and strict discipline from others—the very elements you yourself could not tolerate from your superiors. You may be intensely patriotic and much concerned with the protection of your home or your country.

Sun in Capricorn—Moon in Taurus: The Moon is well placed in Taurus, for here its restless element is stabilized and its reflective nature is emphasized. The Moon is said to be exalted in Taurus. You are generally courteous though conservative in manner. Taurus is a fixed sign, making you somewhat determined. With the Sun in Capricorn, a harmonious combination is formed. The fixed determination of Taurus and the desire of Capricorn for accomplishment make an excellent combination for realizing your desires. There may be many obstacles in your life, but you will enjoy the process of mastering them. You may take an interest in science—material or natural science rather than the speculative or abstract—for both Taurus and Capricorn are earthy. In some cases, you may remain satisfied where you are, without having any higher ambition. You may even be somewhat indulgent of your senses, especially as to diet. As Capricorn is a cautious sign and Taurus rules money, you may develop miserly habits in your efforts to secure and hold your possessions. You may also have that much-sought-after quality of being entertaining without being boring, making you popular.

Sun in Capricorn—Moon in Gemini: The Moon in Gemini indicates an active, investigating mentality, with possibly a superficial interest in numerous subjects rather than any real depth of thought. This is owning to the natural restlessness indicated by the Moon. Combined with the Sun in Capricorn, the superficiality is to a certain extent overcome, for the natural patience and concentration of Capricorn harness the impatience of Gemini to more concrete endeavor and definite accomplishments. This is an excellent Sun-Moon combination for the scientist or research worker whose inquiring mind searches for the secrets of matter. It is also a good combination for the writer, for it indicates a capacity for patient, steady work and serious mental discipline. Being very observant and having an alert mentality, you may become too aware of the imperfections existing about you and, consequently, develop an irritability and intolerance about error. To guard against making yourself unpleasant to others and becoming depressed yourself, you should not allow yourself to wallow in melancholia. You can prevent this by deliberate self-discipline, by striving to control your thinking and directing your thoughts toward acquiring more profound knowledge, more definite information. You will, thus, sweep away your depression and achieve a satisfaction worth striving for. The Capricorn-Gemini combination specifically indicates a possibility for accomplishment through control of the mind. Matters concerning health and the healing profession will be of deep interest to you. You may want to devote some of your time to a study of these fields.

Sun in Capricorn—Moon in Cancer: The Moon is in its own sign in Cancer, indicating an intense patriotism and a fondness for home and parents, but somewhat changeable moods. You will have a restrained and affectionate disposition, with a distinct leaning toward your mother. Combined with the Sun in Capricorn, a potentially inharmonious combination is formed. In Cancer, the domestic interests of the Moon seem to be blocked or opposed by a weight of public responsibility. You may have a difficult problem in balancing your career with your domestic life. Either your career will interfere with your domestic happiness or your home and family may stand in the way of your success in that career. You will need to exercise much effort and patience in order to produce a harmonious blend between the two. As the Moon in Cancer indicates unusual love of home and country, your efforts may be directed toward maintaining and protecting one or both of these. Matters concerning your relationship with others— marriage, partnerships, even war—will claim your attention.

Sun in Capricorn—Moon in Leo: With the Moon in Leo, you are proud but generous. Leo, the "heart" sign of the zodiac, sublimates the love nature of the Moon and stabilizes its restless vacillation. Combined with the Sun in Capricorn, this makes you a practical, capable, and warm-hearted individual. The warmth of the Leo nature softens the hard, cold outlook of Capricorn. Capricorn strives for attainment, while Leo tends to have a kingly bearing. Therefore, you love to shine before the public and will work hard to gain this result. This combination of Sun and Moon suggests practical administrative abilities. You are conservative and cautious, yet considerate. You will be sincere and unshakable in your opinions, tending more toward conventional and established lines of thought than any revolutionary extreme. However, should a new idea impress itself upon your consciousness in some way, you will cling to it through every adversity. You have a powerful creative urge—for good or ill. If it is properly harnessed and controlled, you may achieve lasting fame, probably for your creative or dramatic accomplishments.

Sun in Capricorn—Moon in Virgo: With the Moon in Virgo, you have a practical, analytical mentality. Your concept of the ideal is so strong that you may become very unhappy in noting the imperfections about you. Combined with the Sun in Capricorn, this makes you a capable and painstaking individual. Capricorn promises effort and accomplishment, while Virgo exhibits a love of detailed perfection. With this combination of Sun and Moon, you will work long and patiently to produce the perfection you envision. You may not be overly affectionate or emotional, for the natural austerity of Capricorn blended with the purity of the sign of "the Virgin" does not encourage ordinary emotional expression or attachment. You will be capable of hard, prolonged, and detailed work but will not be very ambitious, unless you try to reverse this tendency. You will probably be content to plod along in the groove life gives to you, without directly seeking fame or fortune. However, honor may come to you—and it will be because you have earned and deserved it. If you are at all religiously or philosophically inclined, it will be in a practical way.

Sun in Capricorn—Moon in Libra: With the Moon in Libra, you will weigh the report of the senses, consider all sides of a problem, and attempt to reach a just conclusion therefrom. The Sun in Capricorn brings in the love of effort, a tendency to struggle for a cause—here, peace, justice, or a balanced position. Libra is the sign indicating one's relationships with others. Capricorn stands for the urge for attainment. In some cases, you will be continually striving to attain a victory. This is an excellent characteristic for the strategist or the lawyer, but it does not yield domestic harmony, for you will too often take your partner as your opponent. When inharmony comes about, the difficulty may also be based on your unvarying tendency to see both sides of any question. You will argue today on one side, tomorrow on the other. You can see the truth on both sides. When opposed, you will seek a balance by bringing up the opposite side. If left unopposed, you can usually arrive at a just and balanced conclusion by yourself. In some cases, you may tend to switch from side to side in an argument, from point to point, with amazing facility. This process should result in an intensive knowledge about a subject of great interest to you, which you then pass on to mankind.

Sun in Capricorn—Moon in Scorpio: With the Moon in Scorpio, you have an enterprising, forceful, and courageous personality. The best lunar qualities are not revealed in this sign, however, for the emotional nature is too greatly emphasized. With the Sun in Capricorn, a very powerful and intense combination is indicated. The emotional element of Scorpio modifies the restrictive coldness of Capricorn, while the austerity of Capricorn checks the more erratic and extreme desires of Scorpio. With the ability of concentration and effort clearly marked, and with the desire active, ambition is naturally present. Within certain limits, whatever you set your mind to do, you may attain, for you have the necessary patience as well as a fixity of purpose. Both death and birth are ruled by Scorpio, which means it would be well for you to set yourself to constructive, creative endeavors. In some cases, you may release destructive forces. This is an excellent combination of Sun and Moon for a physician or surgeon, for Capricorn gives steadiness and patience, while Scorpio denotes a potential capacity for saving lives. The unusual will also claim your attention.

Sun in Capricorn—Moon in Sagittarius: With the Moon in Sagittarius, you will be hopeful, frank, and generous. Your mentality will be alert and farseeing—but with a tendency to cover a host of subjects without delving deeply into any one. With the Sun in Capricorn, the natural optimism of Sagittarius is limited, but patience is shown in a search for fundamentals. If you give any thought to religion or philosophy, it will be from a concrete, utilitarian viewpoint rather than the mystical. There usually is, however, a leaning toward science. Often, there is an ability for clear and forceful expression (sometimes with a note of sadness, melancholy, or even horror) in speech or writing. You may have a problem with drink or drugs, which you may use as a means of escape from responsibility or depression. At its best, the Capricorn-Sagittarius combination shows a keen appreciation of law and order. At the other extreme, it denotes that you may try to take the law into your own hands. Matters concerning places of confinement will claim your attention at some time in life.

Sun in Capricorn—Moon in Capricorn: The coldness of Capricorn makes this an unfavorable place for the moon. Personal happiness and emotional expression are often buried under a sense of responsibility and purpose. With the Sun also in Capricorn, the qualities of this sign are overemphasized. On the one hand, you may be burdened with obligation, and perhaps fear and apprehension as well, plugging away at your work and seldom, if ever, confiding in others. Your nature is too cold and distrustful. On the other hand, you may, by unusual personal effort, achieve something outstanding. You have a vigorous personality and will put forth great efforts in your specific field.

Sun in Capricorn—Moon in Aquarius: With the Moon in Aquarius, you have a friendly, independent, and unconventional personality. Eccentric, original, or unusual subjects hold your attention. With the Sun in Capricorn, you are a very capable individual. The cold, restrictive atmosphere frequently associated with Capricorn is offset by a friendly and tolerant outlook. Aquarius is a sign that indicates the basic friendship theoretically existing between all peoples, and that proposes the essential oneness of humanity. With the Capricorn-Aquarius combination, your efforts will be directed toward achieving a state of peace, either between individuals or nations. You are patient, persevering, and original—qualities that will enable you to accomplish something unique. The nature of Capricorn is to bind, harness, and utilize. With Aquarius, a sign ruling electric power, you may do well in electrical engineering. Matters concerning money, possessions, and financial systems will also interest you.

Sun in Capricorn—Moon in Pisces: With the Moon in Pisces promises a sensitive, sympathetic, and imaginative mentality. Because of your intense sympathy and understanding, you may often take upon yourself the sufferings of others. With the Sun in Capricorn, an outstanding combination is found, especially in the field of mental activity. The sensitivity and understandings of the Pisces Moon are utilized in purposeful strivings toward some achievement. Capricorn provides a solid backbone, a practical, concrete base, stiffening the soft, yielding, and pliable Pisces. You will do your best work in solitude, undisturbed by others. This is a fine combination for one whose work is to delve into the secrets of others and bring them out to public gaze. Or, it may be the secrets of nature you will reveal. In some cases, you may have the ambition and the apparent ability, but lack the energy or drive to accomplish anything. In such a case, you will do better under the auspices of some institution rather than working independently.

Your Combined Ascendant and Sun Sign Portrait: A Blend of Who You Really Are and How Others See You

Your Sun Sign describes that core identity you possess, that source of your sense of self, and the purpose that guides you through life. Your Ascendant is the way in which that self gets expressed, the filter through which you see the world and through which the world sees you. Not only is each combination different, but every person has a unique way of manifesting it. As the length of days and nights varies in different latitudes, the guidelines below may be less than accurate, so try reading the message before or after the one suggested, to see if it is more helpful in deepening your understanding of how you manifest your unique self in the world.

If you were born between 4:00 A.M. and 6:00 A.M., your Ascendant is the same as your Sun—Capricorn. This double influence of the planet Saturn intensifies the seriousness and practicality with which you face the world. The truth is that Capricorn is a sign of great sensitivity, so much so that you need to hide behind all manner of defenses. This often takes the form of work—and overwork—or an exaggerated concern with caution, overintellectualization, and various other self-protective measures.

Knowing this can help you deal with this issue with tenderness and tact and with respect for your own need for privacy. Acknowledge your own deep concern for the rights and protection of others, as well.

If you were born between 6:00 A.M. and 8:00 A.M., your Ascendant is Aquarius. The planet that moves sideways in its very distinct, eccentric orbit, Uranus, rules this sign. Likewise, this individual's manner of viewing the world may seem to others a bit askew. With a basic concern that what is appropriate gets done, this friendly but unpredictable—alternating between domineering and laid back—approach to action meets with a variety of responses; indirect and sometimes a bit arrogant, your manner may be offensive to some. Your lack of judgment of others and apparent, sincere concern for the well-being of all could make your ill-placed global sense of responsibility a laudable, likable trait.

If you were born between 8:00 A.M. and 10:00 A.M., your Ascendant is Pisces. This softens an otherwise harsh view of the world, with Neptune allowing for greater compassion and an intuitive sense of where others are at—and how to connect most gently with them. Heightened sensitivity to the suffering of others, however, means that you take on even more responsibility than the average Capricorn for righting the wrongs of those who are less able to take constructive steps to improve their own situations. Receptive to the suggestions of others, as well, with your enlightened sensibilities, you solicit help as needed.

If you were born between 10:00 A.M. and noon, your Ascendant is Aries. The combined energy of Mars—the planet ruling your Ascendant—and Saturn—governing your Sun Sign—is an unbeatable combination for getting things done. Moving forward to take charge of a situation is very much your forte—and you have the wherewithal to make sure the responsibilities are delegated so that each job gets successfully completed as well. Your instinctive sense of your best next step is coupled with the confidence and daring to pull it off. Beware a somewhat overwhelming impact upon others, who may be startled by the speed and force behind your actions.

If you were born between noon and 2:00 P.M., your Ascendant is Taurus. Venus, ruling this sign, makes you quite able to perceive not only how to approach people to disarm them, but also how to make a situation pleasant for everyone concerned. Taurus is a sign that appreciates comfort and luxury, so your general approach to life is probably a bit less severe and stark than it would be with any other rising sign combined with a Capricorn Sun. You are more stable and certainly attached to the status quo—as long as it is bringing you the personal security, sense of well-being, and comfort that you have become accustomed to enjoying.

If you were born between 2:00 P.M. and 4:00 P.M., your Ascendant is Gemini. Though communicative—with Mercury influencing your approach to others—you are also somewhat indecisive and hesitant about moving forward, let alone taking any big steps. Seeing all sides of an issue, you are less apt to confidently take hold of a situation and move in any one direction; your sensitivity is to all sides of a situation, as you are greatly aware of the many possible directions in which you can go. Adept at conveying your ideas, you make a witty and engaging mental impact upon others you meet.

If you were born between 4:00 P.M. and 6:00 P.M., your Ascendant is Cancer. This sign—opposite your Sun Sign—is ruled by the Moon and as such brings with it a certain emotionality—humanizing your otherwise stern and pragmatic approach to life. Sensitive to the moods of others—and aware of your own as well—you have an instinctive compassion for the travails of people and a sincere concern for their personal well-being. Able to direct your own practical intuitions, you constructively improve the lot of others in a gentle, caring way that makes them appreciative of and well guided by your protective efforts on their behalf.

If you were born between 6:00 P.M. and 8:00 P.M., your Ascendant is Leo. The Sun governs this sign, shining its way on whatever path to success is being followed. With this combination, you are unlikely to fail, as the motivation to construct, build, and protect—stemming from your Capricorn Sun Sign—is given the boost by a sign that represents strength and daring, optimism and the ability to focus on the enjoyment of reaching any goal, playfully and with love: Leo. In every creative situation you invent, you enjoy playing the hero, giving your effort an extra dramatic flair that attracts the applause and adulation that keeps you well satisfied.

If you were born between 8:00 P.M. and 10:00 P.M., your Ascendant is Virgo. Ruled by Mercury, your ascending sign helps you to discern the details in every situation that needs correcting, as well as giving you the wherewithal to make the needed changes. A highly critical eye to the world—and an accurate one—may sometimes do less to serve your cause than you would think. Sometimes your focus on the practical and material imperfections that exist everywhere is merely a defense against your own more human, less fixable feelings. Ease up in always trying to improve a situation and serve others. Instead, try noticing the inherent perfection of life as it already is.

If you were born between 10:00 P.M. and midnight, your Ascendant is Libra. The Venus influence here emphasizes the relationship aspect of life, as you are always trying to harmonize interactions going on around you, no matter what your other goals are or how hard you are working toward achieving them. This sensitivity to the human side of all that goes on around you can be quite helpful to you in achieving your goals because others respond warmly to your sense of fairness. Your deepest wish and most sincere aim are to see that a peaceful atmosphere prevails despite any and all changes being made for the good of all.

If you were born between midnight and 2:00 A.M., your Ascendant is Scorpio. Pluto intensifies your approach to others and makes you even more secretive about your intentions, your personal self, and the inner motivations behind your actions. There may be a willfulness about you that causes others to resist even your most constructive suggestions for improving a situation. It is most helpful to call upon your deepest intuitions to find better ways of approaching others; let go of any suspicious and paranoid thoughts that make interactions and forward motions a fearful and risky enterprise. Avoid overly self-protective and manipulative ways of dealing with the world; they don't serve you.

If you were born between 2:00 A.M. and 4:00 A.M., your Ascendant is Sagittarius. Jupiter ruling your rising sign makes for a lively and enthusiastic approach to the world. Eager to fulfill your social role, you are well-equipped to perform any obligation that is assigned to you or that you yourself choose to take on. You are flexible and easygoing in ways that make the work you are doing move a bit slowly, but more enjoyably to completion, as you find great satisfaction in the process of getting somewhere—almost as much as you do in achieving the results. Somewhat scattered at times in your approach, however, you would do well to appoint able assistants.

Mercury: Intellect and Ideas

Mercury describes your intellect. It indicates the way you communicate your thoughts and feelings as well as how you accept and use information you receive from the world around you. Since information comes through sight, hearing, touch, smell, or taste, Mercury relates to your sensory perceptions. Mercury describes the formal learning process, especially primary school years. Of course, receiving and transmitting information is only part of your intellect process. Do you seek information for its own sake or only when it has practical value? Do you share ideas and knowledge with others? How well do you analyze what you read or hear? Are you intellectually curious or mentally lazy? Mercury has several other associations. It describes your immediate environment which includes neighbors and others who work there. Mercury, ruling the hands and fingers, describes mechanical and technical skills. Associated with transportation as well as communication, Mercury describes how you get around physically as well as mentally. Do you hurry from place to place, or prefer a much slower pace to make sure you don't get lost? Do you like to wander off the beaten path to follow something that strikes your interest, or move only with predetermined direction and purpose?

Mercury in Aries. Mercury in Aries means there is much energy and enthusiasm connected with your thought processes and also in the way you are apt to express ideas and opinions. You enjoy the constant mental stimulation of dealing with ideas and methods, though this is not necessarily an indication you will take time to sufficiently understand or complete one thing before you are off to something else that's new or appears more exciting. Unless other factors in your personality or background provide some mental brakes and organizational ability, you jump to conclusions and say things or present ideas that you have not really planned or thought out. Impatient with long-winded discussions or prolonged investigations, you do not hesitate to make decisions. Aries suggests your mind is sharp and physical perceptions highly alert. However, quick perceptions may be too quick, leaving no time to detect subtleties. You may, for example, be the first one to notice something, but not understand its significance. In emergency and other situations quickness is an asset, but it is also very important to be able to analyze the information at hand. You'd enjoy being one of the first people in a new development, or being in a neighborhood full of energy and vitality, with many youngsters and people constantly coming and going. When it comes to getting around, mentally or physically, you are likely to prefer speed. Impatient with a slow pace, you want to know everything all at once, and to get where you're going ahead of everyone else.

Mercury in Taurus. Mercury in Taurus indicates a deliberate, methodical manner of thinking and communication. Taurus does not mean you are a slow thinker or communicator. It indicates that you prefer to have time to think things over, and you don't want to be rushed or pressured into making decisions before you are ready. Perceptions are subjected to value judgments. What can I do with this idea? Is it threatening? Is personal advantage or physical pleasure associated with it? Because of the sense of worth or practicality associated with thoughts and ideas, you quickly gain knowledge or develop mechanical skills you deem important. Unable to find out immediately what you need to know, or lacking means to communicate what you know, you will not give up until these obstacles are overcome. Your senses are sharply instinctive, since they are the direct links to the physical world, the reality to which your intellect is so closely attuned. You may not, for example, be the first to perceive something, but you may be the first to realize its intrinsic value when you do. Your neighborhood can be a slower-paced rural community or an urban neighborhood of prosperous, socially minded, upwardly mobile neighbors. When it comes to getting from one place to another, mentally or physically, your pace can be fast or slow. The real issue is having definite purpose and definite direction in order to move at all. Once a certain direction is learned you can be very reluctant to try a new route.

Mercury in Gemini. Mercury in Gemini indicates rapid thought processes that effortlessly pick up all sorts of information from the outer world. Though you have a strong orientation for receiving and collecting information, Mercury in Gemini is not an indication of how you will communicate ideas or use what you learn. Mercury is the planetary ruler of Gemini, which indicates particularly sensitive sensory perceptions. Unless other factors in your personality and background focus your concentration and calm your nervous system, you can easily be distracted and suffer from nervousness and irritability. You have a clever mind, quick wit, and above-average mechanical or technical skills. The difficulty with having such a quick mind is that you may not always take time to fully develop ideas or thoroughly understand and acquire all the facts before repeating them. If, however, you develop organizational ability, which is often the case with this Mercury sign position, you exhibit impressive research and investigative skills. Willing and eager to share information and knowledge of particular skills, the emotional influence on your ideas and opinions is apt to be minimal. In turn, this allows objectivity in your judgment and analysis that others may lack. You enjoy busy, stimulating neighborhoods where neighborhood gossip is everyone's pastime and so is interest in community projects. The influence of Gemini can mean you belong to more than one neighborhood. When it comes to getting around, mentally as well as physically, you move quickly, and the more ways you can get there, the better you like it.

Mercury in Cancer. Mercury in Cancer indicates there is a great deal of emotional input on the information your brain perceives. It can mean you sometimes go to extremes in your thinking. When objective decisions must be made, it is difficult to separate your head from your heart. However, emotional influences, if kept under control, add an important sensitivity to the way you analyze thoughts and ideas as well as the manner in which you express them. The passive nature of Cancer means your thoughts are reflective of the environment and those with whom you spend a great deal of time. It does not indicate the lack of original thoughts or ideas. It suggests that you have to be aware when you are expressing your own ideas and when it is the opinions and ideas of others. The influence of Cancer means your intuition is very strong. In turn, intuition greatly heightens sensory perceptions. You may, for example, be aware of the presence of something long before anyone else, including yourself, may actually perceive it. You enjoy a neighborhood where neighbors are like family. Living in a neighborhood close to the ocean or water is soothing as well as intellectually stimulating. When it comes to getting around, mentally as well as physically, the directions you take and how fast you go will largely be influenced by your mood at the time. You may prefer physically traveling by water, and your learning process may be just as dependent on the flow of your emotions.

Mercury in Leo. Mercury in Leo indicates enthusiasm and energy, which are associated with the way you receive information as well as the manner in which you express your ideas and opinions. Whether or not you are outgoing, you are a communicator. If you aren't comfortable expressing thoughts publicly, you find private ways, such as a personal diary. The imagination and creativity of Leo suggests exaggeration and hyperbole, wonderful influences when you need ideas and mannerisms to entertain and inspire. An urge to compete, to be the best, and to have the last word can mean the tendency to dismiss the ideas of others and to develop intellectual snobbery. Much depends on other facets of your background and personality. Mercury in Leo suggests spirituality, interest in the occult, the subconscious, and abstract thought and motivation. Sensory perceptions are quick but also intuitive. You may often get an idea or feeling about something or someone before anything of a physical nature is observed. Two opposite situations concern your immediate environment. Your neighborhood can be of a social, outgoing nature where neighbors sponsor artistic or creative activities, or neighbors are rarely seen, as in a remote area or in a crowded complex where no one knows who lives next door. Getting around physically or mentally is a matter of energy and enthusiasm. Sometimes you travel too fast and pay little attention to details. At other times you are enticed in a certain direction or toward a particular goal by the excitement and pleasurable experiences along the way.

Mercury in Virgo. Mercury in Virgo indicates that you are very aware of your environment. The mental images you form are quickly and sharply analyzed. If other factors in your personality and background support your basic intellectual orientation, this position of Mercury can also mean a high degree of organization. The influence of Virgo implies a certain practicality, which means you are apt to want to put your knowledge and the information you get to some useful purpose. This, however, does not mean you won't take great pleasure in communicating what you know, expressing ideas and opinions, and dispensing gossip and advice, especially concerning family members, neighbors, those you work with, and anyone else who shares your immediate environment. The flexible nature of Mercury in Virgo suggests fickleness in thinking and opinions. Mercury is the planetary ruler of Virgo, which means sensory perceptions are keen, perhaps to the point of making you nervous or irritable, what others consider fussy. The quickness of your mental perceptions is so remarkable, you can appear to be psychic. The influence of Virgo indicates a variety of interests and above-average mechanical or technical skills. Your neighborhood is apt to be a place of much activity and community concerns, with a number of commercial establishments to add flavor and interest. When it comes to getting around, mentally as well as physically, you will go in many different directions, move at different speeds, and are likely to enjoy every place you go and everything you learn along the way.

Mercury in Libra. Mercury in Libra indicates that your thought processes are infused with a need for balance between the physical and the mental world. As your brain receives what your sensory perceptions pick up, you seek to intellectualize or objectively examine the information before applying it in some emotional or practical way. When you communicate thoughts and ideas, you remove your emotional identification with them. How do you this? One way is by doing it in some sort of entertaining or amusing way, using humor, harmless flirtations, or other imaginative methods. Another way is representing ideas or information as impartial judgments rather than as personal statements. You are more apt to share ideas that invite others to judge for themselves rather than issue statements they must accept. Sensory perceptions are balanced by your mental processes. Knocked off balance by one distraction, say, having a discussion or reading a book, your other perceptions are also knocked off kilter and you fail to immediately notice a ringing phone, a headache, the smell of something burning in the oven. Or distracted by pain or other physical distractions, you find it difficult to think or make decisions. There is some measure of Libra influence in the type of neighborhood you enjoy; contacts with neighbors and others who share your immediate environment being neither too close nor too distant. When it comes to getting around, mentally as well as physically, you prefer not to travel alone, and you always arrive at a goal in your imagination way before your physical body and physical experiences catch up.

Mercury in Scorpio. Mercury in Scorpio indicates shrewdness of thought and communication. The influence of Scorpio means there is a strong emotional input but one devoid of sentiment or moral judgment. It is an instinctive process, one you are not necessarily consciously aware of, in which your mental pictures are formed on the basis of such criteria as, how reliable is this information? Is it threatening? How can I understand it in order to control it? You are very good at separating what is important and relevant from what is not. Sensory perceptions are correspondingly sharp and instinctive. The secretive influence of Scorpio suggests that you are not always willing to communicate openly, especially if what you say can leave you vulnerable in any way. For the most part, however, you actively seek interaction and communication with others, if only to satisfy your natural curiosity about people. Whether or not you are a great talker, you are likely to be a good listener. Your mental orientation is attracted to understanding the psychology of human thought and behavior, the occult, and unraveling the mysteries of nature, either through academic research or physical exploration. You may prefer a neighborhood where people are friendly but strictly observe the rules of privacy. No matter how you travel from one place to another, mentally or physically, you are apt to prefer doing it unobserved. You want to control where you go and what you learn. The directions you take or ultimate goals you seek are extremely private matters.

Mercury in Sagittarius. Mercury in Sagittarius indicates independence and curiosity, which are hallmarks of your thought and communication process. Your interest is immediately aroused by the information your brain receives from the outer world. There is no immediate attempt to decide the usefulness or practicality of the information you receive or communicate—as fast as it comes in, it goes back out. If there are no factors in your personality or background to apply some mental brakes, you may find it difficult to be organized or to stick to the facts. The freedom-loving influence of Sagittarius can mean you will find it difficult to tolerate the confinement of classrooms or repetitious lessons. The grandness associated with Sagittarius is apt to mean that exaggeration and hyperbole can easily overtake your thoughts and ideas as well as your mannerisms. Your flexible mentality may result in a flair for imitation and mimicry. Your thoughts and ideas are imbued with humor, irony, and fondness for gossip. Other strong influences of Sagittarius are interest in spirituality and in the arts and entertainment. Rather than being confined to a single neighborhood, you are apt to prefer belonging to many or constantly changing one for another. When it comes to getting around in life, mentally as well as physically, you are a natural traveler. You want to explore as many different directions as possible, using many methods of transportation to get there. When setting out, you often have more than one goal at a time, or develop them along the way.

Mercury in Capricorn. Mercury in Capricorn indicates thought and communication that are subjected to form and structure. This implies that information your brain receives is accepted on the basis of how it fits into the real world. Mental pictures are ambitious, meaning that information you view as useless trivia or silly has little value, and you seek to eliminate such things from influencing your understanding or communication. Capricorn implies worry, and at times, obsessive or extremes in thinking. You may demand perfectionism and attention to detail from others, even if you sometimes fail to comply with such measures yourself. Alertness of sensory perceptions is based on an understanding of the real world. In other words, you immediately perceive what is obvious and meaningful. Perceiving something that doesn't immediately match reality or previous experience may take a bit longer, or may be ignored altogether. Your manner of communication may tend to be authoritative, though you are also quite interested in what others have to say and what the world itself can teach. Your organization, structure, and rhythm may be accompanied by a talent for art and music composition. You are apt to prefer an older, more settled neighborhood of solid citizens who take an interest in the welfare of the entire community as well as their own families and residences. When it comes to getting around, mentally as well as physically, you prefer following very structured, traditional routes, though within that framework you are not opposed to experiencing adventures along the way.

Mercury in Aquarius. Mercury in Aquarius indicates thought and communication processes that follow very traditional lines. However, with Aquarius there is always a potential for suddenly going off in the opposite direction. What you understood or accepted previously can be reversed or rejected, either as a result of a rebellious independence that is unexpectedly provoked, or by events or changes in your personal environment or in society itself. You have a natural inclination toward spirituality, philosophy, or the arts, and you can be extremely opinionated and resistant to change. You are not apt to reject opportunities to communicate in one form or another, since others act as a forum and sounding board for your thoughts and opinions. Sensory perceptions can be remarkably intuitive or dealt with on a practical, physical basis. Perceptions that involve people are particularly keen and intuitive, while other forms of stimulation can pass through your immediate environment virtually ignored. In fact, damage can be done or valuable time lost simply because you were too lazy or preoccupied to pay attention to things you should have perceived and didn't. Given the socially oriented influence of Aquarius, you enjoy a friendly, outgoing neighborhood, especially when your neighbors are from different races, religions, and cultures. When it comes to getting around, mentally as well as physically, the directions you take may be straight and narrow, or precarious with unexpected twists along the way. You are content to plod along at a snail's pace, but given the right motivation, you'll take off with speed and enthusiasm.

Mercury in Pisces. Mercury in Pisces indicates that significant emotional influence on thought and communication gives you a sensitive understanding of the world. It increases potential for creative talents, ability to understand the abstract, and scientific and mathematical brilliance. However, mental laziness, distraction, or depression can also be the result of overloaded emotional input. Not always logical, your sensitivity and imagination can more than make up for lack of objectivity. Certain extremes are possible. You can, for example, become fanatical and delusional, or so bogged down by self-pity or laziness you don't even attempt to use your intellectual potential. You may possess a photographic memory, though it may be obscured by fantasies and inattention. Ideas can be rendered ineffective by lack of confidence, poor organization, and impracticality, or you can be remarkably inspired as well as inspiring, and a master of creativity and disguise when presenting ideas, or in some areas, deliberately obscuring them. Sensory perceptions, like the mental images they engender, are poor when clouded by hysteria, but also intuitive to the point of being psychic. Your neighborhood may be near water or the ocean, and consist of minority groups, or those involved in the arts, entertainment, medicine, or charitable work. When it comes to getting around, mentally as well as physically, you can turn up almost anywhere, by any means, at any time. You enjoy going wherever fancy leads, but when inspired and organized, you proceed with such haste and directness that others have no idea how you got there ahead of them.

How to Find the Place of Mercury in Your Chart

Find your birth year in the left-hand column and read across the chart until you find your birth date. The top of that column will tell you where Mercury lies in your chart.

PLACE OF MERCURY—1880–1891

	ARIES	TAURUS	GEMINI	CANCER	LEO	VIRGO	LIBRA	SCORPIO	SAGIT.	CAPRI.	AQUAR.	PISCES
1880	3/5-5/11	5/12-5/27	5/28-6/10	6/11-6/27	6/28-9/3	9/4-9/19	9/20-10/7	10/8-10/29, 11/25-12/12	1/10, 10/30-11/24, 12/13	1/11-1/30	1/31-2/16	2/17-3/4
1881	4/16-5/4	5/5-5/18	5/19-6/2	6/3-6/28, 7/10-8/10	6/29-7/9, 8/11-8/26	8/27-9/11	9/12-10/1	10/2-12/7	1/3, 12/8-12/26	1/4-1/21, 12/27	1/22-2/8	2/9-4/15
1882	4/10-4/26	4/27-5/10	5/11-5/28	5/29-8/3	8/4-8/18	8/19-9/4	9/5-9/27, 10/23-11/10	9/28-10/22, 11/11-11/30	12/1-12/19	1/14, 12/20	1/15-2/1, 2/26-3/17	2/2-2/25, 3/18-4/9
1883	4/3-4/17	4/18-5/2	5/3-7/10	7/11-7/26	7/27-8/10	8/11-8/29	8/30-11/4	11/5-11/23	11/24-12/12	1/7, 12/13	1/8-3/15	3/16-4/2
1884	3/26-4/8	4/9-4/30, 5/13-6/13	5/1-5/12, 6/14-7/2	7/3-7/16	7/17-8/2	8/3-8/25	8/26-9/16, 10/10-10/27	9/17-10/9, 10/28-11/15	11/16-12/4	1/1, 1/21-2/14, 12/5	1/2-1/20, 2/15-3/7	3/8-3/24
1885	3/17-4/1	4/2-6/9	6/10-6/24	6/25-7/8	7/9-7/27	7/28-10/2	10/3-10/19	10/20-11/8	11/9-11/30, 12/17	2/9, 12/11-12/16	2/10-2/28	3/1-3/16
1886	3/9-5/15	5/16-6/1	6/2-6/15	6/16-7/1	7/2-7/28, 8/7-9/8	7/29-8/6, 9/9-9/24	9/25-10/12	10/13-11/1	11/2, 12/12	1/13-2/3	2/4-2/20	2/21-3/8
1887	3/3-3/22, 4/18-5/9	5/10-5/24	5/25-6/7	6/8-6/26	6/27-9/1	9/2-9/17	9/18-10/5	10/6-10/29, 11/14-12/11	1/7, 10/30-11/13, 12/12-12/31	1/8-1/26	1/27-2/13	2/14-3/2, 3/23-4/17
1888	4/14-4/30	5/1-5/14	5/15-5/30	5/31-8/7	8/8-8/22	8/23-9/8	9/9-9/28	9/29-12/4	12/5-12/23	1/1-1/19, 12/24	1/20-2/5	2/6-4/13
1889	4/7-4/22	4/23-5/6	5/7-5/28, 6/16-7/12	5/29-6/15, 7/13-7/30	7/31-8/14	8/15-9/1	9/2-9/27, 10/9-11/8	9/28-10/8, 11/9-11/27	11/28-12/16	1/10, 12/12	1/11-1/30, 2/12-3/17	1/31-2/11, 3/18-4/6
1890	3/31-4/13	4/14-4/30	5/1-7/1	7/2-7/22	7/23-8/6	8/7-8/26	8/27-11/1	11/2-11/19	11/20-12/9	1/4, 12/10	1/5-3/12	3/13-3/30
1891	3/22-4/5	4/6-6/13	6/14-6/29	6/30-7/13	7/14-7/30	7/31-10/7	10/8-10/24	10/25-11/12	11/13-12/2	1/7-2/13, 12/3	1/2-1/6, 2/14-3/5	3/6-3/21

PLACE OF MERCURY—1892-1905

Year												
1892	3/13-3/30 4/20-5/15	3/31-4/19 5/16-6/5	6/6-6/20	6/21-7/4	7/5-7/25 8/30-9/9	7/26-8/29 9/10-9/29	9/30-10/16	10/17-11/4	1/3-1/13 11/5	1/2 1/14-2/7	2/8-2/25	2/26-3/12
1893	3/6-5/12	5/13-5/28	5/29-6/11	6/12-6/28	6/29-9/5	9/6-9/21	9/22-10/9	10/10-10/30 11/30-12/12	1/10 10/31-11/29 12/13-12/31	1/11-1/30	1/31-2/17	2/18-3/5
1894	4/17-5/5	5/6-5/20	5/21-6/3	6/4-6/26 7/18-8/10	6/27-7/17 8/11-8/28	8/29-9/13	9/14-10/2	10/3-12/8	1/1-1/4 10/29-12/28	1/15 1/5-1/23 12/29	1/24-2/9	2/10-4/16
1895	4/12-4/27	4/28-5/11	5/12-5/28	5/29-8/5	8/6-8/20	8/21-9/5	9/6-9/27	9/28-10/27 11/12-12/1	10/28-11/11 12/2-12/21	1/15 12/22	1/16-2/2 3/4-3/16	2/3-3/3 3/17-4/11
1896	4/4-4/18	4/19-5/3	5/4-7/10	7/11-7/26	7/27-8/10	8/11-8/29	8/30-11/4	11/5-11/23	11/24-12/12	1/8 12/13	1/9-3/15	3/16-4/3
1897	3/27-4/9	4/10-4/29 5/22-6/12	4/30-5/21 6/13-7/4	7/5-7/18	7/19-8/3	8/4-8/25 9/22-10/10	8/26-9/21 10/11-10/28	10/29-11/16	11/17-12/6	1/1 1/25-2/14 12/7	1/2-1/24 2/15-3/9	3/10-3/26
1898	3/19-4/2	4/3-6/10	6/11-6/25	6/26-7/10	7/11-7/27	7/28-10/4	10/5-10/21	10/22-11/9	1/10 11/10-11/30 12/22	2/10 12/1-12/21	2/11-3/1	3/2-3/18
1899	3/11-5/5	5/16-6/3	6/4-6/17	6/18-7/2	7/3-7/26	7/27-8/14 9/10-9/26	8/15-9/9 9/27-10/13	10/14-11/2	1/8 11/3	1/13 1/14-2/4	2/5-2/22	2/23-3/10
1900	3/4-3/29	3/30-4/16 5/11-5/25	4/17-5/10 5/26-6/8	6/9-6/26	6/27-9/2	9/3-9/18	9/19-10/6	10/7-10/29 11/19-12/12	1/8 10/30-11/18 12/13	1/3-1/20 12/26	1/21-2/6	2/7-4/15
1901	4/16-5/3	5/4-5/17	5/18-6/1	6/2-8/9	8/10-8/25	8/26-9/10	9/11-9/30	10/1-12/6	1/2 12/7-12/25	1/3-1/20 12/26	1/21-2/6	2/7-4/15
1902	4/9-4/24	4/25-5/9	5/10-5/28 6/26-7/12	5/29-6/25 7/13-8/2	8/3-8/17	8/18-9/3	9/4-9/27 10/16-11/10	9/28-10/15 11/11-11/30	1/13 11/30-12/18	1/6 12/19	1/14-2/1 2/19-3/18	2/2-2/18 3/19-4/8
1903	4/2-4/16	4/17-5/2	5/3-7/10	7/11-7/25	7/26-8/9	8/10-8/29	8/30-11/3	11/4-11/22	11/23-12/11	1/6 12/12	1/7-3/14	3/15-4/1
1904	3/24-4/7	4/8-6/13	6/14-7/1	7/2-7/15	7/16-8/1	8/2-8/27 9/8-10/8	8/28-9/7 10/9-10/26	10/27-11/14	1/1 11/15-12/4 12/5	1/14-2/14 12/5	1/2-1/13 2/15-3/6	3/7-3/23
1905	3/16-4/1 4/29-5/15	4/2-4/28 5/16-6/8	6/9-6/22	6/23-7/7	7/8-7/26	7/27-10/1	10/2-10/18	10/19-11/7	11/8-12/1 12/10	2/28 12/2-12/29	2/9-2/27	2/28-3/15

PLACE OF MERCURY—1906–1917

	ARIES	TAURUS	GEMINI	CANCER	LEO	VIRGO	LIBRA	SCORPIO	SAGITT.	CAPRI.	AQUAR.	PISCES
1906	3/8–5/14	5/15–5/31	6/1–6/14	6/15–6/30	7/1–9/7	9/8–9/23	9/24–10/11	10/12–11/1 11/7–12/12	1/12 11/2–12/6 12/13	1/13–2/1	2/2–2/19	2/20–3/7
1907	3/4–3/13 4/18–5/8	5/9–5/22	5/23–6/6	6/7–6/26 7/27–8/12	6/27–7/26 8/13–8/30	8/31–9/15	9/16–10/4	10/5–12/10	1/6 12/11–12/30	1/7–1/25 12/31	1/26–2/11	2/12–3/3 3/14–4/17
1908	4/13–4/29	4/30–5/13	5/14–5/29	5/30–8/6	8/7–8/21	8/22–9/11	9/8–9/28 11/2–11/11	9/29–11/1 11/12–12/13	12/4–12/22	1/18 12/23	1/19–2/4	2/5–4/12
1909	4/6–4/20	4/21–5/5	5/6–7/12	7/13–7/29	7/30–8/13	8/14–8/31	9/1–11/7	11/8–11/26	11/27–12/15	1/9 12/16	1/10–3/16	3/17–4/5
1910	3/29–4/12	4/13–4/30 6/2–6/11	5/1–6/1 6/12–7/6	6/29–7/12	7/13–7/30	8/6–8/26 9/29–10/11	8/27–9/28 10/12–10/31	11/1–11/18	11/19–12/8	1/3 1/31–2/15 12/9	1/4–1/30 2/16–3/11	3/12–3/25
1911	3/21–4/4	4/5–6/12	6/13–6/28	6/29–7/12	7/13–7/30	7/31–10/6	10/7–10/23	10/24–11/11	11/12–12/2 12/28	2/12 12/3–12/27	2/13–3/4	3/5–3/20
1912	3/12–5/16	5/17–6/4	6/5–6/18	6/19–7/3	7/4–7/25 8/21–9/10	7/26–8/20 9/11–9/27	9/28–10/15	10/16–11/4	1/14 11/5	1/15–2/6	2/7–2/24	2/25–3/11
1913	3/5–4/7 4/14–5/11	5/12–5/27	5/28–6/10	6/11–6/27	6/28–9/3	9/4–9/19	9/20–10/8	10/9–10/30 11/24–12/12	1/9 10/31–11/23 12/13	1/10–1/29	1/30–2/15	2/16–3/4 4/8–4/13
1914	4/17–5/4	5/5–5/18	5/19–6/2	6/3–8/10	8/11–8/26	8/27–9/12	9/13–10/1	10/2–12/7	1/3 12/8–12/27	1/4–1/22 12/28	1/23–2/8	2/9–4/16
1915	4/11–4/26	4/27–5/10	5/11–5/28	5/29–8/3	8/4–8/18	8/19–9/4	9/5–9/27 10/21–11/11	9/28–10/20 11/12–11/30	12/1–12/19	1/14 12/20	1/15–2/1 2/24–3/19	2/2–2/28 3/20–4/10
1916	4/2–4/16	4/17–5/2	5/3–7/10	7/11–7/25	7/26–8/9	8/10–8/28	8/29–11/4	11/5–11/22	11/23–12/11	1/7 12/12	1/8–3/14	3/15–4/1
1917	3/25–4/8	4/9–6/14	6/15–7/2	7/3–7/17	7/18–8/2	8/3–8/26 9/15–10/9	8/27–9/14 10/10–10/27	10/28–11/15	11/16–12/5	1/1 1/10–2/14 12/6–12/31	1/2–1/17 2/15–3/8	3/9–3/24

PLACE OF MERCURY—1918–1931

Year													
1918	3/17-4/2	4/3-6/9	6/10-6/24	6/25-7/8	7/9-7/27	7/28-10/2	10/3-10/20	10/21-11/8	11/9-12/1 12/16	1/1-2/9 12/2-12/15	2/10-2/28	3/1-3/16	
1919	3/9-5/15	5/16-6/1	6/2-6/15	6/16-7/1	7/2-9/8	9/9-9/25	9/26-10/12	10/13-11/2	(11/13) 11/3	1/14-2/3	2/4-2/21	2/22-3/8	
1920	3/3-3/19 4/18-5/8	5/9-5/23	5/24-6/6	6/7-6/26 8/3-8/9	6/27-8/2 8/10-8/31	9/1-9/16	9/17-10/4	10/5-10/30 11/11-12/10	(1/7) 10/31-11/10 12/11-12/30	1/8-1/27 12/31	1/28-2/13	2/14-3/2 3/20-4/17	
1921	4/14-4/30	5/1-5/14	5/15-5/30	5/31-8/7	8/8-8/23	8/24-9/8	9/9-9/29	9/30-12/4	12/5-12/23	(1/18) 12/24-12/31	1/19-2/4	2/5-4/13	
1922	4/7-4/22	4/23-5/6	5/7-5/30 6/11-7/13	5/31-6/10 7/14-7/31	8/1-8/14	8/15-9/1	9/2-9/30 10/5-11/8	10/1-10/4 10/9-11/27	11/28-12/16	(1/11) 12/17	1/12-2/1 2/9-3/17	2/2-2/8 3/18-4/6	
1923	3/31-4/14	4/15-4/30	5/1-7/8	7/9-7/22	7/23-8/7	8/8-8/27 10/4-10/11	8/28-10/3 10/12-11/1	11/2-11/20	11/21-12/9	(1/4) 2/7-2/13 12/10	1/5-2/6 2/14-3/12	3/13-3/20	
1924	3/22-4/5	4/6-6/12	6/13-6/29	6/30-7/13	7/14-7/30	7/31-10/6	10/7-10/24	10/25-11/11	11/12-12/2	(2/13) 12/3-12/31	2/14-3/4	3/5-3/21	
1925	3/14-4/1 4/16-5/16	4/2-4/15 5/17-6/6	6/7-6/20	6/21-7/5	7/6-7/25 8/27-9/10	7/26-8/26 9/11-9/29	9/30-10/16	10/17-11/3	(1/7) 1/1-1/13 11/6	1/14-2/6	2/7-2/25	2/26-3/13	
1926	3/6-5/12	5/13-5/29	5/30-6/11	6/12-6/28	6/29-9/5	9/6-9/21	9/22-10/9	10/10-10/30 11/28-12/13	(1/10) 10/31-11/27 12/14	1/11-1/30	1/31-2/17	2/18-3/5	
1927	4/18-5/5	5/6-5/20	5/21-6/4	6/5-6/28 7/14-8/11	6/29-7/13 8/12-8/28	8/29-9/13	9/14-10/2	10/3-12/8	(1/4) 12/9-12/28	1/5-1/23 12/29	1/24-2/9	2/10-4/17	
1928	4/11-4/26	4/27-5/10	5/11-5/28	5/29-8/4	8/5-8/19	8/20-9/5	9/6-9/27 10/25-11/10	9/28-10/24 11/11-12/1	12/2-12/20	(1/16) 12/21	(1/7) 12/14	1/17-2/2 2/29-3/17	2/3-2/28 3/18-4/10
1929	4/4-4/18	4/19-5/3	5/4-7/11	7/12-7/27	7/28-8/11	8/12-8/29	8/30-11/5	11/6-11/23	11/24-12/13	(1/7) 12/14	1/8-3/15	3/16-4/3	
1930	3/27-4/10	4/11-4/30 5/17-6/14	5/1-5/16 6/15-7/4	7/5-7/18	7/19-8/3	8/4-8/26 9/20-10/10	8/27-9/19 10/11-10/29	10/30-11/16	11/17-12/6	(1/11)	1/2-1/22 2/16-3/9	3/10-3/26	
1931	3/19-4/3	4/4-6/10	6/11-6/26	6/27-7/10	7/11-7/28	7/29-10/4	10/5-10/21	10/22-11/9	11/10-12/1 (12/20)	(1/11) 1/23-2/15 (12/17)	2/11 12/2-12/19	2/12-3/2	3/3-3/18

PLACE OF MERCURY—1932-1943

	ARIES	TAURUS	GEMINI	CANCER	LEO	VIRGO	LIBRA	SCORPIO	SAGITT.	CAPRI.	AQUAR.	PISCES
1932	3/10–5/15	5/16–6/2	6/3–6/16	6/17–7/1	7/2–7/27 8/10–9/8	7/28–8/9 9/9–9/25	9/26–10/13	10/14–11/2	11/3 ↰1/14	1/15–2/4	2/5–2/22	2/23–3/9
1933	3/3–3/25 4/18–5/9	5/10–5/25	5/26–6/8	6/9–6/26	6/27–9/1	9/2–9/17	9/18–10/6	10/7–10/29 11/16–12/11	10/30–11/15 12/12 ↰1/7	1/8–1/27	1/28–2/13	2/14–3/2 3/26–4/17
1934	4/15–5/2	5/3–5/16	5/17–5/31	6/1–8/9	8/10–8/24	8/25–9/9	9/10–9/30	10/1–12/5	12/6–12/25 ↰1/1	1/2–1/19 12/26	1/20–2/6	2/7–4/14
1935	4/9–4/24	4/25–5/8	5/9–5/29 6/21–7/13	5/30–6/20 7/14–8/1	8/2–8/16	8/17–9/2	9/3–9/28 10/13–11/9	9/29–10/12 11/10–11/28	11/29–12/17 ↰1/12	1/12 12/18	1/13–1/31 2/15–3/18	2/1–2/14 3/19–4/8
1936	3/31–4/14	4/15–4/30	5/1–7/8	7/9–7/23	7/24–8/7	8/8–8/27	8/28–11/1	11/2–11/20	11/21–12/9 ↰1/3	12/10	1/6–3/12	3/13–3/30
1937	3/23–4/6	4/7–6/13	6/14–6/30	7/1–7/14	7/15–7/31	8/1–10/7	10/8–10/25	10/26–11/13	11/14–12/3 ↰1/1	12/4	1/2–1/9 2/14–3/6	3/7–3/22
1938	3/15–4/1 4/24–5/16	4/2–4/23 5/17–6/8	6/9–6/22	6/23–7/6	7/7–7/26 9/3–9/10	7/27–9/2 9/11–9/30	10/1–10/18	10/19–11/6	1/7–1/12 11/7 ↰1/6	1/13–2/8	2/9–2/26	2/27–3/14
1939	3/7–5/14	5/15–5/30	5/31–6/13	6/14–6/29	6/30–9/6	9/7–9/22	9/23–10/10	10/11–10/31 12/3–12/13	11/1–12/2 12/14 ↰1/11	1/12–2/1 ↰1/14	2/2–2/18	2/19–3/6
1940	3/4–3/7 4/17–5/6	5/7–5/21	5/22–6/4	6/5–6/26 7/21–8/11	6/27–7/20 8/12–8/28	8/29–9/13	9/14–10/2	10/3–12/9	12/10–12/28 ↰1/5	1/6–1/24 12/29	1/25–2/11	2/12–3/3 3/8–4/16
1941	4/12–4/28	4/29–5/12	5/13–5/29	5/30–8/5	8/6–8/20	8/21–9/6	9/7–9/27 10/30–11/11	9/28–10/29 11/12–12/2	12/3–12/21 ↰1/6	12/22 ↰1/6	1/17–2/3 3/7–3/15	2/4–3/6 3/16–4/11
1942	4/5–4/20	4/21–5/4	5/5–7/12	7/13–7/28	7/29–8/12	8/13–8/30	8/31–11/6	11/7–11/25	11/26–12/14 ↰1/9	12/15	1/10–3/16	3/17–4/4
1943	3/28–4/11	4/12–4/30 5/26–6/13	5/1–5/25 6/14–7/5	7/6–7/20	7/21–8/4	8/5–8/26 9/25–10/11	8/27–9/24 10/12–10/30	10/31–11/18	11/19–12/7 ↰1/2	1/28–2/15 12/8	1/3–1/27 2/16–3/10	3/11–3/27

PLACE OF MERCURY—1944–1958

Year												
1944	3/19-4/3	4/4-6/10	6/11-6/26	6/27-7/10	7/11-7/28	7/29-10/4	10/5-10/21	10/22-11/9	11/10-12/1, 12/23	12/2-12/22 (2/12)	2/13-3/2	3/3-3/18
1945	3/11-5/16	5/17-6/3	6/4-6/18	6/19-7/3	7/4-7/26, 8/18-9/9	7/27-8/17, 9/10-9/27	9/28-10/13	10/14-11/3	11/4-12/31 (1/13)	1/14-2/4	2/5-2/22	2/23-3/10
1946	3/4-4/1, 4/17-5/11	5/12-5/26	5/27-6/9	6/10-6/27	6/28-9/3	9/4-9/19	9/20-10/7	10/8-10/29, 11/21-12/12	10/30-11/21, 12/13 (1/9)	1/10-1/28	1/29-2/15	2/16-3/3, 4/2-4/16
1947	4/16-5/3	5/4-5/18	5/19-6/2	6/3-8/10	8/11-8/26	8/27-9/10	9/11-10/1	10/2-12/7	12/8-12/26 (1/1)	1/2-1/20, 12/27	1/21-2/7	2/8-4/15
1948	4/9-4/24	4/25-5/8	5/9-5/27, 6/29-7/11	5/28-6/28, 7/12-8/2	8/3-8/16	8/17-9/3	9/4-9/26, 10/17-11/9	9/27-10/16, 11/10-11/29	11/30-12/18 (1/13)	12/19	1/14-2/1, 2/20-3/17	2/2-2/19, 3/18-4/8
1949	4/2-4/16	4/17-5/1	5/2-7/9	7/10-7/24	7/25-8/8	8/9-8/28	8/29-9/11	11/4-11/21	11/22-12/11	12/12 (1/5)	1/6-3/13	3/14-4/1
1950	3/25-4/7	4/8-6/14	6/15-7/2	7/3-7/16	7/17-8/1	8/2-8/27, 9/10-10/9	8/28-9/9, 10/10-10/26	10/27-11/14	11/15-12/4	1/15-2/14, 12/5-12/31	1/2-1/14, 2/15-3/7	3/8-3/24
1951	3/17-4/2, 5/2-5/15	4/3-5/1, 5/16-6/9	6/10-6/24	6/25-7/8	7/9-7/27	7/28-10/2	10/3-10/19	10/20-11/8	11/9-12/1 (1/13)	12/2-12/12	2/10-2/28	3/1-3/16
1952	3/8-5/14	5/15-5/31	6/1-6/14	6/15-6/30	7/1-9/7	9/8-9/23	9/24-10/11	10/12-11/1	11/2-12/1 (1/6)	1/14-2/3	2/4-2/20	2/21-3/7
1953	3/3-3/15, 4/18-5/8	5/9-5/23	5/24-6/6	6/7-6/26, 7/29-8/11	6/27-7/28, 8/12-8/30	8/31-9/15	9/16-10/4	10/5-10/31, 11/7-12/10	11/1-11/6, 12/11-12/30 (1/6)	1/7-1/25, 12/31	1/26-2/11	2/12-3/2, 3/16-4/17
1954	4/14-4/30	5/1-5/14	5/15-5/30	5/31-8/7	8/8-8/22	8/23-9/8	9/9-9/29, 11/5-11/11	9/30-11/4, 11/12-12/4	12/5-12/23 (1/18)	12/24	1/19-2/4	2/5-4/13
1955	4/7-4/22	4/23-5/6	5/7-7/13	7/14-7/30	7/31-8/14	8/15-9/1	9/2-11/8	11/9-11/27	11/28-12/16 (1/10)	12/17	1/11-3/17	3/18-4/6
1956	3/29-4/12	4/13-4/29	4/30-7/6	7/7-7/21	7/22-8/5	8/6-8/26, 9/30-10/11	8/27-9/29, 10/12-10/31	11/1-11/18	11/19-12/8	12/9 (1/4)	1/5-2/2, 2/16-3/11	3/12-3/28
1957	3/21-4/4	4/5-6/12	6/13-6/28	6/29-7/12	7/13-7/30	7/31-10/6	10/7-10/23	10/24-11/11	11/12-12/2, 12/29 (1/14)	12/3-12/28	2/13-3/4	3/5-3/20
1958	3/13-4/2, 4/11-5/17	4/3-4/10, 5/18-6/5	6/6-6/20	6/21-7/4	7/5-7/26, 8/24-9/11	7/27-8/23, 9/12-9/28	9/29-10/16	10/17-11/5	11/6 (1/14)	1/15-2/6	2/7-2/24	2/25-3/12

PLACE OF MERCURY—1959-1969

	ARIES	TAURUS	GEMINI	CANCER	LEO	VIRGO	LIBRA	SCORPIO	SAGITT.	CAPRI.	AQUAR.	PISCES
1959	3/6-5/12	5/13-5/28	5/29-6/11	6/12-6/28	6/29-9/5	9/6-9/21	9/22-10/9	10/10-10/31 / 11/26-12/13	↰1/10 / 11/1-11/25 / 12/14↰	1/11-1/30	1/31-2/17	2/18-3/5
1960	4/17-5/4	5/5-5/19	5/20-6/2	6/3-7/1 / 7/7-8/10	7/2-7/6 / 8/11-8/27	8/28-9/12	9/13-10/1	10/2-12/7	↰1/4 / 12/8-12/27	1/5-1/23 / 12/28-12/31	1/24-2/9	2/10-4/16
1961	4/10-4/25	4/26-5/9	5/10-5/27	5/28-8/3	8/4-8/17	8/18-9/3	9/4-9/26 / 10/22-11/9	9/27-10/21 / 11/10-11/29	11/30-12/19	1/1-1/13 / 12/20↰	1/14-1/31 / 2/24-3/17	2/1-2/23 / 3/18-4/9
1962	4/3-4/17	4/18-5/2	5/3-7/10	7/11-7/25	7/26-8/9	8/10-8/28	8/29-11/4	11/5-11/22	11/23-12/11	↰1/6 / 12/12↰	1/7-3/14	3/15-4/2
1963	3/26-4/8	4/9-5/2 / 5/10-6/13	5/3-5/9 / 6/14-7/3	7/4-7/17	7/18-8/2	8/3-8/25 / 9/16-10/9	8/26-9/15 / 10/10-10/27	10/28-11/15	11/16-12/5	↰1/1 / 1/20-2/14 / 12/6↰	1/2-1/19 / 2/15-3/8	3/9-3/25
1964	3/16-4/1	4/2-4/17	4/18-6/23	6/24-7/8	7/9-7/26	7/27-10/3	10/4-10/19	10/20-11/7	11/8-11/29 / 12/16↰	↰2/9 / 11/30-12/15	2/10-2/28	2/29-3/15
1965	3/9-5/14	5/15-6/1	6/2-6/15	6/16-6/30	7/1-7/30 / 8/3-9/7	7/31-8/2 / 9/8-9/24	9/25-10/11	10/12-11/11	↰1/12 / 11/12↰	1/13-2/2	2/3-2/20	2/21-3/8
1966	3/3-3/21 / 4/17-5/8	5/9-5/23	5/24-6/6	6/7-6/25	6/26-8/31	9/1-9/16	9/17-10/4	10/5-10/29 / 11/13-12/10	↰1/6 / 10/30-11/12 / 12/11-12/31↰	1/7-1/26	1/27-2/12	2/13-3/2 / 3/22-4/16
1967	4/14-4/30	5/1-5/15	5/16-5/30	5/31-8/5	8/6-8/23	8/24-9/8	9/9-9/29	9/30-12/4	12/5-12/23	1/1-1/18 / 12/24↰	1/19-2/5	2/6-4/13
1968	4/7-4/21	4/22-5/5	5/6-5/28 / 6/13-7/12	5/29-6/12 / 7/13-7/30	7/31-8/14	8/15-8/31	9/1-9/27 / 10/7-11/7	9/28-10/6 / 11/8-11/26	11/27-12/15	↰1/11 / 12/16↰	1/12-1/31 / 2/11-3/16	2/1-2/10 / 3/17-4/6
1969	3/30-4/13	4/14-4/29	4/30-7/7	7/8-7/21	7/22-8/6	8/7-8/26 / 10/7-10/8	8/27-10/6 / 10/9-10/31	11/1-11/19	11/20-12/8	↰1/3 / 12/9↰	1/4-3/11	3/12-3/29

PLACE OF MERCURY—1970–1980

1970	3/22-4/5	4/6-6/12	6/13-6/29	6/30-7/13	7/14-7/30	7/31-10/6	10/7-10/24	10/25-11/12	11/13-12/2	↶2/12 12/3-12/31	2/13-3/4	3/5-3/21
1971	3/14-3/31 4/18-5/16	4/1-4/17 5/17-6/6	6/7-6/20	6/21-7/5	7/6-7/25 8/29-9/10	7/26-8/28 9/11-9/29	9/30-10/16	10/17-11/5	1/2-1/13 11/6↶	1/1 1/14-2/6	2/7-2/25	2/26-3/13
1972	3/5-5/11	5/12-5/28	5/29-6/11	6/12-6/27	6/28-9/4	9/5-9/20	9/21-10/8	10/9-10/29 11/29-12/11	↶1/10 10/30-11/28 12/12↶	1/11-1/30	1/31-2/17	2/18-3/4
1973	4/16-5/5	5/6-5/19	5/20-6/3	6/4-6/26 7/16-8/10	6/27-7/15 8/11-8/27	8/28-9/12	9/13-10/1	10/2-12/7	1/3 12/8-12/27	1/4-1/22 12/28↶	1/23-2/8	2/9-4/15
1974	4/11-4/27	4/28-5/11	5/12-5/28	5/29-8/4	8/5-8/19	8/20-9/5	9/6-9/27 10/26-11/10	9/28-10/25 11/11-12/1	12/2-12/20	↶1/15 12/21↶	1/16-2/1 3/2-3/16	2/2-3/1 3/17-4/10
1975	4/5-4/18	4/19-5/3	5/4-7/11	7/12-7/27	7/28-8/11	8/12-8/29	8/30-11/5	11/6-11/24	11/25-12/13	↶1/7 12/14↶	1/8-3/15	3/16-4/3
1976	3/26-4/9	4/10-4/28 5/19-6/12	4/29-5/18 6/13-7/3	7/4-7/17	7/18-8/2	8/3-8/24 9/21-10/9	8/25-9/20 10/10-10/28	10/29-11/15	11/16-12/5	↶2/9 1/25-2/14 12/6↶	1/2-1/24 2/15-3/8	3/9-3/25
1977	3/18-4/2	4/3-6/9	6/10-6/25	6/26-7/9	7/10-7/27	7/28-10/3	10/4-10/20	10/21-11/8	11/9-11/30 12/21↶	↶1/12 11/3↶ 12/1-12/20	2/10-3/1	3/2-3/17
1978	3/10-5/15	5/16-6/2	6/3-6/16	6/17-7/1	7/2-7/26 8/13-9/8	7/27-8/12 9/9-9/25	9/26-10/13	10/14-11/2	↶1/17 10/30-11/17 12/12↶	1/13-2/3	2/4-2/21	2/22-3/9
1979	3/3-3/26 4/17-5/9	5/10-5/25	5/26-6/8	6/9-6/26	6/27-9/1	9/2-9/17	9/18-10/6	10/7-10/29 11/18-12/11	10/30-11/17 12/12↶	1/8-1/27	1/28-2/13	2/14-3/2 3/28-4/16
1980	4/14-5/1	5/2-5/15	5/16-5/30	5/31-8/8	8/9-8/23	8/24-9/9	9/10-9/29	9/30-12/4	↶1/1 12/5-12/24	1/2-1/20 12/25-12/31	1/21-2/6	2/7-4/13

PLACE OF MERCURY—1981-1987

	ARIES	TAURUS	GEMINI	CANCER	LEO	VIRGO	LIBRA	SCORPIO	SAGITT.	CAPRI.	AQUAR.	PISCES
1981	4/8-4/23	4/24-5/7	5/8-5/27, 6/22-7/11	5/28-6/21, 7/12-7/31	8/1-8/15	8/16-9/1	9/2-9/26, 10/13-11/8	9/27-10/12, 11/9-11/27	11/28-12/16	1/1-1/11, 12/17	1/12-1/30, 2/16-3/16	1/31-2/15, 3/17-4/7
1982	3/31-4/14	4/15-4/30	5/1-7/8	7/9-7/23	7/24-8/7	8/8-8/26	8/27-11/1	11/2-11/20	11/21-12/9	1/4, 12/10-12/31	1/5-3/12	3/13-3/30
1983	3/23-4/6	4/7-6/13	6/14-6/30	7/1-7/14	7/15-7/31	8/1-8/28, 9/5-10/7	8/29-9/4, 10/8-10/25	10/26-11/13	11/14-12/3	1/12-2/13, 12/4	1/1-1/11, 2/14-3/5	3/6-3/22
1984	3/14-3/30, 4/25-5/15	3/31-4/24, 5/16-6/6	6/7-6/21	6/22-7/5	7/6-7/25	7/26-9/29	9/30-10/16	10/17-11/5	11/6-11/30, 1/10 12/7	2/7, 12/1-12/6	2/8-2/26	2/27-3/13
1985	3/6-5/12	5/13-5/29	5/30-6/12	6/13-6/28	6/29-9/5	9/6-9/21	9/22-10/9	10/10-10/30, 12/4-12/11	10/31-12/3, 1/10 12/12	1/11-1/31	2/1-2/17	2/18-3/5
1986	3/3-3/10, 4/17-5/6	5/7-5/21	5/22-6/4	6/5-6/25, 7/23-8/10	6/26-7/22, 8/11-8/28	8/29-9/13	9/14-10/2	10/3-12/8	12/9-12/28, 1/4	1/5-1/23, 12/29	1/24-2/10	2/11-3/2, 3/11-4/16
1987	4/12-4/28	4/29-5/12	5/13-5/28	5/29-8/5	8/6-8/20	8/21-9/6	9/7-9/27, 10/31-11/10	9/28-10/30, 11/11-12/2	12/3-12/21	12/22, 4/16	1/17-2/2, 3/11-3/12	2/3-3/10, 3/13-4/11

PLACE OF MERCURY—1988–2000

Year												
1988	4/4-4/19	4/20-5/3	5/4-7/11	7/12-7/27	7/28-8/11	8/12-8/29	8/30-11/5	11/6-11/24	11/25-12/13	12/14 (↳1/9)	1/10-3/15	3/16-4/3
1989	3/27-4/10	4/11-4/28, 5/28-6/11	4/29-5/27, 6/12-7/4	7/5-7/19	7/20-8/3	8/4-8/25, 9/26-10/10	8/26-9/25, 10/11-10/29	10/30-11/16	11/17-12/6	1/28-2/13, 12/7 (↳1/1)	1/2-1/27, 2/14-3/9	3/10-3/26
1990	3/19-4/3	4/4-6/10	6/11-6/26	6/27-7/10	7/11-7/28	7/29-10/4	10/5-10/21	10/22-11/9	11/10-11/30, 12/25	12/1-12/24 (↳2/10)	2/11-3/2	3/3-3/18
1991	3/11-4/15	4/16-6/3	6/4-6/18	7/4-7/25, 8/19-9/9	7/26-8/18, 9/10-9/26	9/27-10/14	10/15-11/3	11/4-12/11	12/12-12/31	12/11-12/31 (↳1/5)	1/14-2/4	2/23-3/10
1992	3/3-4/2, 4/14-5/9	5/10-5/25	5/26-6/8	6/9-6/26	6/27-9/2	9/3-9/18	9/19-10/6	10/7-10/28, 11/21-12/11	10/29-11/20, 12/12	1/9-1/28 (↳1/8)	1/29-2/15	2/16-3/2, 4/3-4/13
1993	4/15-5/2	5/3-5/17	5/18-5/31	6/1-8/9	8/10-8/25	8/26-9/10	9/11-9/29	9/30-12/5	12/6-12/25	12/6-12/25 (↳1/1)	1/21-2/6	2/7-4/14
1994	4/9-4/24	4/25-5/8	5/9-5/27, 7/2-7/9	5/28-7/1, 7/10-8/2	8/3-8/16	8/17-9/2	9/3-9/26, 10/19-11/9	9/27-10/18, 11/10-11/28	11/29-12/18	12/19 (↳1/12)	1/13-3/17	3/18-4/8
1995	4/2-4/16	4/17-5/1	5/2-7/9	7/10-7/24	7/25-8/8	8/9-8/27	8/28-11/3	11/4-11/21	11/22-12/10	12/11-12/31 (↳1/5)	1/6-3/13	3/14-4/1
1996	3/24-4/6	4/7-6/12	6/13-7/1	7/2-7/15	7/16-7/31	8/1-8/25, 9/12-10/7	8/26-9/11, 10/8-10/25	10/26-11/13	11/14-12/3	1/17-2/13, 12/4 (↳2/8)	1/1-1/16, 2/14-3/6	3/7-3/23
1997	3/15-3/31	4/1-6/7	6/8-6/22	6/23-7/7	7/8-7/25	7/26-10/1	10/2-10/18	10/19-11/6	11/7-11/29, 12/13	11/30-12/12 (↳1/11)	2/9-2/26	2/27-3/14
1998	3/8-5/13	5/14-5/31	6/1-6/14	6/15-6/29	6/30-9/6	9/7-9/23	9/24-10/10	10/11-10/31	11/1-11/19	11/20-12/9 (↳1/11)	2/2-2/19	2/20-3/7
1999	3/2-3/17, 4/17-5/7	5/8-5/22	5/23-6/5	6/6-6/25, 7/31-8/9	6/26-7/30, 8/10-8/30	8/31-9/15	9/16-10/4	10/5-10/29, 11/9-12/9	10/30-11/8, 12/10-12/30	12/31 (↳1/5)	1/26-2/11	2/12-3/1, 3/18-4/16
2000	4/12-4/28	4/29-5/13	5/14-5/28	5/29-8/6	8/7-8/21	8/22-9/6	9/7-9/27, 11/5-11/7	9/28-11/6, 11/8-12/2	12/3-12/21	12/22-12/31 (↳1/17)	1/18-2/4	2/5-4/11

YOUR MOST FREQUENT FAULT: ARIES—Haste; TAURUS—Stubbornness; GEMINI—Loquaciousness; CANCER—Inattention; LEO—Boastfulness; VIRGO—Timidity; LIBRA—Vanity; SCORPIO—Lack of sympathy; SAGITTARIUS—Sarcasm; CAPRICORN—Curiosity; AQUARIUS—Procrastination; PISCES—Self-immolation.

Venus: Affection and Attraction

Venus represents social attitudes. It is your capacity to enjoy the society of others, the part of you that relates to others rather than yourself. In addition to describing spontaneous interactions with people in general, Venus represents closer relationships, especially partnership. This includes marriage partner, business partner, and alliances in which you cooperate with others to achieve a common goal. Venus describes other social attributes, such as honor, dignity, respect, and loyalty. It rules affection, love, the romantic side of sex, and romance in the general sense of the word. It is the personal sense of proportion and balance that influences your decisions and preferences. Venus relates to humor, merriment, and other aspects of your disposition. What you value, beauty most likely to appeal to you, and things that give you pleasure are all in the province of Venus. It is descriptive of wealth and luck. Venus is not an indication of physical action. It is based on emotional responses, the power to attract others or be attracted by others. In a male's horoscope, Venus is associated with the type of women to whom he is attracted. In a female's horoscope, Venus is indicative of her own attraction for men.

Venus in Aries. Venus in Aries indicates that your relationships, social attitudes, and contacts are vigorous and enthusiastic. Attraction for or to others is uncomplicated, since your interest, or lack of it, is immediate. You have a spirit of cooperation and easy affection. Though carelessness sometimes overrides it, and other factors in your personality can obscure it, an inner balance causes you to treat others as you want to be treated, and to be as open and honest with others as you want them to be with you. This idealism is often tested by reality when others do not follow the golden rule in their treatment of you. Loss or disappointment in dealing with others is caused by engaging people with too much haste or lack of discrimination. Constantly seeking stimulation and inspiration, you are apt to ignore those without similar social drives, and you get bored and restless when things get too quiet. For you, beauty is active and bold. Energy and vitality are what appeals most in life, which is why you are attracted to whatever conveys the spirit of these two elements: possessions you own, clothes you wear, mannerisms you adopt, situations in which you are involved, and of course, the people you want to spend time with. Men with Venus in Aries are usually attracted to strong, courageous women who don't mind making the first move. Women with Venus in Aries have aggressive social natures, and as a rule find the friendship of men preferable to being with women.

Venus in Taurus. Venus in Taurus indicates that your relationships, social attitudes, and contacts are largely influenced by pleasure and pragmatism. It means that even if you are not outwardly gregarious, you nevertheless enjoy socializing and being around other people. It also means that, consciously or subconsciously, people are regarded as valuable resources. This makes you very selective when it comes to those with whom you socialize as well as those whom you wish to attract. Friendships and contacts with others in general are established for a particular reason, and invariably lead to some advantage or are used in one way or another, even if there was no selfish intent on your part. However, as much as you gain from others, you can be just as generous in giving. While you appreciate high-minded principles and pretty words, you are likely to be more impressed by those who actually live by them. In turn, the affection and love that you give to others is a solid commitment. Attracted to something or someone, you are persistent in your attentions. The Taurus influence suggests natural affinity for material advantages, personal comforts, and beauty in many forms. The beauty of nature and natural things, art, and music are high on the list of your appreciations and priorities. Males with Venus in Taurus are attracted to women with earthy beauty and sensuous natures. Females with Venus in Taurus have hearty, physically down-to-earth attractions, and they do not suffer well, or for very long, those who toy with their affections.

Venus in Gemini. Venus in Gemini indicates that your relationships, social attitudes, and contacts are imbued with wit and enthusiasm. Not likely to remain content with passive acknowledgments, you seek animated involvement with those around you, a quest no doubt aided by your friendly disposition and engaging curiosity. Unless these suggested traits are severely discouraged by other factors in your personality and background, your obvious interest in people is what in turn causes them to be attracted to you. You are a natural and accomplished flirt. Though your important emotional commitments may not lack depth or endurance, you do not, as a rule, find intense interactions with few people as wholly stimulating or satisfying as enjoying more light-hearted associations with many people. Variety and flexibility are two elements necessary to the quality of life you seek. You want, for example, to associate with many different people, and especially enjoy being around those with a sense of humor and interesting personality. You need to be involved in work or other situations that offer changes of pace and scenery from time to time. Your idea of beauty in art or music is apt to match the popular conception. Men with Venus in Gemini invariably have an eye for every pretty woman, but they are also attracted to those who exhibit intelligence and an air of mystery. Women with Venus in Gemini are changeable, what some may consider fickle. Until they settle down to a long-term relationship, they prefer a wide variety of male attendants.

Venus in Cancer. Venus in Cancer indicates that your relationships, social attitudes, and contacts are strongly attended by emotional influences. It is not necessarily indicative of great eagerness (or lack of it) for social contacts. It does mean that when attracted, either platonically or romantically, you must express all your sentiments, good and bad, and the significant emotional involvement that is usually present implies a certain lack of proportion. If, for example, you like something you are not content merely to appreciate it. You embrace it with your heart and soul. This is good in that it encourages those who either create or present whatever you so obviously enjoy, and also reassures those who are mutually attracted to you socially or romantically. However, you can drive everyone around you crazy with your latest craze, and you can become jealous and possessive with regard to possessions and relationships. Venus in Cancer indicates fondness for the domestic environment and enjoyment of family activities. Making others feel at home is one of your basic pleasures and apt to be an integral part of your profession or work. Beauty for you has more than aesthetic appeal. If it fails to convey sensitivity, it gets minimal attention. Men with Venus in Cancer are usually attracted to nurturing women, though they may not wish to be dominated by such females. Women with Venus in Cancer are vulnerable in their attractions, which can mean possessiveness and emotional dependence.

Venus in Leo. Venus in Leo indicates that relationships, social attitudes, and contacts are pursued with energy and enthusiasm. Unless other factors in your background or personality discourage it, Venus in Leo implies significant sociability. The quality of life is considerably diminished when you lack social contacts. Being so enthusiastically people-oriented, you automatically draw others to you. Difficult situations can arise, however, when your enthusiastic attraction for something or someone is misinterpreted as emotional commitment. Though your social nature is not apt to be overloaded from an emotional point of view, there is likely to be significant ego involvement. This means you may be too concerned with social status, too proud to admit rejection, and too stubbornly loyal to those who may not be worthy of it. The pleasure principle is very active when Venus is in Leo, an implication that your capacity for enjoyment is both natural and likely to be prodigious. You are apt to acquire quite a few "toys"— cars, appliances, tools, sports equipment, and so on. There is grandness in your appreciation of beauty, music, and especially art. For you, beauty should not be subdued. You are not attracted to the ordinary or mundane, preferring instead brightness and imagination. Men with Venus in Leo enjoy showing off their women. They are attracted to bold, beautiful ladies who know how to amuse them. Women with Venus in Leo are ambitious in their attractions. They are passionate, though not necessarily sympathetic, and they can be jealous, but not overly possessive.

Venus in Virgo. Venus in Virgo indicates that your relationships, social contacts, and behavior are somewhat subdued and analytical rather than spontaneous or eager. Others may often misjudge this approach, thinking you are either antisocial or just don't know how to have a good time. This is not necessarily true, since however subtle you are about it, you are very fond of luxury, physical comforts, and pleasure. The influence of Virgo does tend to be overly critical and analytical at times, but it also suggests creativity, caring, and friendly curiosity; all of which gives you a more substantial social nature than may be readily apparent. Part of the reason you may seem shy is that the practicality of Virgo makes it difficult to spontaneously interact with others, especially strangers, without having a reason or some common identification as a starting point. There are certain traits you value more than others. You are, for example, drawn to those who exhibit a strong sense of responsibility, and put off by those who constantly look to their own interests. You are not likely to be impressed with art, music, or beauty in any form that is too outrageous or flamboyant. Natural beauty is preferred to artifice and ostentation. Men with Venus in Virgo are usually attracted to women with compassionate natures, earthy beauty, and intelligence. Women with Venus in Virgo are not apt to be overly aggressive in pursuing the affections of others, but once the romance has bloomed they are passionate and down to earth.

Venus in Libra. Venus in Libra indicates that your relationships, social contacts, and attitudes are conducted on an intellectual level. If you are not gregarious or outgoing, you may not aggressively seek to be with others. That doesn't mean you are antisocial. Venus is strong in Libra, an indication of orientation toward people rather than away from them. Spending too much time alone is a mistake, since the stimulation of interactions with others, even on a fleeting basis, is necessary. Unless other factors in your personality discourage it, you have a cooperative spirit and are happiest when doing things with a partner. Being involved socially, academically, or professionally with people-related situations, such as public relations, law, and counseling, suits you quite well. You are attracted to music and art and a luxurious lifestyle. Beauty and harmony are important elements in the quality of your life, though you may not be totally conscious of these deeply ingrained preferences. If, for example, your domestic or working environment is esthetically unappealing or constantly invaded by fractious interactions of those who share it, you may be depressed or unhappy without being aware of the underlying cause. Those with bad manners, violent passions, and aggressive personalities are not apt to find you pursuing their attention or affections. Men with Venus in Libra are attracted to women who are well proportioned physically, mentally, and temperamentally. Women with Venus in Libra find their attractions grow stronger or weaker in direct proportion to the amount of interest that is returned.

Venus in Scorpio. Venus in Scorpio indicates that your relationships, social attitudes, and contacts are influenced by emotional needs. A conscious or unconscious desire for control means you want to know everything there is to know about the inner workings and physical or psychological make-up of whatever attracts you, and that includes people, situations, and things. In addition to enjoying art or music from an esthetic point of view, for example, you'll be likely to dig deeper in order to understand composition and construction. Observing people at close range is an enjoyable pursuit, and you'll be happy to sit and quietly watch the coming and goings of those around you. Though you may outwardly be gregarious and friendly, your interactions can sometimes become too intense, especially when you are attracted to someone. Though capable of being very circumspect in not revealing your attractions, you can also be very explicit and even brutally frank when stating what you want. The potential for developing control over your own desires is matched only by the intensity of the need to obtain what attracts you. Passions are always strong and can easily turn into jealousy, possessiveness, and vengefulness unless diminished by other factors in your personality and background. Even then it will always be difficult for you to give up one thing in order to gain another. Men with Venus in Scorpio are attracted to women who appear mysterious and unobtainable. Women with Venus in Scorpio are apt to be very sensuous with strong and passionate attractions.

Venus in Sagittarius. Venus in Sagittarius indicates that your relationships, social attitudes, and contacts are energetic, accompanied as they are by enthusiasm for travel and learning about people and various religions, cultures, and habitats. Your well-developed capacity for enjoying the good things in life is bound to mean too much generosity or exaggeration somewhere along the line. Your pursuits can deplete your bank account or afflict you with excess weight and other physical complaints related to overindulgence. Social contacts are widespread and varied, though you can be too conscious of wealth and status when selecting those with whom to socialize. Friends are important, and though emotional commitments may not be particularly deep or intense, you enjoy having many friends. Art, design, architecture, or fashion are highly appealing. You are also apt to be an excellent salesperson, teacher, or actor. The open honesty of Sagittarius means you do not beat around the bush or play games when it comes to dealing with who and what attracts you. The idealism associated with Sagittarius means you become discouraged when people fail to live up to your expectations. Dual-natured Sagittarius means you can be spiritual and sensitive as well as fickle and restless. Men with Venus in Sagittarius are attracted to the "ideal woman." More often than not, she turns out to be independent, intelligent, and a better friend than lover. The attractions of women with Venus in Sagittarius are imbued with idealism, sometimes causing them to lose sight of what their men are really like.

Venus in Capricorn. Venus in Capricorn indicates that your relationships, social attitudes, and contacts are imbued with a sense of practicality. Inhibitions or restrictions, either inherent in your approach or in the people you meet, slow things up. This sign position of Venus suggests fear of rejection, so it is not surprising if cautiousness creeps into your attitude toward others. The practicality of Capricorn means your dealings are not superficial. You have a natural tendency to mix business with pleasure. Contacts with others are immediately or eventually used to some advantage. Social contacts, for example, often become business clients, or the other way around. The onus of responsibility or seriousness invades many contacts. Either you take on more responsibility or get more involved than is necessary in your dealings with others, or others seem to automatically expect you to accept responsibility. You are apt to be attracted to those older or more mature. You enjoy politics, tradition, formality, ceremony. You are attracted to the beauty of nature and natural things, though your tastes can also be very ornate at times. You are attracted to those with authority and power, and in turn, you want to attract the respect of others. Though men with Venus in Capricorn have an eye for great beauties, in the long run they want ambitious ladies who will help them in their business or career. Women with Venus in Capricorn find their attractions somewhat inhibited, though not their passion or sensuousness when they are free to express themselves.

Venus in Aquarius. Venus in Aquarius indicates that your relationships, social attitudes, and contacts are frequent and enthusiastic. Venus, the planet that rules social contacts, in Aquarius, the sign associated with humanity and brotherhood, emphasizes the potential eagerness you should have for being part of many social groups. Unless other factors in your personality or background discourage it, you attract a wide variety of friends and associations wherever you go. Communicating with others is a vital element in your life, one that urges you to deal directly with people or the public. The further you get from being in constant contact with people, the more unhappy you will be. The possible problem with such a strong social orientation is that it may be difficult to concentrate on just one person or a few people. Those who have close personal relationships with you may complain that you are not sufficiently attentive. One of the most admirable traits possible with Venus in Aquarius is a truly unbiased attitude toward others. Race, religion, culture, or social level will not get in the way of your interest or affection for another individual. Men with Venus in Aquarius are attracted to women with exotic or unusual beauty or always settle for someone very much like themselves. Women with Venus in Aquarius are extremely social. Their attractions usually cover a wide range, and until the right man comes along, they prefer friendship rather than passion.

Venus in Pisces. Venus in Pisces indicates that there is a great deal of emotional input and sensitivity involved in your relationships, social attitudes, and contacts. You may or may not be gregarious, but you enjoy being in social situations and being around people in general. The friendships you establish are extremely close and can become very spiritual or even psychic in nature. This position of Venus implies an artistic temperament, which can leave you very vulnerable with respect to those who may not be as sensitive in their outlook or approach. You are apt to get maximum enjoyment out of sensual pleasures, though you can also become addicted to them. Unless other factors in your personality and background have given you a more cynical view of life, romance takes first place. Lack of discrimination and a too-compassionate nature can be your biggest downfalls as well as your greatest virtues. You value the small things over the big things in life. Venus in Pisces is very strong and is often the indication of talent as well as deep appreciation for art, music, dance, and other creative endeavors. Beauty is everywhere in your eyes and seldom do you miss seeing it, even where others do not. Men with Venus in Pisces often choose females that bring them sorrow; however, they are most attracted to women of great beauty and delicate manners. Women with Venus in Pisces form sentimental, fanciful attractions, which may often put them at the mercies of false flattery and insincere attentions.

How to Find the Place of Venus in Your Chart

Find your birth year in the left-hand column and read across the chart until you find your birth date. The top of that column will tell you where Venus lies in your chart.

PLACE OF VENUS—1880–1891

	ARIES	TAURUS	GEMINI	CANCER	LEO	VIRGO	LIBRA	SCORPIO	SAGITT.	CAPRI.	AQUAR.	PISCES
1880	4/14–5/7	5/8–6/1	6/2–6/25	6/26–7/20	7/21–8/13	8/14–9/6	9/7–9/30	1/1–1/4 10/1–10/25	1/5–1/30 10/26–11/18	1/31–2/24 11/19–12/13	2/25–3/19 12/14–12/31	3/20–4/13
1881	2/3–3/3	3/4–7/7	7/8–8/5	8/6–9/1	9/2–9/27	9/28–10/21	10/22–11/14	11/15–12/8	12/9–12/31		1/1–1/7	1/8–2/2
1882	3/15–4/7	4/8–5/2	5/3–5/26	5/27–6/20	6/21–7/15	7/16–8/10	8/11–9/6	9/7–10/6	1/1 10/7–12/31	1/2–1/25	1/26–2/18	2/19–3/14
1883	4/28–5/22	5/23–6/16	6/17–7/11	7/12–8/4	8/5–8/29	8/30–9/22	9/23–10/16	10/17–11/9	1/1–2/4 11/10–12/3	2/5–3/6 12/4–12/27	3/7–4/1 12/28–12/31	4/2–4/27
1884	2/15–3/10	3/11–4/5	4/6–5/4	5/5–9/7	9/8–10/7	10/8–11/3	11/4–11/28	11/29–12/22	12/23–12/31		1/1–1/20	1/21–2/14
1885	3/30–4/22	4/23–5/16	5/17–6/10	6/11–7/4	7/5–7/29	7/30–8/23	8/24–9/16	9/17–10/12	1/1–1/16 10/13–11/6	1/17–2/9 11/7–12/4	2/10–3/5 12/5–12/31	3/6–3/29
1886	5/7–6/3	6/4–6/29	6/30–7/25	7/26–8/19	8/20–9/12	9/13–10/7	10/8–10/31	11/1–11/23	11/24–12/17	12/18–12/31	1/1–1/6 2/19–4/1	1/7–2/18 4/2–5/6
1887	2/28–3/24	3/25–4/17	4/18–5/13	5/14–6/8	6/9–7/6	7/7–8/11 9/19–11/5	8/12–9/18 11/6–12/8	12/9–12/31		1/1–1/10	1/11–2/3	2/4–2/27
1888	4/13–5/7	5/8–5/31	6/1–6/25	6/26–7/19	7/20–8/12	8/13–9/6	9/7–9/30	1/1–1/4 10/1–10/24	1/5–1/29 10/25–11/18	1/30–2/23 11/19–12/12	2/24–3/19 12/13–12/31	3/20–4/12
1889	2/3–3/4	3/5–7/7	7/8–8/5	8/6–9/1	9/2–9/26	9/27–10/21	10/22–11/14	11/15–12/8	12/9–12/31		1/1–1/6	1/7–2/2
1890	3/15–4/7	4/8–5/1	5/2–5/26	5/27–6/20	6/21–7/15	7/16–8/10	8/11–9/6	9/7–10/7	1/1 10/8–12/31	1/2–1/25	1/26–2/18	2/19–3/14
1891	4/27–5/22	5/23–6/16	6/17–7/10	7/11–8/4	8/5–8/28	8/29–9/21	9/22–10/15	10/16–11/8	1/1 11/9–12/2	2/6–3/5 12/3–12/26	3/6–4/1 12/27–12/31	4/2–4/26

PLACE OF VENUS—1892–1906

Year												
1892	2/14–3/9	3/10–4/4	4/5–5/4	5/5–9/7	9/8–10/7	10/8–11/2	11/3–11/27	11/28–12/22	12/23–12/31		1/1–1/20	1/21–2/13
1893	3/29–4/22	4/23–5/16	5/17–6/9	6/10–7/4	7/5–7/28	7/29–8/22	8/23–9/16	9/17–10/11	1/1–1/15, 10/12–11/6	1/16–2/8, 11/7–12/4	2/9–3/4, 12/5–12/31	3/5–3/28
1894	5/5–6/2	6/3–6/29	6/30–7/24	7/25–8/18	8/19–9/12	9/13–10/6	10/7–10/30	10/31–11/23	11/24–12/17	12/18–12/31	1/1–1/8, 2/13–4/2	1/9–2/12, 4/3–5/4
1895	2/28–3/23	3/24–4/17	4/18–5/12	5/13–6/7	6/8–7/6	7/7–8/13, 9/13–11/6	8/14–9/12, 11/7–12/8	12/9–12/31		1/1–1/10	1/11–2/3	2/4–2/27
1896	4/13–5/6	5/7–5/31	6/1–6/24	6/25–7/19	7/20–8/12	8/13–9/5	9/6–9/29	1/1–1/3, 9/30–10/24	1/4–1/29, 10/25–11/17	1/30–2/23, 11/18–12/12	2/24–3/18, 12/13–12/31	3/19–4/12
1897	2/2–3/4	3/5–7/7	7/8–8/5	8/6–8/31	9/1–9/26	9/27–10/20	10/21–11/13	11/14–12/7	12/8–12/31		1/1–1/6	1/7–2/1
1898	3/14–4/6	4/7–5/1	5/2–5/25	5/26–6/19	6/20–7/14	7/15–8/10	8/11–9/16	9/17–10/7	10/8–12/31	1/1–1/24	1/25–2/17	2/18–3/13
1899	4/27–5/21	5/22–6/15	6/16–7/10	7/11–8/3	8/4–8/28	8/29–9/21	9/22–10/15	10/16–11/8	1/1–1/25, 11/9–12/2	2/6–3/5, 12/3–12/26	3/6–3/31, 12/27–12/31	4/1–4/26
1900	2/14–3/10	3/11–4/5	4/6–5/5	5/6–9/8	9/9–10/8	10/9–11/3	11/4–11/28	11/29–12/22	12/23–12/31		1/1–1/19	1/20–2/13
1901	3/30–4/22	4/23–5/16	5/17–6/10	6/11–7/4	7/5–7/29	7/30–8/23	8/24–9/16	9/17–10/12	1/1–1/15, 10/13–11/17	1/16–2/9, 11/8–12/5	2/10–3/5, 12/6–12/31	3/6–3/29
1902	5/7–6/3	6/4–6/29	6/30–7/25	7/26–8/19	8/20–9/12	9/13–10/7	10/8–10/30	10/31–11/23	11/24–12/17	12/18–12/31	1/1–1/11, 2/7–4/4	1/12–2/6, 4/5–5/6
1903	2/28–3/23	3/24–4/17	4/18–5/13	5/14–6/8	6/9–7/7	7/8–8/17, 9/7–11/8	8/18–9/6, 11/9–12/9	12/10–12/31		1/1–1/10	1/11–2/3	2/4–2/27
1904	4/13–5/7	5/8–5/31	6/1–6/25	6/26–7/19	7/20–8/12	8/13–9/6	9/7–9/30	1/1–1/4, 10/1–10/24	1/5–1/29, 10/25–11/18	1/30–2/23, 11/19–12/12	2/24–3/19, 12/13–12/31	3/20–4/12
1905	2/3–3/5, 5/9–5/27	3/6–5/8, 5/28–7/7	7/8–8/5	8/6–9/1	9/2–9/26	9/27–10/21	10/22–11/14	11/15–12/8	12/9–12/31		1/1–1/7	1/8–2/2
1906	3/15–4/7	4/8–5/1	5/2–5/26	5/27–6/20	6/21–7/15	7/16–8/10	8/11–9/7	9/8–10/8, 12/16–12/25	1/1, 10/9–12/15, 12/26–12/31	1/2–1/25	1/26–2/18	2/19–3/14

PLACE OF VENUS—1907–1916

	ARIES	TAURUS	GEMINI	CANCER	LEO	VIRGO	LIBRA	SCORPIO	SAGITT.	CAPRI.	AQUAR.	PISCES
1907	4·28–5·22	5·23–6·16	6·17–7·10	7·11–8·3	8·4–8·28	8·29–9·21	9·22–10·15	10·16–11·8	1·1–2·6 11·9–12·2	2·7–3·6 12·3–12·26	3·7–4·1 12·27–12·31	4·2–4·27
1908	2·14–3·9	3·10–4·5	4·6–5·5	5·6–9·8	9·9–10·7	10·8–11·2	11·3–11·27	11·28–12·22	12·23–12·31		1·1–1·20	1·21–2·13
1909	3·29–4·21	4·22–5·16	5·17–6·9	6·10–7·4	7·5–7·28	7·29–8·22	8·23–9·16	9·17–10·11	1·1–1·15 10·12–11·6	1·16–2·8 11·7–12·5	2·9–3·3 12·6–12·31	3·4–3·28
1910	5·7–6·3	6·4–6·29	6·30–7·24	7·25–8·18	8·19–9·12	9·13–10·6	10·7–10·30	10·31–11·23	11·24–12·17	12·18–12·31	1·1–1·15 1·29–4·4	1·16–1·28 4·5–5·6
1911	2·28–3·23	3·24–4·17	4·18–5·12	5·13–6·8	6·9–7·7	7·8–11·8	11·9–12·8	12·9–12·31		1·1–1·10	1·11–2·2	2·3–2·27
1912	4·13–5·6	5·7–5·31	6·1–6·24	6·25–7·18	7·19–8·12	8·13–9·5	9·6–9·30	1·1–1·4 9·31–10·24	1·5–1·29 10·25–11·17	1·30–2·23 11·18–12·12	2·24–3·18 12·13–12·31	3·19–4·12
1913	2·3–3·6 5·2–5·30	3·7–5·1 5·31–7·7	7·8–8·5	8·6–8·31	9·1–9·26	9·27–10·20	10·21–11·13	11·14–12·7	12·8–12·31		1·1–1·6	1·7–2·2
1914	3·14–4·6	4·7–5·1	5·2–5·25	5·26–6·19	6·20–7·15	7·16–8·10	8·11–9·6	9·7–10·9 12·6–12·30	10·10–12·5 12·31	1·1–1·24	1·25–2·17	2·18–3·13
1915	4·27–5·21	5·22–6·15	6·16–7·10	7·11–8·3	8·4–8·28	8·29–9·21	9·22–10·15	10·16–11·8	1·1–2·6 11·9–12·2	2·7–3·6 12·3–12·26	3·7–4·1 12·27–12·31	4·2–4·26
1916	2·14–3·9	3·10–4·5	4·6–5·5	5·6–9·8	9·9–10·7	10·8–11·2	11·3–11·27	11·28–12·21	12·22–12·31		1·1–1·19	1·20–2·13

PLACE OF VENUS—1917-1931

Year												
1917	3/29-4/21	4/22-5/15	5/16-6/9	6/10-7/3	7/4-7/28	7/29-8/21	8/22-9/16	9/17-10/11	1/1-1/14 10/12-11/6	1/15-2/7 11/7-12/5	2/8-3/4 12/6-12/31	3/5-3/28
1918	5/7-6/2	6/3-6/28	6/29-7/24	7/25-8/18	8/19-9/11	9/12-10/5	10/6-10/29	10/30-11/22	11/23-12/16	12/17-12/31	1/1-4/5	4/6-5/6
1919	2/27-3/22	3/23-4/16	4/17-5/12	5/13-6/7	6/8-7/7	7/8-11/8	11/9-12/8	12/9-12/31		1/1-1/9	1/10-2/2	2/3-2/26
1920	4/12-5/6	5/7-5/30	5/31-6/23	6/24-7/18	7/19-8/11	8/12-9/4	9/5-9/30	1/1-1/3 9/31-10/23	1/4-1/28 10/24-11/17	1/29-2/22 11/18-12/11	2/23-3/18 12/12-12/31	3/19-4/11
1921	2/3-3/6 4/26-6/1	3/7-4/25 6/2-7/7	7/8-8/5	8/6-8/31	9/1-9/25	9/26-10/20	10/21-11/13	11/14-12/7	12/8-12/31		1/1-1/6	1/7-2/2
1922	3/13-4/6	4/7-4/30	5/1-5/25	5/26-6/19	6/20-7/14	7/15-8/9	8/10-9/6	9/7-10/10 11/29⌐	10/11-11/28	⌐1/24	1/25-2/16	2/17-3/12
1923	4/27-5/21	5/22-6/14	6/15-7/9	7/10-8/3	8/4-8/27	8/28-9/20	9/21-10/14	10/15-11/7	1/2-2/6 11/8-12/1	2/7-3/5 12/2-12/25	3/6-3/31 12/26⌐	4/1-4/26
1924	2/13-3/8	3/9-4/4	4/5-5/5	5/6-9/8	9/9-10/7	10/8-11/2	11/3-11/26	11/27-12/21	12/22⌐	⌐1/14	1/1-1/19	1/20-2/12
1925	3/28-4/20	4/21-5/15	5/16-6/8	6/9-7/3	7/4-7/27	7/28-8/21	8/22-9/15	9/16-10/11	1/1-1/14 10/12-11/6	1/15-2/7 11/7-12/5	2/8-3/3 12/6⌐	3/4-3/27
1926	5/7-6/2	6/3-6/28	6/29-7/23	7/24-8/17	8/18-9/11	9/12-10/5	10/6-10/29	10/30-11/22	11/23-12/16	12/17-12/31	1/1-4/5	4/6-5/6
1927	2/27-3/22	3/23-4/16	4/17-5/11	5/12-6/7	6/8-7/7	7/8-11/9	11/10-12/8	12/9⌐		⌐1/8	1/9-2/1	2/2-2/26
1928	4/12-5/5	5/6-5/29	5/30-6/23	6/24-7/17	7/18-8/11	8/12-9/4	9/5-9/28	⌐1/3 9/29-10/23	1/4-1/28 10/24-11/16	1/29-2/22 11/17-12/11	2/23-3/17 12/12⌐	3/18-4/11
1929	2/3-3/7 4/20-6/2	3/8-4/19 6/3-7/7	7/8-8/4	8/5-8/30	8/31-9/25	9/26-10/19	10/20-11/12	11/13-12/6	12/7-12/30	12/31⌐	⌐1/5	1/6-2/2
1930	3/13-4/5	4/6-4/30	5/1-5/24	5/25-6/18	6/19-7/14	7/15-8/9	8/10-9/6	9/7-10/11 11/22⌐	10/12-11/21	⌐1/23	1/24-2/16	2/17-3/12
1931	4/26-5/20	5/21-6/14	6/15-7/9	7/10-8/2	8/3-8/26	8/27-9/20	9/21-10/14	⌐1/3 10/15-11/7	1/4-2/6 11/8-12/1	2/7-3/5 12/2-12/25	3/6-3/31 12/26⌐	4/1-4/25

PLACE OF VENUS—1932–1943

	ARIES	TAURUS	GEMINI	CANCER	LEO	VIRGO	LIBRA	SCORPIO	SAGITT.	CAPRI.	AQUAR.	PISCES
1932	2/13–3/8	3/9–4/4	4/5–5/5 7/13–7/27	5/6–7/12 7/28–9/8	9/9–10/6	10/7–11/1	11/2–11/26	11/27–12/20	12/21		↰1/18	1/19–2/12
1933	3/28–4/20	4/21–5/14	5/15–6/8	6/9–7/2	7/3–7/27	7/28–8/21	8/22–9/15	9/16–10/10	↰1/13 10/11–11/6	1/14–2/6 11/7–12/5	2/7–3/2 12/6	3/3–3/27
1934	5/6–6/1	6/2–6/27	6/28–7/23	7/24–8/17	8/18–9/10	9/11–10/4	10/5–10/28	10/29–11/21	11/22–12/15	12/16↰	4/5	4/6–5/5
1935	2/26–3/21	3/22–4/15	4/16–5/11	5/12–6/7	6/8–7/7	7/8–11/9	11/10–12/8	12/9↰		↰1/8	1/9–2/1	2/2–2/25
1936	4/11–5/4	5/5–5/29	5/30–6/22	6/23–7/17	7/18–8/10	8/11–9/3	9/4–9/28	↰1/3 9/29–10/22	1/4–1/28 10/23–11/16	1/29–2/21 11/17–12/11	2/22–3/17 12/12	3/18–4/10
1937	2/2–3/9 4/14–6/3	3/10–4/13 6/4–7/7	7/8–8/4	8/5–8/30	8/31–9/24	9/25–10/19	10/20–11/12	11/13–12/6	12/7–12/30	12/31	↰1/5	1/6–2/1
1938	3/12–4/5	4/6–4/29	4/30–5/24	5/25–6/18	6/19–7/13	7/14–8/9	8/10–9/6	9/7–10/13 11/16↰	10/14–11/15	↰1/22	1/23–2/15	2/16–3/11
1939	4/26–5/20	5/21–6/13	6/14–7/8	7/9–8/2	8/3–8/26	8/27–9/19	9/20–10/13	↰1/4 10/14–11/6	1/5–2/5 11/7–11/30	2/6–3/5 12/1–12/24	3/6–3/30 12/25	3/31–4/25
1940	2/12–3/8	3/9–4/4	4/5–5/6 7/6–7/31	5/7–7/5 8/1–9/8	9/9–10/6	10/7–11/1	11/2–11/26	11/27–12/20	12/21↰		↰1/18	1/19–2/11
1941	3/27–4/19	4/20–5/14	5/15–6/7	6/8–7/2	7/3–7/26	7/27–8/20	8/21–9/14	9/15–10/10	↰1/13 10/11–11/5	1/14–2/6 11/6–12/5	2/7–3/2 12/6	3/3–3/26
1942	5/6–6/1	6/2–6/27	6/28–7/22	7/23–8/16	8/17–9/10	9/11–10/4	10/5–10/28	10/29–11/21	11/22–12/15	12/16↰	↰4/6	4/7–5/5
1943	2/26–3/21	3/22–4/15	4/16–5/10	5/11–6/7	6/8–7/7	7/8–11/9	11/10–12/17	12/8↰		↰1/7	1/8–1/31	2/1–2/25

PLACE OF VENUS—1944–1958

Year												
1944	4/11-5/4	5/5-5/28	5/29-6/22	6/23-7/16	7/17-8/10	8/11-9/3	9/4-9/27	1/2 · 9/28-10/22	1/3-1/27 · 10/23-11/15	1/28-2/21 · 11/16-12/9	2/22-3/16 · 12/10	3/17-4/10
1945	2/2-3/10 · 4/8-6/4	3/11-4/7 · 6/5-7/7	7/8-8/3	8/4-8/30	8/31-9/24	9/25-10/18	10/19-11/11	11/12-12/5	12/6-12/29	1/22 · 12/30	1/5	1/6-2/1
1946	3/12-4/4	4/5-4/28	4/29-5/23	5/24-6/17	6/18-7/13	7/14-8/8	8/9-9/6	11/8 · 9/7-10/15	10/16-11/7	1/22 · 12/6-12/29	1/23-2/15	2/16-3/11
1947	4/25-5/18	5/19-6/13	6/14-7/8	7/9-7/31	8/1-8/25	8/26-9/18	9/19-10/13	1/5 · 10/14-11/6	11/7-11/30	12/1-12/24	3/5-3/30 · 12/25	3/31-4/24
1948	2/12-3/7	3/8-4/4	4/5-5/6 · 6/29-8/2	5/7-6/28 · 8/3-9/8	9/9-10/6	10/7-10/31	11/1-11/25	11/26-12/19	12/20	10/10-11/4	1/17	1/18-2/11
1949	3/26-4/19	4/20-5/13	5/14-6/6	6/7-7/1	7/2-7/26	7/27-8/20	8/21-9/14	9/15-10/9	1/12 · 10/10-11/4	1/13-2/5 · 11/5-12/5	2/6-3/1 · 12/6	3/2-3/25
1950	5/6-6/1	6/2-6/26	6/27-7/22	7/23-8/16	8/17-9/9	9/10-10/3	10/4-10/27	10/28-11/20	11/21-12/14	12/15-12/31	4/6	4/7-5/5
1951	2/25-3/21	3/22-4/15	4/16-5/11	5/12-6/7	6/8-7/8	7/9-11/9	11/10-12/7	12/8 · 9/28-10/22	1/1-1/7	12/15-12/31	1/8-1/31	2/1-2/24
1952	4/10-5/4	5/5-5/28	5/29-6/22	6/23-7/16	7/17-8/9	8/10-9/3	9/4-9/27	1/2 · 9/28-10/22	1/3-1/27 · 10/23-11/15	1/28-2/21 · 11/16-12/10	2/22-3/16 · 12/11	3/17-4/9
1953	2/3-2/14 · 4/1-6/5	2/15-3/31 · 6/6-7/7	7/8-8/4	8/5-8/30	8/31-9/24	9/25-10/18	10/19-11/11	11/12-12/5	12/6-12/29	1/22 · 12/30	1/5	1/6-2/2
1954	3/12-4/4	4/5-4/28	4/29-5/23	5/24-6/17	6/18-7/13	7/14-8/8	8/9-9/6	10/28 · 9/7-10/23	10/13-11/5 · 10/24-10/27	1/6 · 11/26-12/19	1/23-2/15	2/16-3/11
1955	4/25-5/19	5/20-6/13	6/14-7/8	7/9-8/1	8/2-8/25	8/26-9/18	9/19-10/12	1/6 · 10/13-11/5	11/6-11/30	12/1-12/24	3/5-3/30 · 12/25	3/31-4/24
1956	2/12-3/7	3/8-4/4	4/5-5/8 · 6/24-8/4	5/9-6/23 · 8/5-9/8	9/9-10/5	10/6-10/31	11/1-11/25	11/26-12/19	1/12 · 12/20	10/10-11/4	1/17	1/18-2/11
1957	3/26-4/19	4/20-5/13	5/14-6/6	6/7-7/1	7/2-7/26	7/27-8/19	8/20-9/14	9/15-10/9	1/12 · 10/10-11/4	1/13-2/5 · 11/5-12/6	2/6-3/1 · 12/7	3/2-3/25
1958	5/6-6/1	6/2-6/26	6/27-7/22	7/23-8/15	8/16-9/9	9/10-10/3	10/4-10/27	10/28-11/20	11/21-12/14	12/15	4/6	4/7-5/5

PLACE OF VENUS—1959–1969

	ARIES	TAURUS	GEMINI	CANCER	LEO	VIRGO	LIBRA	SCORPIO	SAGITT.	CAPRI.	AQUAR.	PISCES
1959	2/25–3/20	3/21–4/14	4/15–5/10	5/11–6/6	6/7–7/8 / 9/21–9/24	7/9–9/20 / 9/25–11/9	11/10–12/7	12/8		1/7	1/8–1/31	2/1–2/24
1960	4/10–5/3	5/4–5/28	5/29–6/21	6/22–7/15	7/16–8/9	8/10–9/2	9/3–9/27	1/2 / 9/28–10/21	1/3–1/26 / 10/22–11/15	1/27–2/20 / 11/16–12/10	2/21–3/15 / 12/11–12/31	3/16–4/9
1961	2/2–6/4	6/5–7/6	7/7–8/2	8/3–8/28	8/29–9/22	9/23–10/17	10/18–11/10	11/11–12/4	12/5–12/27	12/28	1/1–1/4	1/5–2/1
1962	3/10–4/2	4/3–4/27	4/28–5/22	5/23–6/16	6/17–7/11	7/12–8/7	8/8–9/5	9/6		1/20	1/21–2/13	2/14–3/9
1963	4/24–5/18	5/19–6/11	6/12–7/6	7/7–7/30	7/31–8/24	8/25–9/17	9/18–10/11	1/5 / 10/12–11/4	1/6–2/4 / 11/5–11/28	2/5–3/3 / 11/29–12/22	3/4–3/29 / 12/23	3/30–4/23
1964	2/10–3/6	3/7–4/3	4/4–5/8 / 6/17–8/4	5/9–6/16 / 8/5–9/7	9/8–10/4	10/5–10/30	10/31–11/24	11/25–12/18	12/19		1/16	1/17–2/9
1965	3/25–4/17	4/18–5/11	5/12–6/5	6/6–6/29	6/30–7/24	7/25–8/18	8/19–9/12	9/13–10/8	1/11 / 10/9–11/4	1/12–2/4 / 11/5–12/6	2/5–2/28 / 12/7	3/1–3/24
1966	5/5–5/30	5/31–6/25	6/26–7/20	7/21–8/14	8/15–9/7	9/8–10/2	10/3–10/26	10/27–11/19	11/20–12/12	2/6–2/24 / 12/13	2/25–4/5	4/6–5/4
1967	2/23–3/19	3/20–4/13	4/14–5/9	5/10–6/5	6/6–7/7 / 9/9–9/30	7/8–9/8 / 10/1–11/8	11/9–12/6	12/7–12/31		1/5	1/6–1/29	1/30–2/22
1968	4/8–5/2	5/3–5/26	5/27–6/20	6/21–7/14	7/15–8/7	8/8–9/1	9/2–9/25	9/26–10/20	1/1–1/25 / 10/21–11/13	1/26–2/19 / 11/14–12/8	2/20–3/14 / 12/9	3/15–4/7
1969	2/2–6/5	6/6–7/5	7/6–8/2	8/3–8/28	8/29–9/22	9/23–10/16	10/17–11/9	11/10–12/3	12/4–12/27	12/28	1/3	1/4–2/1

PLACE OF VENUS—1970–1980

Year												
1970	3/10-4/2	4/3-4/26	4/27-5/21	5/22-6/15	6/16-7/11	7/12-8/7	8/8-9/6	9/7-12/31		↳1/20	1/21-2/13	2/14-3/9
1971	4/23-5/17	5/18-6/11	6/12-7/5	7/6-7/31	8/1-8/23	8/24-9/16	9/17-10/10	1/1-1/6 / 10/11-11/4	1/7-2/4 / 11/15-11/28	2/5-3/3 / 11/29-12/22	3/4-3/28 / 12/23↳	3/29-4/22
1972	2/10-3/7	3/8-4/2	4/3-5/9 / 6/11-8/5	5/10-6/10 / 8/6-9/6	9/7-10/4	10/5-10/29	10/30-11/23	11/24-12/17	12/18↳		↳1/15	1/16-2/9
1973	3/24-4/17	4/18-5/11	5/12-6/4	6/5-6/29	6/30-7/24	7/25-8/18	8/19-9/12	9/13-10/8	↳1/10 / 10/9-11/4	1/11-2/3 / 11/5-12/6	2/4-2/27 / 12/7↳	2/28-3/23
1974	5/4-5/30	5/31-6/24	6/25-7/20	7/21-8/13	8/14-9/7	9/8-10/1	10/2-10/25	10/26-11/18	11/19-12/12	1/29-2/27 / 12/13↳	↳1/28 / 2/28-4/5	4/6-5/3
1975	2/23-3/18	3/19-4/12	4/13-5/8	5/9-6/5	6/6-7/8	7/9-9/1 / 10/4-11/8	9/2-10/3 / 11/9-12/6	12/7-12/31		↳1/5	1/6-1/29	1/30-2/22
1976	4/8-5/1	5/2-5/26	5/27-6/19	6/20-7/13	7/14-8/7	8/8-8/31	9/1-9/25	1/1-1/10 / 9/26-10/19	1/11-1/25 / 10/20-11/13	1/26-2/18 / 11/14-12/8	2/19-3/14 / 12/9↳	3/15-4/7
1977	2/2-6/5	6/6-7/5	7/6-8/1	8/2-8/27	8/28-9/21	9/22-10/16	10/17-11/9	11/10-12/3	12/4-12/26	12/27↳	↳1/3	1/4-2/1
1978	3/9-4/1	4/2-4/26	4/27-5/21	5/22-6/15	6/16-7/11	7/12-8/7	8/8-9/6	9/7-12/31		↳1/19	1/20-2/12	2/13-3/8
1979	4/23-5/17	5/18-6/10	6/11-7/5	7/6-7/29	7/30-8/23	8/24-9/16	9/17-10/10	1/1-1/6 / 10/11-11/3	1/7-2/4 / 11/4-11/27	2/5-3/2 / 11/28-12/21	3/3-3/28 / 12/22↳	3/29-4/22
1980	2/9-3/5	3/6-4/2	4/3-5/11 / 6/5-8/5	5/12-6/4 / 8/6-9/6	9/7-10/3	10/4-10/29	10/30-11/23	11/24-12/17	12/18-12/31		↳1/15	1/16-2/8

PLACE OF VENUS—1981–1987

	ARIES	TAURUS	GEMINI	CANCER	LEO	VIRGO	LIBRA	SCORPIO	SAGITT.	CAPRI.	AQUAR.	PISCES
1981	3/24–4/16	4/17–5/10	5/11–6/4	6/5–6/28	6/29–7/23	7/24–8/17	8/18–9/11	9/12–10/7	1/1–1/10 10/8–11/4	1/11–2/3 11/5–12/7	2/4–2/27 12/8↱	2/28–3/23
1982	5/4–5/29	5/30–6/24	6/25–7/19	7/20–8/13	8/14–9/6	9/7–9/30	10/1–10/24	10/25–11/17	11/18–12/11	1/22–3/1 12/12↱	↰1/21 3/2–4/5	4/6–5/3
1983	2/22–3/18	3/19–4/12	4/13–5/8	5/9–6/5	6/6–7/9 8/27–10/4	7/10–8/26 10/5–11/8	11/9–12/5	12/6–12/30	12/31↱	↰1/4	1/5–1/28	1/29–2/21
1984	4/7–4/30	5/1–5/25	5/26–6/18	6/19–7/13	7/14–8/6	8/7–8/31	9/1–9/24	9/25–10/19	↰1/24 10/20–11/12	1/25–2/17 11/13–12/7	2/18–3/13 12/8↱	3/14–4/6
1985	2/2–6/5	6/6–7/5	7/6–8/1	8/2–8/26	8/27–9/20	9/21–10/15	10/16–11/8	11/9–12/2	12/3–12/26	12/27↱	↰1/3	1/4–2/1
1986	3/8–4/1	4/2–4/25	4/26–5/20	5/21–6/14	6/15–7/10	7/11–8/6	8/7–9/6	9/7↱		↰1/19	1/20–2/11	2/12–3/7
1987	4/22–5/16	5/17–6/10	6/11–7/4	7/5–7/29	7/30–8/22	8/23–9/15	9/16–10/9	↰1/6 10/10–11/2	1/7–2/3 11/3–11/26	2/4–3/2 11/27–12/21	3/3–3/27 12/22↱	3/28–4/21

PLACE OF VENUS—1988–2000

Year													
1988	2/9–3/5	3/6–4/2	4/3–5/16 5/27–8/5	5/17–5/26 8/6–9/6	9/7–10/3	10/4–10/28	10/29–11/22	11/23–12/16	12/17	1/10–2/2 11/5–12/8	2/3–2/26 12/9	↪1/14	1/15–2/8
1989	3/23–4/15	4/16–5/10	5/11–6/3	6/4–6/28	6/29–7/22	7/23–8/16	8/17–9/11	9/12–10/7	↪1/9 10/8–11/4	11/5–12/8			2/27–3/22
1990	5/3–5/29	5/30–6/23	6/24–7/18	7/19–8/12	8/13–9/6	9/7–9/30	10/1–10/24	10/25–11/17	11/18–12/11	12/12	1/16–3/2 12/12	↪1/15 3/3–4/5	4/6–5/2
1991	2/22–3/17	3/18–4/11	4/12–5/7	5/8–6/4	6/5–7/10 8/21–10/5	7/11–8/20 10/6–11/8	11/9–12/5	12/6–12/30	12/31	1/25–2/17 11/13–12/7	1/5–1/27	↪1/4	1/28–2/21
1992	4/7–4/30	5/1–5/24	5/25–6/18	6/19–7/12	7/13–8/6	8/7–8/30	8/31–9/23	9/24–10/18	↪1/24 10/19–11/12	1/25–2/17 11/13–12/7	2/18–3/12 12/8		3/13–4/6
1993	2/2–6/5	6/6–7/4	7/5–7/31	8/1–8/26	8/27–9/20	9/21–10/14	10/15–11/7	11/8–12/1	12/2–12/25	12/26		↪1/2	1/3–2/1
1994	3/8–3/31	4/1–4/25	4/26–5/19	5/20–6/14	6/15–7/10	7/11–8/6	8/7–9/6	9/7	↪1/6 10/10–11/2	11/22–12/16	12/26	↪1/18 1/19–2/11	2/12–3/7
1995	4/21–5/15	5/16–6/9	6/10–7/4	7/5–7/28	7/29–8/21	8/22–9/15	9/16–10/9	10/10–11/2	11/3–11/26	11/27–12/20	↪1/7 1/7–2/3	3/2–3/27 12/21	3/28–4/20
1996	2/8–3/4	3/5–4/2	4/3–8/6	8/7–9/6	9/7–10/2	10/3–10/28	10/29–11/21	11/22–12/16	12/17	1/10–2/1 11/5–12/10	2/2–2/25 12/11	↪1/13	1/14–2/7
1997	3/23–4/15	4/16–5/9	5/10–6/2	6/3–6/27	6/28–7/22	7/23–8/16	8/17–9/10	9/11–10/7	↪1/9 10/8–11/4	11/5–12/10	1/9–3/3 12/11		2/26–3/22
1998	5/3–5/28	5/29–6/23	6/24–7/18	7/19–8/12	8/13–9/5	9/6–9/29	9/30–10/23	10/24–11/16	11/17–12/10	12/11	1/9–3/3 12/11	↪1/8 3/4–4/5	4/6–5/2
1999	2/21–3/17	3/18–4/11	4/12–5/7	5/8–6/4	6/5–7/11 8/15–10/6	7/12–8/14 10/7–11/7	11/8–12/4	12/5–12/29	12/30	1/24–2/16 11/12–12/7	1/4–1/27	↪1/3	1/28–2/20
2000	4/6–4/29	4/30–5/24	5/25–6/17	6/18–7/12	7/13–8/5	8/6–8/29	8/30–9/23	9/24–10/18	↪1/23 10/19–11/11	1/24–2/16 11/12–12/7	2/17–3/12 12/8–12/30		3/13–4/5

YOUR MOST CONSPICUOUS TRAIT: ARIES—Courage; TAURUS—Fortitude; GEMINI—Alertness; CANCER—Loyalty; LEO—Magnanimity; VIRGO—Efficiency; LIBRA—Friendliness; SCORPIO—Determination; SAGITTARIUS—Fidelity; CAPRICORN—Sincerity; AQUARIUS—Cooperation; PISCES—Compassion.

Mars: Drive and Ego

Mars is associated with your physical actions as they are directed by your ego, emotions, and intellect. It is physical energy. It is the energy that fuels intellectual endeavors. And finally, as the passionate expression of emotions, it fires sexual activities, gives birth to the anger of disappointment or frustration, engenders the elation from joy and success, and heightens the merriment of laughter. In a male's chart, Mars describes his masculine identity, the aggressiveness of his male spirit. In a female's chart, Mars relates to the important men in her life, her attitude toward men and relationships with them.

Mars in Aries. Mars in Aries indicates raw energy. Mars, the planet that rules Aries, is very potent when in its own sign. Potent or not, there is no guarantee you will make full or proper use of its potential energy. Mars in Aries might be compared to a tightly wound spring, poised and ready to move. If its direction and purpose have not been planned in advance, when the energy is released, it can go off in any number of unpredictable directions or simply wander around in circles, accomplishing nothing at all. Aries is the sign of the warrior, increasing the potential for being openly combative, a daredevil and gambler. Not putting enough thought behind your actions, or caring about their consequences, you let yourself in for many regrets, and starting over more times than you'd like to admit. On the other hand, if you possess a more subdued approach, or at least managed to develop one, you will enjoy a steady pace, incredible stamina, and more than likely, a much better rate of success. Men with Mars in Aries have strong physical drives. Though not all overtly macho, they invariably leave unmistakable masculine imprints on their efforts. Women with Mars in Aries have strong male influences in their lives. Relationships with men are passionate, which includes hate and anger as well as love.

Mars in Taurus. When Mars is in Taurus, desires become a very high priority, which means that much energy is focused on obtaining something rather than doing, thinking, or feeling. The influence of Taurus is, above all, pragmatic. Activities that, at least as far as you are concerned, waste energy are not likely to be viewed with enthusiasm. Consciously or unconsciously, your energy is always expended in a particular direction and for a specific reason. This does not mean you are lazy or selfish, since Mars rules only actions, not morality or judgment. You may, for example, be quite generous in sharing whatever you gain. You are not quick to anger, but when you do get mad, you nurse a grudge longer than anyone. However, you are also very appreciative and never forget favors and other generosities you receive. Compromise can be difficult, and giving up one thing in order to gain another can stymie you for unseemly lengths of time, and perhaps be impossible after all. Men with Mars in Taurus are passionate, but not very subtle. For the most part, they aptly fit the description of the strong, silent type. Women with Mars in Taurus have the protection and strength of the men in their lives, but not the interest or excitement they may prefer. Relationships with men are stable, but can be destroyed by possessiveness and jealousy.

Mars in Gemini. Gemini is the sign associated with communication and information. For the most part, Mars in Gemini means that much of your energy is directed toward these two goals. In turn, this increases the potential that many of your efforts are likely to involve sales, teaching, or writing. Intellectual energy and curiosity can be wasted absorbing superficial trivia and buzz words that make you seem to know much more than you actually do. However, it is also possible that mental energy at your disposal is used more profitably in serious study and research. The inherent restlessness of Gemini suggests problems that result from being constantly distracted, as well as doing too many things at one time, and in the end, accomplishing nothing. You probably enjoy and do get around quite a bit, in your own community as well as long distance. Cars or other vehicles of transport may be a passion, and you are apt to possess clever artistic or mechanical skills. A strong masculine image is often not of singular importance to men with Mars in Gemini. While their sexual preferences may be entirely heterosexual, the rest of their outlook and approach is likely to be as feminine as it is masculine. Though physical attachments may be minimal, women with Mars in Gemini have communication and intellectual rapport with the men in their lives.

Mars in Cancer. Mars in Cancer means there is a great emotional influence behind your energy and actions. Cancer is the sign identified with the family, so it is not unreasonable to think that many of your efforts involve family and those you think of as family. You are also likely to pay a lot of attention to your domestic environment, engaging wholeheartedly in domestic activities, such as gardening, cooking, or raising animals (or children, as the case may be). The sensitivity of Cancer makes this Mars position vulnerable—a vulnerability, however, that does nothing to discourage a very energetic pursuit when it comes to getting your own way or accomplishing important goals. Your emotional energy is sometimes negative when you resort to possessiveness or hysterics. Artistic or other creative talents exhibit passion and sensitivity, but care must be taken to avoid too much sentimentality. Men with Mars in Cancer have as much nurturing ability as any mother could wish to possess. Most of them are not ordinarily emasculated by their sensitivities, but may nevertheless be ruined by romantic or other personal rejections. Women with Mars in Cancer have strong emotional identifications with the important men in their lives. However, the ladies can often become too possessive and smothering toward their men on the one hand, or completely dominated by the demands of their men on the other.

Mars in Leo. Mars in Leo indicates that much of your energy is ego-centered. It doesn't mean, of course, that you are selfish or megalomaniac. It can mean, for example, that you take such personal pride in what you do, from small things to great accomplishments, that you inspire admiration and emulation in others. When ego involvement becomes too inflated, however, you waste energy seeking attention and trying to become a legend in your own time. The exaggeration of Leo suggests overestimation of your own strength or ability to accomplish something. Mars in Leo signifies strong creative spirit, and whether or not you possess artistic talent yourself, you generously encourage and support those who do. The influence of Leo also implies kindness in giving your time and talents to help others. At times, however, your actions in this respect can be self-serving, too hasty, or overly dramatic. Rushing ahead with flourish and enthusiasm, you don't always care about or take time to find out what is actually needed or wanted by those you think you are helping. Men with Mars in Leo invariably trip over their masculine egos. Creative energy is equated with masculinity. Developing maturity to overcome this concept is difficult but not impossible. Women with Mars in Leo usually take great pride in their men, and in turn, their men enjoy showing these ladies off.

Mars in Virgo. Mars in Virgo indicates that organization and analysis are behind many of your efforts. Unless other factors in your personality or background promote laziness, this position of Mars suggests you are an excellent worker. In fact, you may be a workaholic or put in many hours of work in order to avoid other areas of life you don't want to deal with. Perfectionism is prominent when Mars is in Virgo. You demand excellence from yourself and others. If you aren't aggressive enough to demand it from others, you may find yourself redoing everyone else's work, or doing everything yourself. When it comes to your own efforts, there may be more dedication than enthusiasm, more technical talent and professionalism than originality. Mars in Virgo suggests tendencies to go overboard. For example, you may be concerned with health to the point of hypochondria, so concerned with cleanliness you are forever washing your hands, and so meticulous a housekeeper no one dares to get comfortable. Paying too much attention to unimportant details distracts you from the overall picture. Not ones to flaunt their masculinity, or anything else for that matter, men with Mars in Virgo are usually fastidious and precise in dress and manner. Though male relationships are not overly passionate, women with Mars in Virgo maintain devoted enduring friendships with the men in their lives.

Mars in Libra. Mars in Libra is a difficult situation. The physical energy of Mars tends to run in Libran cycle. Sometimes you have abundant energy, and other times you become practically inert, waiting for a renewed burst of energy to get things going again. Aggressive Mars does not flourish in Libra, a sign that prefers nonconfrontational maneuvers. You would rather make use of polite manners and objective reviews of available information than endure heated debates or threatening physical abuse. You simply avoid people or situations that are contentious and disagreeable. When angry, you are more likely to walk away than fight. It's a little like playing ball. When people throw insults or challenges your way, you win the game by refusing to throw the ball back in their court. When it comes down to actually getting things done on a physical basis, you are good at furnishing detailed plans and strategy, but whenever possible will arrange to let others physically carry them out. Men with Mars in Libra find it difficult to develop a strong masculine image. Some of them will overcompensate by being overly macho, while others remain quite content to substitute brains for brawn. Women with Mars in Libra seek equality with the men in their lives. They tend to give in like manner and proportion to what is given them in these relationships.

Mars in Scorpio. Mars in Scorpio indicates formidable energy and stamina. Formidable because of the potential concentration and intensity you can put behind any or all of your efforts. There is also a great deal of emotional influence behind your actions. Desires are difficult to ignore and only your ability to develop self-control can keep things from getting out of hand. There are deep creative forces with Mars in Scorpio and you are apt to use them to understand the mysteries of nature and the psychology of human motivation and behavior. No one can be more determined than you when it comes to getting something accomplished, if not by physical strength then by force of will. Scorpio is a sign that seeks to control, the unfortunate result of which may be your tendency to constantly engage in power struggles, and to manipulate people or situations in order to gain an advantage. Anger and revenge can destroy what you have built up, unless other forces in your personality and background have softened these tendencies. Men with Mars in Scorpio often associate failure or loss of power and status with loss of masculinity. They hardly ever find it necessary or even possible to compromise. Women with Mars in Scorpio have intense, even psychic relationships with their men, though at times these relationships can be afflicted with unreasonable possessiveness and jealousy.

Mars in Sagittarius. Mars in Sagittarius enhances the spirit of freedom, making it difficult to accept constraints and restrictions. There is much potential energy, but how or if it will be used depends on other factors in your background and personality. For example, Sagittarius is associated with enjoyment and prodigious appetites, so it is not unreasonable to suppose that many efforts include the energetic pursuit of pleasures and the good life. Sports are apt to be high on your list of activities. Riding, racing, or breeding of horses are often among the favorite activities of those with Mars in Sagittarius. Sagittarius also directs you in a number of other directions, which include writing, education, art, religion, politics, and acting. With you, passion adds fuel to idealism just as easily as idealism fuels your passion. Too much haste and inattention to details are potential faults of this Mars position. Patience and organization can save you, not only from ill-advised actions but from repeating things you've already done. You are apt to get around quite a bit, mentally as well as physically, learning about different people, places, and cultures. Men with Mars in Sagittarius flex their masculinity through sports, the cars they drive, or the importance they have achieved. Women with Mars in Sagittarius tend to be very independent of, though somewhat competitive with, the men in their lives.

Mars in Capricorn. Mars in Capricorn means ambitious energy. Once you set a goal, you work as long and hard as necessary to attain it. Goals energize your ambitions, and ambitions expand your goals. Of course, this freight train can be derailed by other factors in your personality or background, but if encouraged, you can achieve almost anything. There are potential problems even with success.

For one thing, ambition, pushed ever onward by a strong competitive streak, can get so far ahead of practicality or values that you resort to the dangerous philosophy that the end justifies the means. Or you may get so caught up in attaining material goals that you neglect important relationships. Given the structured, purposeful nature of Capricorn, few of your efforts are pointless or wasted. All efforts, however, are not orientated toward business. One of the implications of this sign position of Mars suggests that your pursuits of pleasure are accomplished with great and passionate enthusiasm. Men with Mars in Capricorn equate masculinity with material success. They can also be proverbial old goats, since their masculine image is also equated with powers of procreation. Women with Mars in Capricorn have strong, stable relationships. They want their men to be as successful as the men seem to want to be. At times, these relationships are based on their own ambitions to get ahead.

Mars in Aquarius. Mars in Aquarius means energy is focused on communicating with others. Your use of the telephone is likely to be such a constant and consistent part of your life that others assume you have perished when they don't hear from you. This highly social energy covers much more enthusiasm for socializing. It indicates that you probably make better use of your energy when involved with people than you do when you are alone. Friends are important. You regard them as a sort of fraternity, and yourself, more often than not, the unofficial leader. With minimum encouragement you become active in sports and religious, political, and civic associations. You may also develop keen interest in international communities and trade organizations. Mars in Aquarius suggests you can become stubborn and opinionated to the point that it stymies personal growth and progress you might otherwise attain. Whether or not others express willingness to comply, or interest in the social reforms or philosophies you espouse, it in no way dampens your zeal.

A humanitarian at heart, you generally share your resources or talent to help others. Men with Mars in Aquarius often idealize their masculinity, sometimes going so far as to abandon physical passion for higher realms of consciousness. Women with Mars in Aquarius are often as good or better friends as anything else to their men.

Mars in Pisces. Mars in Pisces means emotional influences are behind many of your actions. Mars in Pisces suggests vulnerability that can paralyze productivity and make you into your own worst enemy. Sensitive Pisces is hard-pressed to correctly direct the too hasty and aggressive energy of Mars. This dilemma is handled according to the relative strength or weakness of other factors in your personality or background. You may, for example, over-compensate for vulnerability by racing cars or boats or engaging in other death-defying pursuits. Another possibility is to fantasize so much about what you want to do, that you never actually get around to doing it. There is promotional talent, though it may be long on imagination and short on facts. Mars in Pisces suggests mathematical ability, remarkable artistic talent, psychic energy, and a high level of spirituality. It may be difficult to get recognition for your efforts, but on the other hand, you may work best alone or unobserved. The biggest key to your success is developing the self-discipline to channel talents and energy productively and consistently. Men with Mars in Pisces can be extremely sensitive about their masculinity, suffering irreparable damage if it is impugned, especially when they are young. Women with Mars in Pisces have close spiritual relationships with their men, but they are also apt to drown them in pure fantasy.

How to Find the Place of Mars in Your Chart

Find your birth year in the left-hand column and read across the chart until you find your birth date. The top of that column will tell you where Mars lies in your chart.

PLACE OF MARS—1880–1891

	♈ ARIES	♉ TAURUS	♊ GEMINI	♋ CANCER	♌ LEO	♍ VIRGO	♎ LIBRA	♏ SCORP.	♐ SAGITT.	♑ CAPRI.	♒ AQUAR.	♓ PISCES
1880		2/13	2/14-4/11	4/12-6/1	6/2-7/20	7/21-9/5	9/6-10/21	10/22-12/3	12/4⟲			
1881	5/13-6/21	6/22-8/3	8/4-9/23	⟲9/24					⟲1/13	1/14-2/22	2/23-4/2	4/3-5/12
1882			1/12-2/25	2/26-5/7	5/8-6/30	7/1-8/18	8/19-10/2	10/3-11/14	11/15-12/25	12/26⟲		
1883	4/21-5/29	5/30-7/10	7/11-8/23	8/24-10/14	10/15⟲					⟲2/2	2/3-3/12	3/13-4/20
1884					⟲6/4	6/5-7/27	7/28-9/12	9/13-10/25	10/26-12/5	12/6⟲		
1885	3/31-5/8	5/9-6/18	6/19-7/31	8/1-9/16	9/17-11/8	11/9⟲				⟲1/12	1/13-2/19	2/20-3/30
1886						⟲7/1	7/2-8/21	8/22-10/5	10/6-11/14	11/15-12/23	12/24⟲	
1887	3/11-4/18	4/19-5/29	5/30-7/11	7/12-8/26	8/27-10/13	10/14-12/5	12/6⟲				⟲1/30	1/31-3/10
1888							⟲2/26 / 3/10-7/21	2/27-3/9 / 7/22-9/10	9/11-10/22	10/23-12/1	12/2⟲	
1889	2/17-3/28	3/29-5/9	5/10-6/22	6/23-8/6	8/7-9/22	9/23-11/10	11/11-12/31				⟲1/9	1/10-2/16
1890								1/1-2/28 / 6/17-7/21	3/1-6/16 / 7/22-9/23	9/24-11/5	11/6-12/16	12/17⟲
1891	1/26-3/7	3/8-4/19	4/20-6/3	6/4-7/19	7/20-9/4	9/5-10/21	10/22-12/7	12/8⟲				⟲1/25

PLACE OF MARS—1892–1906

	♈ ARIES	♉ TAURUS	♊ GEMINI	♋ CANCER	♌ LEO	♍ VIRGO	♎ LIBRA	♏ SCORP.	♐ SAGITT.	♑ CAPRI.	♒ AQUAR.	♓ PISCES
1892	12/28 ς							ς 1/24	1/25–3/13	3/14–5/6	5/7–11/8	11/9–12/27
1893	ς 2/10	2/11–3/28	3/29–5/13	5/14–6/29	6/30–8/15	8/16–10/1	10/2–11/16	11/17–12/31				
1894	6/23–8/18 / 10/13–12/30	8/19–10/12 / 12/31 ς							1/1–2/13	2/14–3/27	3/28–5/9	5/10–6/22
1895		ς 3/1	3/2–4/21	4/22–6/10	6/11–7/28	7/29–9/13	9/14–10/29	10/30–12/11	12/12 ς			
1896	5/22–7/1	7/2–8/15	8/16–12/31						ς 1/22	1/23–3/2	3/3–4/11	4/12–5/21
1897			1/1–3/21	3/22–5/17	5/18–7/8	7/9–8/25	8/26–10/9	10/10–11/21	11/22 ς			
1898	4/29–6/6	6/7–7/18	7/19–9/2	9/3–10/30	10/31 ς				ς 1/1	1/2–2/10	2/11–3/20	3/21–4/28
1899				1/16–4/14	ς 1/15 / 4/15–6/15	6/16–8/5	8/6–9/20	9/21–11/2	11/3–12/13	12/14 ς		
1900	4/8–5/16	5/17–6/26	6/27–8/9	8/10–9/26	9/27–11/22	11/23 ς				ς 1/21	1/22–2/28	3/1–4/7
1901					3/2–5/10	ς 3/1 / 5/11–7/13	7/14–8/31	9/1–10/14	10/15–11/23	11/24 ς		
1902	3/19–4/26	4/27–6/6	6/7–7/20	7/21–9/4	9/5–10/23	10/24–12/19	12/20 ς			ς 1/1	1/2–2/8	2/9–3/18
1903		6/7–7/20				4/20–5/30	ς 4/19 / 5/31–8/6	8/7–9/22	9/23–11/2	11/3–12/11	12/12 ς	
1904	2/27–4/6	4/7–5/17	5/18–6/30	7/1–8/14	8/15–10/1	10/2–11/19	11/20 ς				ς 1/19	1/20–2/26
1905							ς 1/13	1/14–8/21	8/22–10/7	10/8–11/17	11/18–12/27	12/28 ς
1906	2/5–3/16	3/17–4/28	4/29–6/11	6/12–7/27	7/28–9/12	9/13–10/29	10/30–12/16	12/17 ς				ς 2/4

PLACE OF MARS—1907–1923

Year												
1907								℞2/4	2/5-4/1	4/2-10/13	10/14-11/28	11/29 ℞1/10
1908	1/11-2/22	2/23-4/6	4/7-5/22	5/23-7/7	7/8-8/23	8/24-10/9	10/10-11/25	11/26℞				
1909	7/21-9/26 11/21℞	℞1/22						℞1/9			4/10-5/25	9/27-11/20 5/26-7/20
1910	1/23-3/13	3/14-5/1	5/2-6/18	6/19-8/5	8/6-9/21	9/22-11/6	11/7-12/19	12/20	1/10-2/23	2/24-4/9		
1911	6/3-7/15	7/16-9/5 11/30℞	9/6-11/29					℞1/31		2/1-3/13	3/14-4/22	4/23-6/2
1912	℞1/30	1/31-4/4	4/5-5/27	5/28-7/16	7/17-9/2	9/3-10/17	10/18-11/29	11/30℞	℞1/10	1/11-2/18	3/14-4/22	
1913	5/8-6/16	6/17-7/28	7/29-9/15	9/16℞ 5/1				10/18-11/10	11/11-12/21	12/22 ℞1/29	2/19-3/29	3/30-5/7
1914	4/17-5/25	5/26-7/5	7/6-8/18 8/19-10/7		5/28		8/15-9/28	9/29-11/10	11/11-12/21	12/22 ℞1/29	1/30-3/9	3/10-4/16
1915	5/26-7/5	7/6-8/18	8/19-10/7 10/8 ℞5/28			7/23-9/8	9/9-10/21	10/22-12/1	12/2 ℞1/9	1/29	1/30-3/9	3/10-4/16
1916	5/5-6/14	6/15-7/27	7/28-9/11 9/12-11/1	11/2 ℞1/10 2/26-6/23		7/23-9/8	9/9-10/21	10/22-12/1	10/1-11/10	11/11-12/19 12/20	1/10-2/16	2/17-3/26
1917	3/27-5/4	5/5-6/14	6/15-7/27 7/28-9/11	9/12-11/1	11/2			8/17-9/30	10/1-11/10	11/11-12/19	1/10-2/16	2/17-3/26
1918				1/11-2/25 6/24-8/16	10/10-11/29					℞1/9	12/20 ℞1/26	1/27-3/6
1919	3/7-4/14	4/15-5/25	5/26-7/8	7/9-8/22	8/23-10/9	10/10-11/29	11/30℞	2/1-4/23 7/11-9/4	9/5-10/18	10/19-11/27	11/28	1/27-3/6
1920	4/15-5/25	5/26-7/8	7/9-8/22	8/23-10/9	9/19-11/6	11/30℞	2/1-4/23 4/24-7/10		9/5-10/18	10/19-11/27	12/20 ℞1/26	1/5-2/12
1921	2/13-3/24	3/25-5/5	5/6-6/18	6/19-8/2	8/3-9/18	9/19-11/6	11/7-12/25	12/16	2/19-9/13		11/28 11/4	1/5-2/12
1922					8/3-9/18	11/7-12/25	12/16	2/18℞		2/19-9/13	1/4	12/12
1923	1/21-3/3	3/4-4/15	4/16-5/30	5/31-7/15	7/16-8/31	9/1-10/17	10/18-12/3	12/4-12/31		9/14-10/30	10/31-12/11 12/12	℞1/20

PLACE OF MARS—1924–1933

	♈ ARIES	♉ TAURUS	♊ GEMINI	♋ CANCER	♌ LEO	♍ VIRGO	♎ LIBRA	♏ SCORP.	♐ SAGITT.	♑ CAPRI.	♒ AQUAR.	♓ PISCES	•♂ Retrograde R — D
1924	12/19							1/1–1/19	1/20–3/6	3/7–4/24	4/25–6/24, 8/25–10/19*	6/25–8/24*, 10/20–12/18	5♓7/24–25♒9/22
1925	2/4	2/5–3/23	3/24–5/9	5/10–6/25	6/26–8/12	8/13–9/28	9/29–11/13	11/14–12/27	12/28				
1926	6/15–7/31	8/1*							2/8	2/9–3/22	3/23–5/3	5/4–6/14	19♉9/29–4♉12/7
1927		2/21	2/22–4/16	4/17–6/5	6/6–7/24	7/25–9/10	9/11–10/25	10/26–12/7	12/8				
1928	5/17–6/25	6/26–8/8	8/9–10/2, 12/20	10/3–12/19*					1/18	1/19–2/27	2/28–4/7	4/8–5/16	9♋11/12
1929			3/10*	3/11–5/12	5/13–7/3	7/4–8/21	8/22–10/5	10/6–11/18	11/19–12/28	12/29			20♊1/27
1930	4/25–6/2	6/3–7/14	7/15–8/27	8/28–10/20	10/21*					2/6	2/7–3/16	3/17–4/24	17♌12/19
1931				2/17–3/29*	2/16, 3/30–6/10	6/11–8/1	8/2–9/16	9/17–10/30	10/31–12/9	12/10			27♋3/9
1932	4/3–5/11	5/12–6/21	6/22–8/4	8/5–9/30	10/1–11/13	11/14				1/17	1/18–2/24	2/25–4/2	
1933						7/6	7/7–8/25	8/26–10/8	10/9–11/18	11/19–12/27	12/28		20♍1/21–1♍4/13

PLACE OF MARS—1934–1944

Year											
1934	3/14-4/22	4/23-6/2	6/3-7/15	7/16-8/30	8/31-10/17	10/18-12/10	12/11 ℞			℞2/3	2/4-3/13
1935							℞7/29	7/30-9/16	9/17-10/29	10/30-12/7	12/8 ℞1/15
1936	2/23-4/2	4/3-5/13	5/14-6/26	6/27-8/10	8/11-9/27	9/28-11/15	11/16 ℞	℞1/6	10/1-11/12	11/13-12/22	1/16-2/22
1937		8/25* ℞				1/7-3/13 / 5/16-8/9*	3/14-5/15* / 8/10-9/30		12/23	12/23	
1938	2/1-3/13	3/14-4/24	4/25-6/8	6/9-7/23	7/24-9/8	9/9-10/26	10/27-12/12	12/13 ℞1/6		℞1/31	
1939							1/30	1/31-3/22	3/23-5/25 / 7/23-9/25*	5/26-7/22* / 9/26-11/20	11/21 ℞1/4
1940	1/5-2/18	2/19-4/2	4/3-5/18	5/19-7/4	7/5-8/20	8/21-10/6	10/7-11/21	11/22 ℞	1/5		
1941	7/4* ℞1/12							1/6-2/18	2/19-4/3	4/4-5/17	5/18-7/3
1942	1/13-3/8 / 7/9-8/24	3/9-4/27	4/28-6/15	6/16-8/2	8/3-9/18	9/19-11/2	11/5-12/16	12/17 ℞1/27			24♈♈9/7-11♈11/11
1943	5/29-7/8							11/27 ℞	1/28-3/9	3/10-4/18	4/19-5/28
1944	℞3/29*	3/30-5/23	5/24-7/13	7/14-8/30	8/31-10/14	10/15-11/26	11/27 ℞				22π10/30

PLACE OF MARS—1945–1958

	♈ ARIES	♉ TAURUS	♊ GEMINI	♋ CANCER	♌ LEO	♍ VIRGO	♎ LIBRA	♏ SCORP.	♐ SAGITT.	♑ CAPRI.	♒ AQUAR.	♓ PISCES	Retrograde R — D
1945	5/4–6/12	6/13–7/24	7/25–9/8	9/9–11/12, 12/28*	11/13–12/27*					1/7–2/15	2/16–3/26	3/27–5/3	3♌12/5
1946				☞4/23*	4/24–6/21	6/22–8/10	8/11–9/25	9/26–11/7	11/8–12/18	12/19			14♋2/22
1947	4/13–5/22	5/23–7/2	7/3–8/14	8/15–10/2	10/3–12/2	12/3 ☞				☞1/26	1/27–3/5	3/6–4/12	
1948					2/14–5/19*	☞2/13*, 5/20–7/18	7/19–9/4	9/5–10/18	10/19–11/27	11/28			8♏1/9–18♌3/30
1949	3/23–5/1	5/2–6/11	6/12–7/24	7/25–9/8	9/9–10/28	10/29–12/27	12/28			☞1/5	1/6–2/12	2/13–3/22	
1950						3/30–6/12*	3/29*, 6/13–8/11	8/12–9/26	9/27–11/7	11/8–12/16	12/17–12/31		11♎2/13–22♍5/5
1951	3/2–4/10	4/11–5/21	5/22–7/3	7/4–8/18	8/19–10/4	10/5–11/24	11/25				1/11–1/22	1/23–3/1	13♏1/2
1952								1/21–8/27	8/28–10/12	10/13–11/21	11/22–12/30	12/31 ☞	1♐3/25–1♏6/11
1953	2/9–3/20	3/21–5/1	5/2–6/14	6/15–7/29	7/30–9/14	9/15–11/1	11/2–12/20	12/21					8♈5/23–25♐7/30
1954		2/27–4/10						2/9 ☞	2/10–4/12, 7/4–8/24*	4/13–7/3*, 8/25–10/21	10/22–12/4	12/5 ☞	
1955	1/16–2/26	2/27–4/10	4/11–5/26	5/27–7/11	7/12–8/27	8/28–10/13	10/14–11/29	11/30	1/15–2/28		4/15–6/3	1/15 ☞	23♊8/11–13♈10/11
1956	12/7 ☞	1/29–3/17						1/14 ☞	1/15–2/28	2/29–4/14	4/15–6/3	6/4–12/6*	
1957	☞1/28	1/29–3/17	3/18–5/4	5/5–6/21	6/22–8/8	8/9–9/24	9/25–11/8	11/9–12/23	12/24 ☞		3/18–4/27	1/25 ☞	2♊10/11–6♉12/21
1958	6/8–7/21	7/22–9/21, 10/30*	9/22–10/29*						2/3 ☞	2/4–3/17	3/18–4/27	4/28–6/7	2♊10/11–6♉12/21

PLACE OF MARS—1959–1971

Year											Station / Sign
1959	℞2/10	2/11-4/10	4/11-6/1	6/2-7/20	7/21-9/5	9/6-10/21	10/22-12/3	12/4		4/3-5/11	18♒11/21
1960	5/12-6/20	6/21-8/2	8/3-9/21	9/22-12/31*		10/1-11/12	11/13-12/23	12/24℞	1/15-2/23	2/24-4/2	0♒5/27
1961	4/19-5/27			1/1-5/5*	10/1-11/12	11/13-12/23	℞1/14	2/1-3/11	3/12-4/18		24♑12/26
1962	5/28-7/8	7/9-8/21	8/22-10/10	10/11	℞6/2*	9/12-10/24	10/25-12/4	12/5℞	1/13-2/19	2/20-3/28	5♑3/17
1963	5/7-6/16	6/17-7/29	7/30-9/14	9/15-11/5	11/6	℞6/28*	7/27-9/11	℞1/12			
1964	3/29-5/6					6/29-8/19	8/20-10/3	10/4-11/13	11/14-12/22	1/13-2/19	28♍1/28 / 8♍4/20
1965	3/9-4/16	4/17-5/27	5/28-7/10	7/11-8/24	8/25-10/11	10/12-12/3	℞12/4	10/4-11/13	12/23	1/29	
1966						12/4	2/11	9/10-10/22	10/23-11/30	1/21	3♏3/9 / 15♒5/26
1967		5/8-6/20	6/21-8/4	8/5-9/20	9/21-11/8	11/9-12/28	2/12-9/9*	1/29	℞12/1	1/30-3/8	3♏3/9 / 15♒5/26
1968	2/17-3/26	3/27-5/7	5/8-6/20	6/21-8/4	8/5-9/20	9/21-11/8	11/9-12/28	12/29℞	℞2/24	1/9-2/16	16♐4/27 / 1♐1/8
1969	1/24-3/6	3/7-4/17	4/18-6/1	6/2-7/17	7/18-9/2	9/3-10/19	2/25-9/20*	12/6-12/31	11/4-12/14	12/15	
1970	3/7-4/17	4/18-6/1			10/20-12/5	12/6-12/31	9/21-11/3	11/4-12/14	℞1/23		1/23
1971	12/26℞			5/3-11/5*		1/1-1/22	1/23-3/11	3/12-5/2	5/3-11/5*	11/6-12/25	21♒7/10♓ / 11♒9/8♑

PLACE OF MARS—1972-1980

	♈ ARIES	♉ TAURUS	♊ GEMINI	♋ CANCER	♌ LEO	♍ VIRGO	♎ LIBRA	♏ SCORP.	♐ SAGITT.	♑ CAPRI.	♒ AQUAR.	♓ PISCES	♂ Retrograde R / D
1972	↳2/9	2/10-3/26	3/27-5/11	5/12-6/27	6/28-8/14	8/15-9/29	9/30-11/14	11/15-12/29	12/30				
1973	6/20-8/11, 10/29-12/23*	8/12-10/28*, 12/24↴							↳2/11	2/12-3/25	3/26-5/7	5/8-6/19	9♊9/19℞, 25♈11/25D
1974		↳2/26	2/27-4/19	4/20-6/8	6/9-7/26	7/27-9/11	9/12-10/27	10/28-12/9	12/10				
1975	5/21-6/30	7/1-8/13	8/14-10/16, 11/25↴	10/17-11/24*					↳1/20	1/21-3/2	3/3-4/10	4/11-5/20	2♏11/6℞
1976			↳3/17	3/18-5/15	5/16-7/5	7/6-8/23	8/24-10/7	10/8-11/19	11/20-12/31				14♊1/20D
1977	4/27-6/5	6/6-7/16	7/17-8/31	9/1-10/25	10/26↴					1/1-2/8	2/9-3/19	3/20-4/26	11♋12/12℞
1978				1/26-4/9*	↳1/25*, 4/10-6/13	6/14-8/3	8/4-9/18	9/19-11/1	11/2-12/11	12/12↴			22♌5/10
1979	4/7-5/15	5/16-6/25	6/26-8/7	8/8-9/23	9/24-11/18	11/19				↳1/19	1/20-2/26	2/27-4/6	
1980					3/11-5/3*	↳3/10*, 5/4-7/9	7/10-8/28	8/29-10/11	10/12-11/21	11/22-12/29	12/30-12/31		15♍16℞, 25♌6D

*In these periods, Mars (♂) is Retrograde during some or all of the time. See right-hand Column.

PLACE OF MARS—1981–1990

	♈ ARIES	♉ TAURUS	♊ GEMINI	♋ CANCER	♌ LEO	♍ VIRGO	♎ LIBRA	♏ SCORP.	♐ SAGITT.	♑ CAPRI.	♒ AQUAR.	♓ PISCES
1981	3/16–4/24	4/25–6/4	6/5–7/17	7/18–8/31	9/1–10/19	10/20–12/14	12/15				1/1–2/5	2/6–3/15
1982							℞8/2	8/3–9/18	9/19–10/30	10/31–12/9	12/10℞	
1983	2/24–4/4	4/5–5/15	5/16–6/28	6/29–8/12	8/13–9/28	9/29–11/17	11/18℞				℞1/16	1/17–2/23
1984							℞1/9	1/10–8/16	8/17–10/4	10/5–11/14	11/15–12/24	12/25℞
1985	2/2–3/14	3/15–4/25	4/26–6/8	6/9–7/23	7/24–9/8	9/9–10/26	10/27–12/13	12/14℞				℞2/1
1986								℞2/1	2/2–3/26	3/27–10/7	10/8–11/24	11/25℞
1987	1/8–2/19	2/20–4/4	4/5–5/19	5/20–7/5	7/6–8/21	8/22–10/7	10/8–11/22	11/23℞				℞1/7
1988	7/13–10/22 11/1℞							℞1/7	1/8–2/21	2/22–4/5	4/6–5/21	5/22–7/12 10/23–10/31
1989	℞1/18	1/19–3/9	3/10–4/27	4/28–6/15	6/16–8/2	8/3–9/18	9/19–11/3	11/4–12/16	12/17℞			
1990	5/31–7/11	7/12–8/30 12/14℞							℞1/28	1/29–3/10	3/11–4/19	4/20–5/30

PLACE OF MARS—1991–2000

	♈ ARIES	♉ TAURUS	♊ GEMINI	♋ CANCER	♌ LEO	♍ VIRGO	♎ LIBRA	♏ SCORP.	♐ SAGITT.	♑ CAPRI.	♒ AQUAR.	♓ PISCES
1991		↳1/20	1/21–4/1	4/2–5/25	5/26–7/14	7/15–8/31	9/1–10/15	10/16–11/27	11/28			
1992	5/5–6/13	6/14–7/25	7/26–9/11	9/12 ↱					↳1/8	1/9–2/16	2/17–3/26	3/27–5/4
1993				↳4/26	4/27–6/22	6/23–8/10	8/11–9/25	9/26–11/7	11/8–12/18	12/19 ↱		
1994	4/14–5/22	5/23–7/2	7/3–8/15	8/16–10/3	10/4–12/11	12/12 ↱				↳1/26	1/27–3/6	3/7–4/13
1995					1/22–5/23	↳1/21 5/24–7/20	7/21–9/6	9/7–10/19	10/20–11/29	11/30 ↱		
1996	3/24–5/1	5/2–6/11	6/12–7/24	7/25–9/8	9/9–10/29	10/30 ↱				↳1/7	1/8–2/14	2/15–3/23
1997						↳1/2 3/8–6/18	1/3–3/7 6/19–8/13	8/14–9/27	9/28–11/8	11/9–12/17	12/18 ↱	
1998	3/4–4/11	4/12–5/22	5/23–7/5	7/6–8/19	8/20–10/6	10/7–11/26	11/27 ↱				↳1/24	1/25–3/3
1999							5/5–7/3	1/26–5/4 7/4–9/1	9/2–10/15	10/16–11/25	11/26 ↱	
2000	2/11–3/21	3/22–5/2	5/3–6/15	6/16–7/30	7/31–9/15	9/16–11/12	11/13–12/22	12/23–12/31			↳1/2	1/3–2/10

YOUR RULING PLANET: ARIES—Mars; TAURUS—Venus; GEMINI—Mercury; CANCER—The Moon; LEO—The Sun; VIRGO—Mercury; LIBRA—Venus; SCORPIO—Mars; SAGITTARIUS—Jupiter; CAPRICORN—Saturn; AQUARIUS—Uranus; PISCES—Neptune.

Jupiter: Luck and Opportunity

Jupiter describes the potential for your personal growth and expansion on material and nonmaterial levels. It relates to how you may gain material prosperity and social status. Another of Jupiter's associations is the potential for broadening your intellectual horizons, which includes knowledge, understanding, and specialized training beyond primary education and basic skills. Jupiter describes your potential spiritual and esthetic awareness, and development of artistic talent. Along with Venus, Jupiter describes your potential happiness and capacity for enjoyment, including the lack of these elements in your life. You may be optimistic and quite content with what you attain, or as the case may be, you may lack the capacity to be happy or satisfied with anything, constantly searching for greener pastures.

Jupiter in Aries. The expansive nature of Jupiter is greatly encouraged when this planet is in the energetic environment of Aries. Unfortunately, expansion can sometimes occur too fast. Given Jupiter's association with abundance and good fortune, the idea of quick prosperity does not seem like a negative prospect. However, as many people who experience sudden wealth or status sadly learn, too much too soon can be detrimental, especially for those who have not acquired the perspective of maturity and experience. Vitality and enthusiasm are singularly positive influences of Jupiter in Aries. These dynamic forces encourage bold, pioneering efforts and philanthropic gestures. On the other hand, they can lead to overindulgence and indiscriminate use of wealth, talent, and other resources. Jupiter in Aries indicates a gambler's instinct, the enterprising spirit that has been responsible for the making of more than one person's fortune as well as other, equally impressive, accomplishments. However, taking unnecessary physical risks or gambling with financial assets that you cannot afford to lose are darker potentials of Jupiter in Aries. Avoiding overeagerness and unwarranted enthusiasm while taking advantage of the positive potentials associated with Jupiter in Aries leads to your personal growth and development, perhaps even to material prosperity. Enthusiasm for higher education or special training may steer you into law, medicine, design, entertainment, or advertising. Spirituality and idealism are likely to be strong, though like everything else associated with Jupiter in Aries, they can get out of control when the passionate flames of inspiration turn into raging fanaticism. Jupiter in Aries implies creative imagination and artistic talent as well as the ability to work well with youngsters. Seeking material wealth and social status is likely to take second place to your desire to experience the pleasures and enjoyment of life.

Jupiter in Taurus. The environment of Taurus imbues Jupiter with characteristic physical orientation and value consciousness. There is bound to be conscious or subconscious striving for material assets, or at least the advantages that accompany wealth. If inherited fortune is not your fate, you are no doubt ready and willing to work for it yourself. Furthermore, the benevolence of Jupiter is not usually subdued in Taurus, which means you are probably also quite willing to share your prosperity. The influence of Taurus implies a strong temptation to gauge progress by monetary worth. This is not always the best method for judging personal success, but no matter what other yardsticks you apply, you will always be aware of how much money and other material assets you earn or accumulate. When it comes to broadening your intellectual horizons, the effect of Jupiter in Taurus inspires the urge to apply whatever advanced degrees or special training you acquire to some useful, hopefully lucrative purpose. While Taurus is associated with appreciation for beauty and possession of artistic talents, here, too, you will likely be aware of intrinsic values as well as aesthetic beauty. Jupiter in Taurus suggests you are attracted to institutions of higher learning, museums, the courtroom, or international diplomacy and trade. Your spirituality inclines to the traditional, and if not the traditional, at least the practical. Spiritual doctrines that impose impractical dietary, social, or other ritual requirements may find you heading for more liberal ground. In spite of the potential for being overfond of material wealth or too impressed with personal status, Jupiter in Taurus also means happiness can be found by learning to conserve assets, finding value where others do not, and making the best possible use of all your resources.

Jupiter in Gemini. The mental and communication orientation, singular elements associated with the sign Gemini, are stimulated by the presence of Jupiter, planet of understanding and knowledge. This means that no matter what other successes you experience in life, a significant part of your personal growth occurs as a result of the development of communication skills, learning, sharing thoughts and ideas. Jupiter in Gemini also indicates development and use of mechanical abilities, and correspondingly, a special talent for such things as illustration and design, developing computer software and hardware. Mechanical skills may include building and repair of machinery, typing, shorthand, tailoring, and various other arts and crafts. In the matter of material prosperity, Jupiter in Gemini suggests you are apt to seek your fortune through trade, transportation, writing, education, printing, travel, or sales. There is nonphysical identification with wealth and status, an identification that can inspire you to measure personal growth and success by honorary or administrative titles, deeds of ownership, bank books, and patents. Jupiter, planet of spirituality, in Gemini, sign of ideas and information, may mean you are attracted to the doctrine and dogma of religion, though it must be said that your ideas in this respect are flexible. Should other factors in your background or personality encourage religious zeal, you are apt to be a most active writer or teacher, as well as participant. Jupiter in Gemini suggests facility for languages, music composition, or talent for more than one musical instrument. For you, variety may indeed be the most important spice of life. Maintaining a network of associations, communications, and constant mental stimulation may in the end be the key to your success, as well as the source of your happiness and productivity as an individual.

Jupiter in Cancer. The expansiveness of Jupiter can be a two-edged sword when this planet occupies the emotional environment of Cancer. The combination can inspire undesirable extremes in thought and ideas, while on the other hand promote the most positive elements of creativity and imagination. Jupiter in Cancer is a strong indication that your progress and growth as an individual relies heavily on developing emotional maturity. One of the influences associated with Jupiter is independence, while almost the opposite influence, the need to belong to a family or group, is enhanced in Cancer. This contributes to making Jupiter in Cancer an uneasy alliance. The emotional maturity you ultimately gain may result from effectively reconciling your own independence and growth with your relationships and responsibilities related to home and family. Family connections, family assistance, and family influence are likely to play a significant role in your personal growth and success, and that includes material prosperity. There is apt to be strong desire to keep income and other possessions and property within the family, or the responsibility of managing such assets may fall to you. Jupiter in Cancer can also mean your economic success may come through the construction, sales, design, or development of homes, or through products or services specifically for women. There is increased potential for acquisitiveness, which means you may be a collector of valuable art, antiques, or coins, or it may just mean that you never throw anything away. Overblown emotionalism of Jupiter in Cancer can mean that sensitivity and sentimentality get out of hand at times, but it is also an increased implication of artistic talent. Material possessions, intellectual accomplishments, social status, and even relationships that fail to engender emotional satisfaction will ultimately fail to make you happy.

Jupiter in Leo. Jupiter's associations with knowledge and truth and the affinity for art and beauty are greatly enhanced when this planet occupies the creative, idealistic environment of Leo. On a personal level, this means your growth and some of your success in life involves the use not only of your own artistic talent, creativity, and imagination, but helping others develop their talents as well. The combination of expansive Jupiter in the enthusiastic sign of Leo suggests that exaggeration, overestimation, and a certain flamboyancy accompanies many of your efforts as well your enjoyments. Your personal progress in many instances is greatly aided when you exploit the overblown nature of Jupiter in Leo to good effect when such theatrics are called for, but tone it down to merely being inspirational when situations require a more sedate approach. When Jupiter is in Leo, social status and material advantages can become overly important criteria for measuring individual worth and success. However, any temptation to use such yardsticks may easily be mitigated by stronger factors in your personality and background that inspire the development of higher values. Material success or other types of personal growth you experience may come through the arts, entertainment, sports, higher education, politics, advertising, publishing, marketing, languages, or foreign trade. Jupiter in Leo implies abundant capacity for enjoyment and happiness. However, it must also be said that too much indulgence and emphasis on pleasure and self-satisfaction can create insatiability that, once given expression, denies happiness and also inhibits personal growth and productivity. On the positive side, Jupiter in Leo engenders a strong spirit of philanthropy, which means you are likely to share whatever material prosperity you have, as well as your time and talents in order to benefit and encourage others.

Jupiter in Virgo. The nature of Jupiter promotes the idea of self-importance, being an inspirational, perhaps even imperial, guiding force. This association with self-aggrandizement is necessarily subdued when Jupiter occupies the more self-effacing, service-oriented environment of Virgo. The combination is an uneasy alliance, and according to other factors in your personality and background, your personal growth and success in life may depend on how well you learn to handle Jupiter in Virgo. It may mean, for example, that if you desire to be a leader, you are willing to work for the privilege. If you attain a position of leadership, you must then be a capable administrator, not a figurehead who shows up to be admired and does nothing to inspire the loyalty or productivity in those for whom you are responsible. The old saying, "Do as I say, not as I do," will never work in your case. On the positive side, Jupiter in Virgo indicates the potential for becoming a singularly effective negotiator and unparalleled inspiration in working to improve education, physical environment, or working conditions. Though not above seeking material wealth, you may be prone to measure success by your public status or popularity; that is, how much your efforts are recognized and the position of authority you attain. In spite of the dissimilarity between the influence of Jupiter and the characteristic influence of Virgo, there are certain areas of compatibility. For example, the spirituality of Jupiter is often enhanced in the idealistic environment of Virgo. Whether or not this means you are particularly religious, you may nevertheless possess an altruistic, compassionate nature, evidence of a high level of human maturity and development. For you, happiness is in pursuing, and ultimately attaining, what you believe is your ultimate destiny.

Jupiter in Libra. Jupiter's nature is to encourage independence, a characteristic that must be curtailed when this planet inhabits the relationship-oriented environment of Libra. On a personal level it means part of your capacity for growth, and perhaps some of the material success you experience in life, is based on how well you balance the need to promote your own individuality and goals while also relating to the needs and rights of others. Jupiter in Libra is a signal that personal ambition should only take you so far. Acceptance and acknowledgment of assistance and inspiration you receive from others, and the help and inspiration you give to others are the positive potentials of Jupiter in Libra. A singular spirit of justice and social equality is its admirable asset, though not an easy one to acquire. It will never be enough to say you believe in social equality—you will be required to live up to this principle, or risk losing an important part of your personal growth. Economic gain and other successes may come through your friendships, social contacts, activities related to various civic and corporate associations, club memberships, fund-raising for the arts and humanities, social work, and counseling. Jupiter's association with knowledge and affinity for beauty and art are well served in the environment of Libra. Supported by other factors in your personality and background, the combination of Jupiter in Libra enhances the enjoyment of intellectual pursuits and encourages fondness for books, travel, art, and other cultural activities. It also suggests a strong desire for luxury and material wealth is substantially apt to motivate many of your efforts. There are limitations with respect to material prosperity making you truly happy, unless there is equal emphasis on relationships and other nonmaterial values.

Jupiter in Scorpio. The nature of Jupiter is expansive and generous, elements that unfortunately can have a difficult time surfacing when Jupiter occupies the more restrictive, cautious environment of Scorpio. Jupiter is identified with openness, while Scorpio inspires secretiveness. On a personal level this means part of your development and growth, and perhaps other successes you experience in life, occur as a result of reconciling the dissimilar characteristics of Jupiter in Scorpio. Since Scorpio is an emotionally oriented influence and Jupiter tends to inspire extremes, it may mean you have to avoid letting desires grow into jealousy and possessiveness, or allowing overzealous to turn into fanaticism. Both Jupiter and Scorpio are associated with fondness for power. This implies there is temptation to measure personal worth and success according to the power attained through career or social status. Though not adverse to material wealth for its own sake, you may consciously or subconsciously view wealth as the means to manipulate and control others. These inclinations, however, may be easily mitigated by other factors in your personality and background—factors that in all probability will contribute to a healthier perspective of how power should be used to improve the quality of life for yourself and for others. Jupiter in Scorpio suggests that your income or personal growth may occur through psychological study and counseling, research and investigation, or investment and finance. You may possess artistic and mechanical skills, especially for converting, developing, and conserving raw materials. You are not likely to take matters of enjoyment or happiness lightly. You will pursue what gives you pleasure or happiness with concentration and seriousness. For you, happiness is based on deep emotional satisfaction, a satisfaction that comes more often than not from gaining control over yourself.

Jupiter in Sagittarius. Jupiter is the planetary ruler of Sagittarius and thus likely to be stronger when it inhabits this sign than any other. On a personal level it means your growth and development, and even other successes you may experience in life, result from continual efforts to broaden not only your own intellectual horizons but those of others. Jupiter in Sagittarius also implies that significant growth and development may occur as a result of long-distance travel or living with those of a different race or culture. It stimulates and encourages talent or interest in art and music. Jupiter in Sagittarius has an unfortunate association with promoting form over substance. There is little to inhibit the development of a strong desire for material wealth and status as a motivating force behind your efforts. Intellectual brilliance, merry disposition, and great generosity in sharing your enjoyment and prosperity are all prominent and positive influences when Jupiter is in Sagittarius. Languages, religion, politics, advertising, marketing, writing, and publishing are some of the possible sources that may contribute to your income and other types of personal gain. Spirituality is another emphasized influence of Jupiter in Sagittarius, and an indication of fondness for the pomp and ceremony of religious rite as much as for its dogma and doctrine. Whether or not you are particularly religious, you will nevertheless be interested in finding some way to increase your spiritual awareness. Love of drama is enhanced, and even if you do not possess special talent yourself, you are apt to attend and support the theater enthusiastically. Unless it is severely discouraged by other factors in your personality and background, your capacity for enjoyment and happiness is boundless. If material wealth is denied, you'll find a way of living well anyway.

Jupiter in Capricorn. Jupiter is not weak, but some of its influence is limited when this planet is under the restrictive influence of Capricorn. On a personal level it implies that the growth and development and important successes you experience in life involve attaining Jupiter's nonmaterial goals, such as knowledge, spirituality, philosophy, art and beauty, within the structured, physical reality of Capricorn. This means, for example, that knowledge is not sought for its own sake, but to serve some definite purpose and tangible gain. Your spiritual and philosophical ideas are apt to be traditional. Even a departure from traditional thinking is not likely to be whimsically undertaken and you adopt a serious, organized framework in which to operate. Income or other personal growth may come through government service, family trusts, real estate, and business. When it comes to the arts, Jupiter in Capricorn is more of an asset than a limitation. It promotes the discipline to develop your own talent as well as that of others, it inspires organization and structure in artistic efforts, and aggressiveness to promote and perform. Jupiter's association with desire for authority and status is well served when this planet inhabits the ambitious environment of Capricorn. Jupiter implies the opportunity to get ahead, while Capricorn suggests you will accept responsibilities that accompany elevated status. Desire for material wealth is hard to deny when Jupiter is in Capricorn. However, it is not an implication that you will abuse such a lifestyle if it is attained. If other factors in your personality and background support it, you are inclined to handle assets and income wisely. In the long run, you are likely to be happier with what you have worked for and earned rather than that which is obtained with no effort.

Jupiter in Aquarius. Jupiter is associated with freedom, a characteristic apt to be emphasized when this planet is found in the independence-loving environment of Aquarius. One of the strongest potentials of Jupiter in Aquarius is that your personal capacity for growth and prosperity involves development of intellectual and communicative skills. It implies, however, that in order to attain the most positive influence of this combination, you are not only required to gain knowledge and skills but also to share ideas, information, and methods. Communication with others, social contacts, friendships, and organizations are networks you must establish and maintain. Jupiter in Aquarius often signals the ability to come up with clever, original solutions. It also suggests the ability to organize and disseminate information and statistics in such a way that they are more easily understood, and thereby rendered more useful to a greater number of people. Your income and other areas of personal growth may come through social work, international finance, technological research and development, medicine, fund-raising, social work, transportation, and travel. Jupiter provides intellectual curiosity, which in the environment of Aquarius is likely to stimulate interest in things that are original, unique, or unusual. It may also be fondness for history and antiques. Jupiter in Aquarius means you do not measure either your own success or that of others by wealth or social status. The important keys to your happiness and success lie in developing your own uniqueness and individuality and helping to inspire others with a similar sense of themselves. If material wealth is elusive, you rationalize why you don't need it. It is not apt to be distressful if your circumstances or status are not acceptable to others, since your response is merely to find more congenial company.

Jupiter in Pisces. The spiritual nature of Jupiter is particularly strong when this planet inhabits the emotional environment of Pisces. Creativity and imagination have no restrictions here. The potential consequences of such a limitless environment include the development of remarkable psychic power, artistic talent, and the ability to think in the abstract, not only in artistic terms but with mathematical and scientific perspective. Jupiter's association with overabundance in the ultrasensitive environment of

Pisces can lead to addictive or fanatical thought and behavior patterns, laziness, impracticality, and ideas and concepts that are so obscure as to be meaningless. Your personal growth is a matter of gaining emotional maturity to avoid the negative extremes of Jupiter in Pisces while taking advantage of the positive opportunities it brings. A certain karmic link to home and family associated with the influence of Jupiter in Pisces suggests that part of your emotional maturity may also involve understanding the past and overcoming any negative childhood conditioning. It indicates that income or other types of personal success you experience in life may come through religion, art, music, dance, acting, maritime services, photography, and charitable institutions and activities. You may have desire for material wealth, but whether you are willing to put forth sustained efforts to acquire material assets or manage them wisely depends on other factors in your personality and background. Your own progress as well as that of others is not measured in terms of wealth or status unless you have learned to identify such standards with emotional security. Even if material wealth or status is attained, they will fail to inspire gladness in your heart or motivate your actions for very long. The key to your happiness lies in your own sense of self-worth and spiritual awareness.

Saturn: Discipline and Organization

Saturn is the planet that describes the most likely areas of restriction and frustration. These obstacles represent the particular lessons you were meant to learn in order to succeed. Saturn is associated with hard work, organization, planning, maturity, and getting rid of what is wasteful. It is the universal timekeeper, the discipline and reality of your life. Though Saturn's associations may seem to be negative, this is not the case. Saturn's ultimate description can be compared to a balance sheet. On one side, you must learn patience, acceptance of responsibilities and deprivation, and overcome sorrow and loss. On the other side, you will receive the recognition you deserve, reap the rewards of your sustained efforts, and gain strength and character.

Saturn in Aries. Saturn in Aries means that learning to let maturity and experience overrule aggressiveness, unwarranted enthusiasm, and haste is one of your most important keys to success. Starting new ventures, for example, may require great patience and determination, since such attempts are often beset with delays and other obstacles. Other frustrations you are likely to encounter are failures that result either from acting too fast when you should have been more deliberate, or being unsuccessful because you responded too slowly when quick actions or decisions were needed. Acceptance of responsibilities and circumstances related to home and family and ridding yourself of negative childhood conditioning are two other likely influences of Saturn in Aries. Getting along with authority and developing self-discipline may be difficult unless other factors in your personality and background give you a more positive outlook and strength of character. One of the most promising advantages of combining the determination of Saturn with the energetic environment of Aries is the astonishing endurance you can develop. Reconciling reality with idealism is your constant reminder that anything worth doing is worth doing well, and anything (or anyone) worth having is worth working for.

Saturn in Taurus. Saturn in Taurus implies affinity for the material world and physical reality and that your lessons in life involve these specific orientations. There is potential, for example, that factors in your personality or background may discourage your capacity for enjoyment, and you must ultimately come to realize the importance this element has in the quality of life. On the other hand, physical pleasures may be deeply enjoyed, but they are rarely experienced without accompanying responsibilities. Overindulgence in food and drink invariably leads to appropriate physical complaints. Ready or not, your innocent flirtations turn into romance, romance is pursued by commitment, and romantic commitment soon requires serious consideration of children and marriage. Speculation demands hedging your bets, and when your gambles do pay off, the best philosophy is to take the money and run. Saturn in Taurus implies difficulty in gaining recognition for your creative and artistic talent, or that constant frustrations and obstacles beset their development. Saturn in Taurus can mean you have quite a successful ability to mix business with pleasure, though it can also mean you expect every social event to result in some sort of tangible gain.

Saturn in Gemini. Saturn in Gemini is on the whole thought to be a positive combination, since its influence encourages organization and stability of thoughts and ideas. On the other hand, there are negative associations that cause frustration, and through overcoming the frustration, ultimately bring success. Communication may be restricted by shyness or lack of imagination. Paying too much attention to unnecessary details, and either failing to delegate responsibility to others or delegating too much responsibility and not being sufficiently involved yourself, are some of the possible frustrations to be overcome. Your work may entail endless responsibilities and tasks that net little thanks or remuneration. Relating successfully to coworkers presents potential for still other limitations. You may, for example, be in the unenviable position of correcting their mistakes or supervising them. Chronic health problems are another potential that may limit your productivity and enthusiasm. Getting tasks done on time may be a constant frustrating pattern, whether or not the delays are your fault. Even getting to the job on time may prove frustrating. All of these matters pose problems, to be sure, but overcoming them leads to the rewards of recognition and accomplishment.

Saturn in Cancer. Saturn in Cancer is an indication that you will experience limitations or inhibitions in dealing with others. Cancer is identified with home and family, and when the restrictive influence of Saturn is in this sign it presents the potential for frustrations to be confronted and overcome with respect to these areas. One possibility, for example, is that negative childhood conditioning may be an inhibiting influence on you as an adult. The even broader association connected with Saturn in Cancer suggests that dealing with other people in general, not just family members, may be problematical in your life. Establishing satisfactory partnerships and alliances, eliciting the cooperation of others, and being able to derive stimulation and inspiration from being with others are situations in which you have to make more than a little effort to succeed. On the one hand, relationships can be the biggest obstacles to your goals, while on the other hand, they are what you need to get ahead. Conscious or subconscious fear of being rejected by others can limit your ability to deal with them effectively in order to satisfy another need, which is to gain their acceptance.

Saturn in Leo. Saturn in Leo indicates struggles related to joint funds, inherited wealth, or money and property you handle for others. Using the assets of others for personal gain, failure to repay debts, and unwise loans are invitations to disaster. Attempts to manipulate others invariably work to your disadvantage. Should the reverse occur, and you are the victim of manipulation, it then becomes your responsibility to overcome such restrictive circumstances. Jealousy, greed, and revenge, though not always on your part, are apt to interfere with success until they are met and conquered. Saturn in Leo also suggests that if you exploit others to increase your social status or shoulder your economic burdens, you will pay a high price for the privilege. One of the strongest influences associated with Saturn in Leo is the admonition to develop personal assets—your intellectual, artistic, and physical skills. Developing your own potential also means gaining inner strength and independence. Given the nature of Saturn, there are apt to be inhibitions or restrictions related to personal development. However, obstacles you encounter should only serve as a reminder that personal assets are your most valuable resources.

Saturn in Virgo. Saturn's lessons in Virgo mean that you are likely to struggle with situations that involve the demand for perfection, idealism without imagination, and tradition without warmth. These situations, however, do not necessarily stem from your own feelings and attitudes, but one way or another, your personal environment will be restricted or limited by them. Scholarliness, organization, and impressive mechanical skills are some of the rewards of Saturn in Virgo, though it is not surprising if you have to work unusually hard or overcome difficulties in order to gain them. The serious nature of Saturn combined with Virgo, a sign associated with anxiousness or worry, can mean that fear or caution are obstacles to be conquered. One ramification of this potential is that you will use fear or guilt as an emotional weapon in order to elicit the cooperation or affections of others, or that you are the victim of those who use such methods. Saturn in Virgo suggests you will encounter more than your fair share of delays and frustrations related to travel, mechanical problems, and weather difficulties—in some cases even missing out on important opportunities due to these problems.

Saturn in Libra. Saturn in Libra is considered to be a positive association, though there are always going to be certain limitations connected with Saturn. This particular combination implies that significant accomplishments and recognition of your efforts are possible. However, the problem you continually encounter when you reach out for something is that doing so threatens the loss of something else. Sometimes it is possible to strike a balance between opposing forces in your life, but for the most part you are left to struggle with having to decide between two equally important goals. You may, for example, be in the unhappy position of having to balance the demand of a career or other important long-range goals with the responsibilities related to home and family. Other potential frustrations that must be overcome with Saturn in Libra may occur in your dealings with other people. Eliciting the cooperation of others may be difficult; partnerships and other alliances may be disappointing. Once your relationships or associations with people are established, they can become solid and long-lasting, but initially even the most fleeting of interactions can be accompanied by some sort of discouraging restriction.

Saturn in Scorpio. Saturn in Scorpio implies that struggles you encounter are apt to involve fierce ambition, a force that can mean important accomplishments, but can also destroy what has been gained. Particular sources of struggle and other life lessons to be learned include friendships, social contacts, and membership in fraternal, civic, or political groups. People with whom you associate in these various situations are valuable resources, and thus a way for you to get ahead, but there is bound to be something in these dealings that gives rise to frustration and restriction. If you are unwilling to undertake the responsibility of making friends or establishing a social circle, you may later regret not being able to enjoy the positive benefits such relationships can bring. Your career or long-range goals may be much harder to achieve due to lack of connections or a network of friends who might have helped your progress. Other implications are that you may be guilty of driving friends and associates away because you shamelessly use them for personal gain and never give anything in return, or the reverse occurs and you are the victim of such exploitations.

Saturn in Sagittarius. Saturn in Sagittarius indicates that restrictions you may be obliged to overcome involve dealing with deception or loss, confronting hidden fears, and letting go of the past. Part of your struggle may include the desire to hold on to tradition, while realizing that certain changes must be made. Saturn's association with reticence in communicating information is not comfortable in Sagittarius, a sign that encourages openness and honesty. There are many different situations in which this difficulty presents an obstacles. You may, for example, find yourself in circumstances that require secrecy, even though you wish it could be otherwise. Delays and restrictions in such matters as higher education, long-distance travel, and court decisions are other areas where Saturn's lessons may force you to accept responsibility and learn the virtues of prudent actions and a patient disposition. Saturn in Sagittarius can be a positive combination in promoting spirituality and high principles. However, the negative potential suggests intolerance and bigotry embedded in inflexible moral righteousness. Whether this represents your own limited attitude or a negative inclination in those around you depends on other factors in your personality and background.

Saturn in Capricorn. Saturn is the planetary ruler of Capricorn and thus has strong influence in this sign. This combination indicates that restraint and self-discipline are apt to play significant roles in the lessons you learn in life. Whether you lack these traits and are forced to develop them or possess them to such a high degree as to limit your growth and success in other areas is determined by other factors in your personality and background. Strong ambition is greatly encouraged by Saturn in Capricorn, a valuable motivation in attaining success. However, as with all Saturn's influences, there is a negative potential that ambition can become totally self-serving and manipulative. Saturn's pessimism and fearfulness can be assets when it comes to assessing accurately the potential danger of certain situations, but these negative traits can be turned inward, an indication that you should take pains to avoid a poor self-image. Inner feelings of inferiority lead to aggressiveness and inability to accept anyone's authority but your own. Saturn in Capricorn makes it easy to make the rules or enforce them, but it is not always accompanied by willingness to abide by them yourself.

Saturn in Aquarius. The influence of Saturn in Aquarius may inspire a mature, reliable disposition and talent for finance or scientific pursuits. However, it also indicates that some of the restrictions you may encounter involve monetary concerns and inflexible priorities. For example, it may mean you must overcome monetary loss or poverty, or develop too great a concern with amassing material assets and improving your personal status. Fixing on a goal or set of priorities, you pursue them with such determination and focus that you become heedless of relationships and other important elements in your life. Saturn in Aquarius can be extremely humane in some respects, but if you allow interest in groups and societal problems to overwhelm your private relationships, you may have gained nothing in the way of personal growth or understanding. Another of Saturn's lessons you may be obliged to learn deals with friendships. If Saturn's restrictive influence is indicated by your unwillingness to establish friendships, you suffer the loss of benefits that such relationships bring. If Saturn's ambitiousness is indicated by the fact that you exploit friendships to improve your social status, this, too, becomes a negative situation to overcome.

Saturn in Pisces. Saturn in Pisces indicates that frustrations you encounter may include difficulty in developing basic physical skills and acquiring or applying information. This potential suggests, for example, that early schooling may be a restrictive influence, or circumstances may prevent or interrupt elementary education. Unwillingness to share ideas and information, or allowing yourself to become depressed and unproductive through unnecessary worry or cynicism, are other situations you may have to meet and conquer. Saturn in Pisces presents the possibility of being obliged to overcome loss, chronic illness, or hypochondria, or to accept responsibility for others with such afflictions. Lack of charity on your part will net you exactly the same response from others. The influence of Saturn in Pisces suggests you may be tempted to use guilt as an emotional weapon to obtain the cooperation or affection of others, or being the victim of those who employ such methods, it becomes your responsibility to end this negative situation.

Some rewards of Saturn in Pisces include remarkable intuition and timing, mathematical ability, and the ability to give substance and reality to vision and imagination. These rewards, however, are sure to exact a price.

Uranus: Originality and Rebellion

Uranus is the planet associated with freedom and the instigation of big changes. It takes approximately eighty-four years between the time Uranus is seen in one sign until it is again in the same sign. Since the influence of Uranus in one sign spans several generations until it is once again in the same sign, its effect in that sign is generational rather than personal. However general the influence of Uranus in a sign may seem, its description is nonetheless valuable, since it reveals conditions in society that may considerably affect your private life.

Uranus in Aries (1929–1935). Attraction to that which is new and different inspired by Uranus in Aries means society is prepared to accept change for its own sake as much as anything else. Your generation experiences a complete change in lifestyle from that of your parents, as a result of research and technology.

Uranus in Taurus (1936–1942). Uranus is very stable in the cautious environment of Taurus. Radical ideas and innovative methods will not be accepted in society unless they can be applied to practical purpose. Your generation will be more concerned with material growth and upholding tradition than in outrageous lifestyles and demanding revolutionary actions.

Uranus in Gemini (1943–1949). Uranus in the communication-oriented sign of Gemini indicates your generation is concerned with freedom of speech. Society takes an active interest in new ideas and innovations. Research and technology produced many methods and inventions in the field of communications. Unstructured learning and other less traditional educational methods are promoted.

Uranus in Cancer (1950–1956). Uranus in Cancer means your generation concerns itself with domestic life and family. Promotion of nontraditional ideas introduces communal living, radical approaches to basic nurturing, and new information and methods concerned with diet and food. You are apt to adopt a completely different domestic lifestyle from that of your parents.

Uranus in Leo (1956–1961). There is concern with the creative arts when Uranus is in Leo. Your generation defies many traditional concepts and methods. Bold innovation is encouraged. A larger-than-life approach stirs up love of nature, the spirit of humanitarianism, social reforms, and enthusiasm for flamboyancy in fashions as well as behavior.

Uranus in Virgo (1962–1968). The influence of Uranus in Virgo is not concerned with discovering or promoting anything unique or original. Your generation's forte is in coming up with new ways to handle existing problems. Traditional institutions, including government, education, labor, and armed forces are reorganized. Technology produces more efficient methods for routine tasks.

Uranus in Libra (1968–1974). Traditional concepts regarding relationships are apt to be discarded when Uranus is found in Libra. Your generation takes a radically different view of marriage and partnership roles than that of your parents. There is also concern with individual freedom, and changes in the law result from dramatic new legal precedents.

Uranus in Scorpio (1975–1981). Uranus in Scorpio produces a generation concerned with research and investigation. Unlocking the mysterious forces of nature, human psychology and motivation, and conservation of resources are the targets of this generation. Prevailing societal attitudes regarding sex are altered and the scientific understanding of human sexuality gains new perspective and insight.

Uranus in Sagittarius (1898–1904), (1982–1988). Political groups, religious organizations, and international corporations are the targets of society's interest when Uranus occupies the sign of Sagittarius. This generation also concerns itself with innovative marketing and advertising strategies, finding new approaches to higher education, publishing, and international diplomacy and trade. New ideologies promote the spirit of nationalism.

Uranus in Capricorn (1905–1912), (1988–1996). Reorganization and restructure are the compelling actions inspired by Uranus in Capricorn in getting rid of waste and mismanagement in government, business, and other traditional institutions. Consolidation of needs and goals, and establishing a new authority to replace what has been unworkable or impractical are the aspirations of this generation.

Uranus in Aquarius (1913–1920). Independence and emancipation are wildly urged when Uranus is in Aquarius, which means that this generation will go to war in order to protect or gain their freedom. Not all is chaos, however. Unnecessary or unfair restrictions will be thrown off, while those which traditionally have been useful are kept.

Uranus in Pisces (1921–1928). Uranus in Pisces produces tolerance toward anything that is different or unusual. Dramatic change in fashion, attitudes, and behavior are allowed free expression. This generation is concerned with higher levels of creativity, imagination, spirituality, and the subconscious, through application of scientific methods. Abstract theories are greatly expanded during this period.

Neptune: Illusion and Imagination

Neptune is the planet associated with dreams and fantasies, illusion and disillusion, spirituality, the real and the unreal, the victim and the victimizer. In society it is the disenfranchised, disadvantaged, the orphans and minorities, the artistic and compassionate. Slow-moving Neptune takes about 164 years to travel through all twelve signs, which means that its influence in any one of the signs must be viewed as generational rather than personal. However, its influence in each of the signs describes the conditions in society that can have a considerable effect on your private lifestyle.

Neptune in Aries (1861–1875). Though no one living now was born with Neptune in Aries, it is interesting to note some historical consequences. Neptune-ruled issues gain active expression in Aries. Slavery and the question of emancipation were partly responsible for the Civil War, and the spirit of charity gave rise to the Salvation Army and the Red Cross.

Neptune in Taurus (1874–1889). Taurus is associated with materialism, reality, and the physical world. During the latter half of the nineteenth century, Neptune inspired a markedly Taurean atmosphere. Ignoring spirituality, materialism in philosophy and realism in literature and art attempted to explain everything solely in terms of what could be detected by human senses.

Neptune in Gemini (1887–1902). Gemini is associated with communication and transportation. At the turn of the century, Neptune in Gemini witnessed the automobiles of Karl Benz and Henry Ford, Ferdinand von Zeppelin's airship, the airplane trials of the Wright brothers, Guglielmo Marconi's radio telegraph, and R. A. Fessenden's first transmittal of human speech via radio waves.

Neptune in Cancer (1901–1916). Cancer is associated with family. During this century's first two decades sentiments stirred by Neptune in Cancer resulted in official recognition of Mother's Day and Father's Day. Other sentiments regarding family life were not so popular. Margaret Sanger was jailed for writing *Family Limitation,* the first book on birth control.

Neptune in Leo (1914–1929). The Neptune-ruled movie industry began its phenomenal growth during the 1920s with Neptune in Leo, the sign that also rules entertainment. Neptune in Leo also produced the Dada artistic and literary movement, which led to surrealism. Russia's monarchy (Leo) ended because it failed to respond to its impoverished people (Neptune).

Neptune in Virgo (1928–1943). Virgo's association with perfectionism and idealism reached extremes with Neptune in Virgo from the late twenties through the early forties. On the highest level were the writings and work of Albert Schweitzer. On the lowest level was Hitler's tragic plan to create a master race by eradicating those he considered inferior.

Neptune in Libra (1942–1957). Libra is the peacemaker and Neptune in Libra during the forties and fifties witnessed establishment of the United Nations. However, the influence of Neptune is more inspirational than actual. Efforts to promote world peace and cooperation have received attention, but real solutions or strength have often proved to be illusive.

Neptune in Scorpio (1955–1970). Neptune in Scorpio from the mid-fifties through the sixties impacted society's attitude toward sex (Scorpio). Traditional sexual codes began to erode (Neptune's influence) as sexually explicit material invaded the media and everyday life. Spying and secret surveillance, another Neptune-in-Scorpio influence, became a feature of public and private life.

Neptune in Sagittarius (1970–1984). Neptune and Sagittarius involve spirituality and idealism. The seventies witnessed the recognition of the ordination of women in the Episcopal Church and the rise of the Jesus Movement. The nation's tragic waste of natural resources became increasingly apparent during the energy crisis inspired by increased oil prices (Neptune rules oil).

Neptune in Capricorn (1984–1998). Neptune rules spirituality and Capricorn rules not only organized religion but authority figures connected with any enterprise or institution. Recent scandals involving the TV evangelists are good examples of Neptune's disillusionment in Capricorn. Though the outcome is not yet apparent, the war against drugs (Neptune) by the government (Capricorn) continues.

Neptune in Aquarius (1834–1848), (1999–2011). Neptune inspires idealism and Aquarius promotes independence. During the 1830s and '40s, with Neptune in Aquarius, Karl Marx urged workers to revolt against the ruling class. Unrest among the oppressed increased until it culminated in what is called the year of revolutions, which included the first convention of women's rights.

Neptune in Pisces (1847–1862). Neptune in Pisces encourages imagination and spirituality, but also inspires illusion and disillusionment. Spiritualism, for example, became popular during the late 1840s. *Great Expectations,* written by Charles Dickens in this period, is an excellent description of Neptune in Pisces. Speculation in the unrealistic Neptune-Pisces environment caused economic crisis throughout Europe.

Pluto: Power and Transformation

Pluto is identified with intense energy and concentration. It is mysterious rather than mystical, the past and future rather than the present. It represents sources of power and manipulation that can be used for good or evil. Pluto is the slowest moving planet, taking approximately 248 years to complete one cycle through each of the signs. Though its influence is interpreted as generational rather than personal, the description of Pluto in the signs is an indication of how the private lives of those born in a given sign can be affected.

Pluto in Aries (1822–1852). Pluto in Aries brings renewed cycles of investigation and energy. During Pluto in Aries from the 1820s to 1850s, experimentation and discoveries in electricity, thermodynamics, and other physical forces occurred. Explorers pushed into Africa and the polar region while American explorers and pioneers began to settle the vast western wilderness.

Pluto in Taurus (1851–1884). Pluto was in Taurus from the 1850s to early 1880s. During the previous period in Aries, great strides in science and technology created the industrial revolution. The influence of Pluto in pragmatic Taurus was to make use of the unprecedented growth of industry for material gain, giving rise to capitalism.

Pluto in Gemini (1885–1913). Gemini rules transportation and communication. At the turn of the century both Pluto and Neptune were in Gemini, a combined influence resulting in the automobiles built by Karl Benz and Henry Ford and the flight of the Wright brothers. Communications were improved by introduction of the radio and the telegraph.

Pluto in Cancer (1914–1939). Cancer is associated with family. The transforming influence of Pluto in Cancer from 1912 through 1930 changed domestic life in America. What was a social demand by women for more freedom and work outside the home in the twenties became a financial necessity during the economic collapse of the thirties.

Pluto in Leo (1937–1958). Leo is associated with individuality and enjoyment. Pluto's influence in Leo during the forties and fifties resulted in society being increasingly made to accommodate the individual. Modern medicine helped prolong life, and science and technology produced ways to make work easier. People were given more leisure time to enjoy themselves.

Pluto in Virgo (1956–1972). Virgo is associated with the armed services, health care, and the work force. During the sixties, with Pluto in Virgo, the Vietnam War inspired dramatic changes in our country's willingness to go to war, health care became completely transformed by skyrocketing insurance rates, and once-powerful labor unions lost considerable influence.

Pluto in Libra (1971–1984). Libra is associated with equality, and Pluto represents power and manipulation. During the seventies and early eighties the demands of Third

World nations for nuclear energy and other power in the world increased. Civil rights were strong issues in America and world sentiment developed against apartheid in South Africa.

Pluto in Scorpio (1983–1995). Scorpio's association with sex and the power of Pluto to transform is apparent in the current transit that began in 1984. Doing what no religious or philosophical dictates have ever accomplished in the history of man, the AIDS virus has completely altered the sexual behavior of people throughout the world.

Pluto in Sagittarius (1749–1762), (1995–   ). Sagittarius is associated with knowledge; it encourages spiritual, political, and philosophical ideas. Though Pluto will not transit Sagittarius until 1995, its influence during the 1700s inspired the Enlightenment. This was an age of advancement in scientific and political thought, the proliferation of newspapers, and increased higher education for all social classes.

Pluto in Capricorn (1762–1778). Capricorn represents organization and structure, and Pluto represents power. Though Pluto in Capricorn will not occur until the next century, we can note that the last time it happened, an organized group of men were inspired to draft the Declaration of Independence, a document that changed the course of history.

Pluto in Aquarius (1778–1798). Aquarius represents the common man. Pluto in Aquarius does not occur until the next century, but at the end of the nineteenth century it resulted in the newly formed American government being changed from one controlled by the upper class to the more democratic form advocated by Thomas Jefferson.

Pluto in Pisces (1799–1823). Pluto rules investigation and intense energy. Pisces rules the ocean and religion. Pluto

in Pisces at the beginning of the eighteenth century resulted in some appropriately related events. Robert Fulton
produced the submarine, John Dalton introduced atomic
theory, Egyptian hieroglyphics were deciphered, and Mary
Baker Eddy founded Christian Science.

How to Find the Place of Jupiter, Saturn, Uranus, Neptune, and Pluto in Your Chart

Find your birth year in the left-hand column and read across the chart until you find your birth date. The top of that column will tell you where Jupiter, Saturn, Uranus, Neptune, and Pluto lie in your chart.

Key: ♈ ARIES | ♉ TAURUS | ♊ GEMINI | ♋ CANCER | ♌ LEO | ♍ VIRGO | ♎ LIBRA | ♏ SCORPIO | ♐ SAGITT. | ♑ CAPRI. | ♒ AQUAR. | ♓ PISCES | Retrograde ℞

PLACE OF JUPITER, SATURN, URANUS, NEPTUNE, AND PLUTO—1880–1885

FIND YOUR BIRTH YEAR HERE	TABLE I-♃-Find Period including birthday. Your Jupiter is in — Sign	TABLE II-♄-Find Period including birthday. Your Saturn is in — Sign	TABLE III-♅-Find. Your Uranus is in — Sign	TABLE IV-♆ Your Neptune is in — Sign	TABLE V-♇ Your Pluto is in — Sign
1880	1/1–4/2 ♓ 4/3–12/31 ♈	All Yr. ♈	All Yr. ♍	All Yr.	All Yr. ♉
1881	1/1–4/11 ♈ 4/12–12/31 ♉	1/1–4/5 ♈ 4/6–12/31 ♉	All Yr. ♍	All Yr.	All Yr. ♉
1882	1/1–4/21 ♉ 4/22–9/19 ♊ 9/20–11/17 ♋ 11/18–12/31 ♊	All Yr. ♉	All Yr. ♍	All Yr.	All Yr. ♉
1883	1/1–5/4 ♊ 5/5–9/26 ♋ 9/27–12/31 ♌	1/1–5/23 ♉ 5/24–12/31 ♊	All Yr. ♍	All Yr.	All Yr. ♉
1884	1/1–1/16 ♋ 1/17–5/21 ♋ 5/22–10/17 ♌ 10/18–12/31 ♍	All Yr. ♊	1/1–10/13 ♍ 10/14–12/31 ♎	All Yr.	All Yr. ♊
1885	1/1–2/25 ♍ 2/26–6/14 ♌ 6/15–11/15 ♍ 11/16–12/31 ♎	1/1–7/5 ♊ 7/6–12/31 ♋	1/1–4/11 ♎ 4/12–7/28 ♍ 7/29–12/31 ♎	All Yr.	All Yr. ♊

PLACE OF JUPITER, SATURN, URANUS, NEPTUNE, AND PLUTO—1886–1893

Year	Jupiter	Saturn	Uranus	Neptune	Pluto
1886	1/1–3/29 ♌ 3/30–7/15 ♍ 7/16–12/16 ♌ 12/17–12/31 ♍	All Yr. ♋	All Yr. ♎	All Yr. ♉	All Yr. ♊
1887	1/1–4/28 ♍ 4/29–8/15 ♎ 8/16–12/31 ♍	1/1–8/18 ♋ 8/19–12/31 ♌	All Yr. ♎	1/1–8/15 ♉ 8/16–9/21 ♊ 9/22–12/31 ♉	All Yr. ♊
1888	1/1–1/14 ♎ 1/15–6/2 ♏ 6/3–9/10 ♎ 9/11–12/31 ♏	1/1–3/9 ♌ 3/10–4/20 ♋ 4/21–12/31 ♌	All Yr. ♎	1/1–5/25 ♉ 5/26–12/31 ♊	All Yr. ♊
1889	1/1–2/5 ♏ 2/6–7/23 ♐ 7/24–9/25 ♏ 9/26–12/31 ♐	1/1–10/6 ♌ 10/7–12/31 ♍	All Yr. ♎	1/1–3/20 ♉ 3/21–12/31 ♊	All Yr. ♊
1890	1/1–2/22 ♐ 2/23–12/31 ♑	1/1–2/24 ♍ 2/25–6/27 ♌ 6/28–12/31 ♍	1/1–12/9 ♎ 12/10–12/31 ♏	All Yr. ♊	All Yr. ♊
1891	1/1–3/7 ♑ 3/8–12/31 ♒	1/1–12/26 ♍ 12/27–12/31 ♎	1/1–4/4 ♏ 4/5–9/25 ♎ 9/26–12/31 ♏	All Yr. ♊	All Yr. ♊
1892	1/1–3/16 ♒ 3/17–12/31 ♓	1/1–1/22 ♎ 1/23–8/29 ♍ 8/30–12/31 ♎	All Yr. ♏	All Yr. ♊	All Yr. ♊
1893	1/1–2/24 ♓ 3/25–8/20 ♈ 8/21–10/19 ♓ 10/20–12/31 ♈	All Yr. ♎	All Yr. ♏	All Yr. ♊	All Yr. ♊

PLACE OF JUPITER, SATURN, URANUS, NEPTUNE, AND PLUTO—1894–1900

FIND YOUR BIRTH YEAR HERE	TABLE I-♃ — Find Period including birthday. Your Jupiter is in	Sign	TABLE II-♄ — Find Period including birthday. Your Saturn is in	Sign	TABLE III-♅ — Your Uranus is in	Sign	TABLE IV-♆ — Your Neptune is in	Sign	TABLE V-♇ — Your Pluto is in	Sign
1894	1/1–4/1 4/2–8/13 8/14–12/31	♉ ♓ ♋	1/1–11/6 11/7–12/31	♎ ♏	All Yr.	♏	All Yr.	♊	All Yr.	♊
1895	1/1–4/10 4/11–9/4 9/5–12/31	♊ ♋ ♌	All Yr.	♏	All Yr.	♏	All Yr.	♊	All Yr.	♊
1896	1/1–2/29 3/1–4/17 4/18–9/27 9/28–12/31	♌ ♋ ♌ ♍	All Yr.	♏	All Yr.	♏	All Yr.	♊	All Yr.	♊
1897	1/1–10/27 10/28–12/31	♍ ♎	1/1–2/16 2/7–4/9 4/10–10/26 10/27–12/31	♏ ♐ ♏ ♐	1/1–12/1 12/2–12/31	♏ ♐	All Yr.	♊	All Yr.	♊
1898	1/1–11/26 11/27–12/31	♎ ♏	All Yr.	♐	1/1–7/3 7/4–9/10 9/11–12/31	♐ ♏ ♐ ♐	All Yr.	♊	All Yr.	♊
1899	1/1–12/25 12/26–12/31	♏ ♐	All Yr.	♐	All Yr.	♐	All Yr.	♊	All Yr.	♊
1900	All Yr.	♐	1/1–1/20 1/21–7/18 7/19–10/16 10/17–12/31	♐ ♑ ♐ ♑	All Yr.	♐	All Yr.	♊	All Yr.	♊

PLACE OF JUPITER, SATURN, URANUS, NEPTUNE, AND PLUTO—1901–1911

Year	Jupiter	Saturn	Uranus	Neptune	Pluto
1901	1/1–1/18 ♐ 1/19–12/31 ♑	All Yr. ♑	All Yr. ♐	1/1–7/19 ♊ 7/20–12/25 ♋ 12/26–12/31 ♊	♊
1902	1/1–2/6 ♑ 2/7–12/31 ♒	All Yr. ♑	All Yr. ♐	1/1–5/20 ♊ 5/21–12/31 ♋	♊
1903	1/1–2/19 ♒ 2/20–12/31 ♓	1/1–1/19 ♑ 1/20–12/31 ♒	All Yr. ♐	All Yr. ♋	♊
1904	1/1–2/29 ♓ 3/1–8/6 ♈ 8/9–8/31 ♉ 9/1–12/31 ♈	All Yr. ♒	1/1–12/19 ♐ 12/20–12/31 ♑	All Yr. ♋	♊
1905	1/1–3/7 ♈ 3/8–7/20 ♉ 7/21–12/4 ♊ 12/5–12/31 ♉	1/1–4/12 ♒ 4/13–8/16 ♓ 8/17–12/31 ♒	All Yr. ♑	All Yr. ♋	♊
1906	1/1–3/9 ♉ 3/10–7/30 ♊ 7/31–12/31 ♋	1/1–1/7 ♒ 1/8–12/31 ♓	All Yr. ♑	All Yr. ♋	♊
1907	1/1–8/18 ♋ 8/19–12/31 ♌	All Yr. ♓	All Yr. ♑	All Yr. ♋	♊
1908	1/1–9/11 ♌ 9/12–12/31 ♍	1/1–3/18 ♓ 3/19–12/31 ♈	All Yr. ♑	All Yr. ♋	♊
1909	1/1–10/11 ♍ 10/12–12/31 ♎	All Yr. ♈	All Yr. ♑	All Yr. ♋	♊
1910	1/1–11/11 ♎ 11/12–12/31 ♏	1/1–5/16 ♈ 5/17–12/14 ♉ 12/15–12/31 ♈	All Yr. ♑	All Yr. ♋	♊
1911	1/1–12/9 ♏ 12/10–12/31 ♐	1/1–1/19 ♈ 1/20–12/31 ♉	All Yr. ♑	All Yr. ♋	♊

PLACE OF JUPITER, SATURN, URANUS, NEPTUNE, AND PLUTO—1912–1920

FIND YOUR BIRTH YEAR HERE	TABLE I-♃-Find Period including birthday. Your Jupiter is in	Sign	TABLE II-♄-Find Period including birthday. Your Saturn is in	Sign	TABLE III-♅ Your Uranus is in	Sign	TABLE IV-♆ Your Neptune is in	Sign	TABLE V-♇ Your Pluto is in	Sign
1912	All Yr.	♐	1/1–7/6 7/17–11/30 12/1–12/31	♉ ♊ ♉	1/1–1/30 1/31–9/4 9/5–11/11 11/12–12/31	♑ ♒ ♑ ♒	All Yr.	♋	All Yr.	♊
1913	1/1 + 2 1/3–12/31	♐ ♑	1/1–3/25 3/26–12/31	♉ ♊	All Yr.	♒	All Yr.	♋	All Yr.	♊
1914	1/1–1/21 1/22–12/31	♑ ♒	1/1–8/24 8/25–12/6 12/7–12/31	♊ ♋ ♊	All Yr.	♒	1/1–9/22 9/22–12/14 12/15–12/31	♋ ♌ ♋	All Yr.	♋
1915	1/1–2/3 2/4–12/31	♒ ♓	1/1–5/11 5/12–12/31	♊ ♋	All Yr.	♒	1/1–7/18 7/19–12/31	♋ ♌	All Yr.	♋
1916	1/1–2/11 2/12–6/25 6/26–10/26 10/27–12/31	♓ ♈ ♉ ♈	1/1–10/16 10/17–12/7 12/8–12/31	♋ ♌ ♋	All Yr.	♒	1/1–3/19 3/20–5/1 5/2–12/31	♌ ♋ ♌	All Yr.	♋
1917	1/1–2/12 2/13–6/29 6/30–12/31	♈ ♉ ♊	1/1–7/23 7/24–12/31	♋ ♌	All Yr.	♒	All Yr.	♌	All Yr.	♋
1918	1/1–6/12 6/13–12/31	♊ ♋	All Yr.	♌	All Yr.	♒	All Yr.	♌	All Yr.	♋
1919	1/1–8/1 8/2–12/31	♋ ♌	1/1–8/11 8/12–12/31	♌ ♍	1/1–3/31 4/1–8/16 8/17–12/31	♒ ♓ ♒	All Yr.	♌	All Yr.	♋
1920	1/1–8/26 8/27–12/31	♌ ♍	All Yr.	♍	1/1–1/21 1/22–12/31	♒ ♓	All Yr.	♌	All Yr.	♋

PLACE OF JUPITER, SATURN, URANUS, NEPTUNE, AND PLUTO—1921–1931

Year	Jupiter		Saturn		Uranus		Neptune		Pluto	
1921	1/1–9/25 9/26–12/31	♍ ♎	1/1–10/7 10/8–12/31	♍ ♎	All Yr.	♓	All Yr.	♌	All Yr.	♋
1922	1/1–10/26 10/27–12/31	♎ ♏	All Yr.	♎	All Yr.	♓	All Yr.	♌	All Yr.	♋
1923	1/1–11/24 11/25–12/31	♏ ♐	1/1–12/19 12/20–12/31	♎ ♏	All Yr.	♓	All Yr.	♌	All Yr.	♋
1924	1/1–12/17 12/18–12/31	♐ ♑	1/1–4/5 4/6–9/13 9/14–12/31	♏ ♎ ♏	All Yr.	♓	All Yr.	♌	All Yr.	♋
1925	All Yr.	♑	All Yr.	♏	All Yr.	♓	All Yr.	♌	All Yr.	♋
1926	1/1–1/5 1/6–12/31	♑ ♒	1/1–12/2 12/3–12/31	♏ ♐	All Yr.	♓	All Yr.	♌	All Yr.	♋
1927	1/1–1/17 1/18–6/5 6/6–9/10 9/11–12/31	♒ ♓ ♈ ♓	All Yr.	♐	1/1–3/30 3/31–11/4 11/5–12/31	♓ ♈ ♓	All Yr.	♌	All Yr.	♋
1928	1/1–1/22 1/23–6/3 6/4–12/31	♓ ♈ ♉	All Yr.	♐	1/1–1/12 1/13–12/31	♓ ♈	1/1–9/20 9/21–12/31	♌ ♍	All Yr.	♋
1929	1/1–6/11 6/12–12/31	♈ ♊	1/1–3/14 3/15–5/4 5/5–11/29 11/30–12/31	♐ ♑ ♐ ♑	All Yr.	♈	1/1–2/19 2/20–7/23 7/24–12/31	♍ ♌ ♍	All Yr.	♋
1930	1/1–6/26 6/27–12/31	♊ ♋	All Yr.	♑	All Yr.	♈	All Yr.	♍	All Yr.	♋
1931	1/1–7/17 7/18–12/31	♋ ♌	All Yr.	♑	All Yr.	♈	All Yr.	♍	All Yr.	♋

PLACE OF JUPITER, SATURN, URANUS, NEPTUNE, AND PLUTO—1932–1939

FIND YOUR BIRTH YEAR HERE	TABLE I-♃-Find Period Including birthday. Your Jupiter is in	Sign	TABLE II-♄-Find Period Including birthday. Your Saturn is in	Sign	TABLE III-♅ Your Uranus is in	Sign	TABLE IV-♆ Your Neptune is in	Sign	TABLE V-♇ Your Pluto is in	Sign
1932	1/1–8/11 8/12–12/31	♌ ♍	1/1–2/23 2/24–8/13 8/14–11/19 11/20–12/31	♑ ♒ ♑ ♒	All Yr.	♈	All Yr.	♍	All Yr.	♋
1933	1/1–9/10 9/11–12/31	♍ ♎	All Yr.	♒	All Yr.	♈	All Yr.	♍	All Yr.	♋
1934	1/1–10/11 10/12–12/31	♎ ♏	All Yr.	♒	1/1–6/6 6/7–10/10 10/11–12/31	♈ ♉ ♈	All Yr.	♍	All Yr.	♋
1935	1/1–11/9 11/10–12/31	♏ ♐	1/1–2/14 2/15–12/31	♒ ♓	1/1–3/28 3/29–12/31	♈ ♉	All Yr.	♍	All Yr.	♋
1936	1/1–12/2 12/3–12/31	♐ ♑	All Yr.	♓	All Yr.	♉	All Yr.	♍	All Yr.	♋
1937	1/1–12/20 12/21–12/31	♑ ♒	1/1–4/25 4/26–10/18 10/19–12/31	♓ ♈ ♓	All Yr.	♉	All Yr.	♍	10/7–11/26 11/27–12/31	♌ ♋
1938	1/1–5/14 5/15–7/30 7/31–12/29 12/30–12/31	♒ ♓ ♒ ♓	1/1–1/14 1/15–12/31	♓ ♈	All Yr.	♉	All Yr.	♍	1/1–8/3 8/4–12/31	♋ ♌
1939	1/1–5/11 5/12–10/30 10/31–12/20 12/21–12/31	♓ ♈ ♓ ♈	All Yr.	♈	All Yr.	♉	All Yr.	♍	1/1–2/7 2/8–6/13 6/14–12/1	♌ ♋ ♌

PLACE OF JUPITER, SATURN, URANUS, NEPTUNE, AND PLUTO—1940–1949

Year	Jupiter	Saturn	Uranus	Neptune	Pluto
1940	♈ 1/1–5/16; ♉ 5/17–12/31	♈ 1/1–3/20; ♉ 3/21–12/31	♉ All Yr.	♍ All Yr.	♌ All Yr.
1941	♉ 1/1–5/26; ♊ 5/27–12/31	♉ All Yr.	♉ 1/1–8/7; ♊ 8/8–10/5; ♉ 10/6–12/31	♍ All Yr.	♌ All Yr.
1942	♊ 1/1–6/10; ♋ 6/11–12/31	♉ 1/1–5/8; ♊ 5/9–12/31	♉ 1/1–5/14; ♊ 5/15–12/31	♍ 1/1–10/3; ♎ 10/4–12/31	♌ All Yr.
1943	♋ 1/1–6/30; ♌ 7/1–12/31	♊ All Yr.	♊ All Yr.	♎ 1/1–4/18; ♍ 4/19–8/2; ♎ 8/3–12/31	♌ All Yr.
1944	♌ 1/1–7/26; ♍ 7/27–12/31	♊ 1/1–6/20; ♋ 6/21–12/31	♊ All Yr.	♎ All Yr.	♌ All Yr.
1945	♍ 1/1–8/25; ♎ 8/26–12/31	♋ All Yr.	♊ All Yr.	♎ All Yr.	♌ All Yr.
1946	♎ 1/1–9/25; ♏ 9/26–12/31	♋ 1/1–8/2; ♌ 8/3–12/31	♊ All Yr.	♎ All Yr.	♌ All Yr.
1947	♏ 1/1–10/24; ♐ 10/25–12/31	♌ All Yr.	♊ All Yr.	♎ All Yr.	♌ All Yr.
1948	♐ 1/1–11/15; ♑ 11/16–12/31	♌ 1/1–9/19; ♍ 9/20–12/31	♊ 1/1–8/30; ♋ 8/31–11/12; ♊ 11/13–12/31	♎ All Yr.	♌ All Yr.
1949	♑ 1/1–4/12; ♒ 4/13–6/27; ♑ 6/28–11/30; ♒ 12/1–12/31	♍ 1/1–4/3; ♌ 4/4–5/29; ♍ 5/30–12/31	♊ 1/1–6/10; ♋ 6/11–12/31	♎ All Yr.	♌ All Yr.

PLACE OF JUPITER, SATURN, URANUS, NEPTUNE, AND PLUTO—1950–1957

FIND YOUR BIRTH YEAR HERE	TABLE I-♃-Find Period including birthday. Your Jupiter is in	Sign	TABLE II-♄-Find Period including birthday. Your Saturn is in	Sign	TABLE III-♅ Your Uranus is in	Sign	TABLE IV-♆ Your Neptune is in	Sign	TABLE V-♇ Your Pluto is in	Sign
1950	1/1-4/14 4/15-9/13 9/14-11/30 12/1-12/31	≈ ✕ ≈ ✕	1/1-11/20 11/21-12/31	♍ ♎	All Yr.	♋	All Yr.	♎	All Yr.	♌
1951	1/1-4/21 4/22-12/31	✕ ♈	1/1-3/7 3/8-8/13 8/14-12/31	♎ ♍ ♎	All Yr.	♋	All Yr.	♎	All Yr.	♌
1952	1/1-4/28 4/29-12/31	♈ ♉	All Yr.	♎	All Yr.	♋	All Yr.	♎	All Yr.	♌
1953	1/1-5/9 5/10-12/31	♉ ♊	1/1-10/22 10/23-12/31	♎ ♏	All Yr.	♋	All Yr.	♎	All Yr.	♌
1954	1/1-5/24 5/25-12/31	♊ ♋	All Yr.	♏	All Yr.	♋	1/1-12/23 12/24-12/31	♎ ♏	All Yr.	♌
1955	1/1-6/12 6/13-11/17 11/18-12/31	♋ ♌ ♍	All Yr.	♏	1/1-8/24 8/25-12/31	♋ ♌	1/1-3/11 3/12-10/18 10/19-12/31	♏ ♎ ♏	1/1-10/19	♌
1956	1/1-1/18 1/19-7/7 7/8-12/12 12/13-12/31	♍ ♌ ♍ ♎	1/1-1/12 1/13-5/14 5/15-10/10 10/11-12/31	♏ ♐ ♏ ♐	1/1-1/28 1/29-6/9 6/10-12/31	♌ ♋ ♌	1/1-6/16 6/17-8/4 8/5-12/31	♏ ♎ ♏	10/20-12/31	♍
1957	1/1-2/19 2/20-8/6 8/7-12/31	♎ ♏ ♎	All Yr.	♐	All Yr.	♌	All Yr.	♏	1/1-1/15 1/16-8/18 8/19-12/31	♍ ♌ ♍

PLACE OF JUPITER, SATURN, URANUS, NEPTUNE, AND PLUTO—1958–1965

Year	Jupiter	Saturn	Uranus	Neptune	Pluto
1958	1/1–1/13 ♏ 1/14–3/20 ♎ 3/21–9/7 ♏ 9/8–12/31 ♏	All Yr. ♐	All Yr. ♌	All Yr. ♏	1/1–4/12 ♍ 4/13–6/10 ♌ 6/11–12/31 ♍
1959	1/1–2/10 ♏ 2/11–4/24 ♐ 4/25–10/5 ♏ 10/6–12/31 ♐	1/1–1/5 ♐ 1/6–12/31 ♑	All Yr. ♌	All Yr. ♏	All Yr. ♍
1960	1/1–3/1 ♐ 3/2–6/10 ♑ 6/11–10/25 ♐ 10/26–12/31 ♑	All Yr. ♑	All Yr. ♌	All Yr. ♏	All Yr. ♍
1961	1/1–3/14 ♑ 3/15–8/11 ♒ 8/12–11/3 ♑ 11/4–12/31 ♒	All Yr. ♑	1/1–10/31 ♌ 11/1–12/31 ♍	All Yr. ♏	All Yr. ♍
1962	1/1–3/24 ♒ 3/25–12/31 ♓	1/1–1/2 ♑ 1/3–12/31 ♒	1/1–1/9 ♍ 1/10–8/8 ♌ 8/9–12/31 ♍	All Yr. ♏	All Yr. ♍
1963	1/1–4/3 ♓ 4/4–12/31 ♈	All Yr. ♒	All Yr. ♍	All Yr. ♏	All Yr. ♍
1964	1/1–3/23 ♈ 3/24–9/16 ♓ 9/17–12/15 12/16–12/31	1/1–3/23 ♒ 3/24–9/16 ♓ 9/17–12/15 ♒ 12/16–12/31 ♓	All Yr. ♍	All Yr. ♏	All Yr. ♍
1965	1/1–4/21 ♉ 4/22–9/20 ♊ 9/21–11/16 ♋ 11/17–12/31 ♊	All Yr. ♓	All Yr. ♍	All Yr. ♏	All Yr. ♍

PLACE OF JUPITER, SATURN, URANUS, NEPTUNE, AND PLUTO—1966–1971

FIND YOUR BIRTH YEAR HERE	TABLE I-♃ Find Period including birthday, Your Jupiter is in	Sign	TABLE II-♄ Find Period including birthday, Your Saturn is in	Sign	TABLE III-♅ Your Uranus is in	Sign	TABLE IV-♆ Your Neptune is in	Sign	TABLE V-♇ Your Pluto is in	Sign
1966	1/1–5/4 5/5–9/26 9/27–12/31	♊ ♋ ♌	All Yr.	♓	All Yr.	♍	All Yr.	♏	All Yr.	♍
1967	1/1–1/15 1/16–5/22 5/23–10/18 10/19–12/31	♌ ♋ ♌ ♍	1/1–3/2 3/3–12/31	♓ ♈	All Yr.	♍	All Yr.	♏	All Yr.	♍
1968	1/1–2/26 2/27–6/14 6/15–11/14 11/15–12/31	♍ ♌ ♍ ♎	All Yr.	♈	1/1–9/27 9/28–12/31	♍ ♎	All Yr.	♏	All Yr.	♍
1969	1/1–3/29 3/30–7/14 7/15–12/15 12/16–12/31	♎ ♍ ♎ ♏	1/1–4/28 4/29–12/31	♈ ♉	1/1–5/20 5/21–6/23 6/24–12/31	♎ ♍ ♎	All Yr.	♏	All Yr.	♍
1970	1/1–4/30 5/1–8/14 8/15–12/31	♏ ♎ ♏	All Yr.	♉	All Yr.	♎	1/1–1/3 1/4–5/2 5/3–11/5 11/6–12/31	♏ ♐ ♏ ♐	1/1–12/31	♍
1971	1/1–1/13 1/14–6/4 6/5–9/10 9/11–12/31	♏ ♐ ♏ ♐	1/16–6/17 6/18–12/31	♉ ♊	All Yr.	♎	All Yr.	♐	1/1–10/5 10/6–12/31	♍ ♎

PLACE OF JUPITER, SATURN, URANUS, NEPTUNE, AND PLUTO—1972–1980

Year	Jupiter	Saturn	Uranus	Neptune	Pluto
1972	1/1–2/5 ♐ 2/6–7/23 ♑ 7/24–9/24 ♐ 9/25–12/31 ♑	1/1–1/9 ♊ 1/10–2/20 ♉ 2/21–12/31 ♊	All Yr. ♎	All Yr. ♐	1/1–4/17 ♎ 4/18–6/30 ♍ ♎ 6/31–12/31 ♎
1973	1/1–2/22 ♑ 2/23–12/31 ♒	1/1–7/31 ♊ 8/1–12/31 ♋	All Yr. ♎	All Yr. ♐	All Yr. ♎
1974	1/1–3/7 ♒ 3/8–12/31 ♓	1/1–1/6 ♋ 1/7–4/17 ♊ 4/18–12/31 ♋	1/1–11/20 ♎ 11/21–12/31 ♏	All Yr. ♐	All Yr. ♎ ♏
1975	1/1–3/17 ♓ 3/18–12/31 ♈	1/1–9/16 ♋ 9/17–12/31 ♌	1/1–4/30 ♏ 5/1–9/7 ♎ 9/8–12/31 ♏	All Yr. ♐	All Yr. ♏
1976	1/1–3/25 ♈ 3/26–8/22 ♉ 8/23–10/15 ♈ 10/16–12/31 ♉	1/1–1/13 ♌ 1/14–6/4 ♋ 6/5–12/31 ♌	All Yr. ♏	All Yr. ♐	All Yr. ♎
1977	1/1–4/2 ♉ 4/3–8/19 ♊ 8/20–12/31 ♋	1/1–11/15 ♌ 11/16–12/31 ♍	All Yr. ♏	All Yr. ♐	All Yr. ♎
1978	1/1–4/10 ♋ 4/11–9/4 ♌ 9/5–12/31 ♌	1/1–1/4 ♍ 1/5–7/25 ♌ 7/26–12/31 ♍	All Yr. ♏	All Yr. ♐	All Yr. ♎
1979	1/1–2/28 ♌ 3/1–4/19 ♋ 4/20–9/28 ♌ 9/29–12/31 ♍	All Yr. ♍	All Yr. ♏	All Yr. ♐	All Yr. ♎
1980	1/1–10/26 ♍ 10/27–12/31 ♎	1/1–9/20 ♍ 9/21–12/31 ♎	All Yr. ♏	All Yr. ♐	All Yr. ♎

PLACE OF JUPITER, SATURN, URANUS, NEPTUNE, AND PLUTO—1981–1989

FIND YOUR BIRTH YEAR HERE	TABLE I-♃-Find Period including birthday. Your Jupiter is in	Sign	TABLE II-♄-Find Period including birthday. Your Saturn is in	Sign	TABLE III-♅ Your Uranus is in	Sign	TABLE IV-♆ Your Neptune is in	Sign	TABLE V-♇ Your Pluto is in	Sign
1981	1/1–11/25 11/26–12/31	♎ ♏	All Yr.	♎	1/1–2/16 2/17–3/19 3/20–11/15 11/16–12/31	♏ ♐ ♏ ♐	All Yr.	♐	All Yr.	♎
1982	1/1–12/24 12/25–12/31	♏ ♐	1/1–11/28 11/29–12/31	♎ ♏	All Yr.	♐	All Yr.	♐	All Yr.	♎
1983	All Yr.	♐	1/1–5/5 5/6–8/23 8/24–12/31	♏ ♎ ♏	All Yr.	♐	All Yr.	♐	1/1–11/5 11/6–12/31	♎ ♏
1984	1/1–1/18 1/19–12/31	♐ ♑	All Yr.	♏	All Yr.	♐	1/1–1/17 1/18–6/21 6/22–11/20 11/21–12/31	♐ ♑ ♐ ♑	1/1–5/19 5/20–8/27 8/28–12/31	♏ ♎ ♏
1985	1/1–2/5 2/6–12/31	♑ ♒	1/1–11/15 11/16–12/31	♏ ♐	All Yr.	♐	All Yr.	♑	All Yr.	♏
1986	1/1–2/19 2/20–12/31	♒ ♓	All Yr.	♐	All Yr.	♐	All Yr.	♑	All Yr.	♏
1987	1/1–3/1 3/2–12/31	♓ ♈	All Yr.	♐	All Yr.	♐	All Yr.	♑	tAll Yr.	♏
1988	1/1–3/7 3/8–7/20 7/21–11/29 11/30–12/31	♈ ♉ ♊ ♉	1/1–2/12 2/13–6/9 6/10–11/11 11/12–12/31	♐ ♑ ♐ ♑	1/1–2/13 2/14–5/25 5/26–12/2 12/2–12/31	♐ ♑ ♐ ♑	All Yr.	♑	All Yr.	♏
1989	1/1–3/9 3/10–7/29 7/30–12/31	♉ ♊ ♋	All Yr.	♑	All Yr.	♑	All Yr.	♑	All Yr.	♏

PLACE OF JUPITER, SATURN, URANUS, NEPTUNE, AND PLUTO—1990–2000

Year	Jupiter	Saturn	Uranus	Neptune	Pluto
1990	1/1–8/17 ♋; 8/18–12/31 ♌	All Yr. ♑	All Yr. ♑	All Yr. ♑	All Yr. ♏
1991	1/1–9/11 ♌; 9/12–12/31 ♍	1/1–2/5 ♑; 2/6–12/31 ♒	All Yr. ♑	All Yr. ♑	All Yr. ♏
1992	1/1–10/9 ♍; 10/10–12/31 ♎	All Yr. ♒	All Yr. ♑	All Yr. ♑	All Yr. ♏
1993	1/1–11/9 ♎; 11/10–12/31 ♏	1/1–5/20 ♒; 5/21–6/29 ♓; 6/30–12/31 ♒	All Yr. ♑	All Yr. ♑	All Yr. ♏
1994	1/1–12/8 ♏; 12/9–12/31 ♐	1/1–1/27 ♒; 1/28–12/31 ♓	All Yr. ♑	All Yr. ♑	1/1–12/31 ♏
1995	All Yr. ♐	All Yr. ♓	1/1–3/31 ♑; 4/1–6/7 ♒; 6/8–12/31 ♑	All Yr. ♑	1/1–1/16 ♏; 1/17–4/21 ♐; 4/22–11/8 ♏; 11/9–12/31 ♐
1996	1/1–1/2 ♐; 1/3–12/31 ♑	1/1–4/6 ♓; 4/7–12/31 ♈	1/1–1/11 ♑; 1/12–12/31 ♒	All Yr. ♑	All Yr. ♐
1997	1/1–1/20 ♑; 1/21–12/31 ♒	All Yr. ♈	All Yr. ♒	All Yr. ♑	All Yr. ♐
1998	1/1–2/3 ♒; 2/4–12/31 ♓	1/1–6/8 ♈; 6/9–10/24 ♉; 10/25–12/31 ♈	All Yr. ♒	1/1–1/27 ♑; 1/28–8/21 ♒; 8/22–11/26 ♑; 11/27–12/31 ♒	All Yr. ♐
1999	1/1–2/11 ♓; 2/12–6/27 ♈; 6/28–10/22 ♉; 10/23–12/31 ♈	1/1–2/27 ♈; 2/28–12/31 ♉	All Yr. ♒	All Yr. ♒	All Yr. ♐
2000	1/1–2/13 ♈; 2/14–6/29 ♉; 6/30–12/31 ♊	1/1–8/8 ♉; 8/9–10/14 ♊; 10/15–12/31 ♉	All Yr. ♒	All Yr. ♒	All Yr. ♐

Moon Sign Activity Guide

"Where is the Moon?" is a question enlightened thinkers of all ages, irrespective of Sun Sign, have asked before coming to a decision or beginning a venture. You, too, should have the benefit of using the wisdom of ancient lunar science. The paragraphs that follow reveal the activities that can be pursued when the Moon occupies a certain sign and is favorably aspected.

Moon in Aries (♈): Begin new enterprises or ventures; make job applications; hire employees; bargain; pioneer some new idea or article; purchase objects made of metal; participate in sports; inspire others with your enthusiasm.

Moon in Taurus (♉): Begin things you desire to be permanent or want to last a long time; buy durable clothing; boost personal income; add to possessions; deal with bankers; open accounts.

Moon in Gemini (♊): Take short journeys; write letters; prepare articles for publication; advertise; give public speeches; make changes that are not apt to be permanent; interview employees; make contacts.

Moon in Cancer (♋): Deal with family matters or women in business or in the home, especially in connection with commodities, food, furniture; plan ocean trips; take care of domestic and property needs; purchase antiques.

Moon in Leo (♌): Contact persons in authority; ask for favors; buy and sell, especially jewelry, gold ornaments, quality clothes and articles; pursue love, social life, entertainment; attend the theater; display executive ability.

Moon in Virgo (♍): Pursue studies that will enhance your skills; seek employment; find improvements in health, hygiene; study statistics; stress the quality of services rendered to others; tend to the needs of pets or dependents.

Moon in Libra (♎): Strengthen marital ties; pursue partnership and cooperative affairs; purchase perfumes, jewelry, home decorations, beauty items, art objects; attend cultural events.

Moon in Scorpio (♏): Take care of tax and estate matters; boost joint resources; exploit hidden talents; make decisions, especially when shrewdness is required; rejuvenate valuable possessions; pursue confidential transactions.

Moon in Sagittarius (♐): Engage in outdoor activities, such as horse racing, hiking, sports, exercise in general; make realistic plans for the future; deal with lawyers, physicians, religious leaders, professional people; plan long journeys or academic goals.

Moon in Capricorn (♑): Be attentive to duties and responsibilities; engage in business related to management or organization, government interests, parental concerns; see influential people; undertake business and career pursuits.

Moon in Aquarius (♒): Pursue hopes and wishes, friendships, social contacts; enjoy clubs or fraternal societies, or seek membership in them; boost revenues from business, occupation; stress humanitarianism; engage in politics.

Moon in Pisces (♓): Overcome limitations and problems; express charitable and sympathetic leanings; pursue peaceful and spiritual interests; boost self-confidence; find the causes for fears, worries, doubts; take care of confidential matters; visit those who are ill, convalescing, or confined.

Daily Predictions

(All times listed in the following section are EST)

October 1991

Tuesday, October 1 (Moon in Cancer). There's lots of steam but little substance to a job or business dispute today, so try to avoid a showdown that could jeopardize a close relationship—whether business or personal. On the other hand, your social life can be rewarding as you accurately size up new people you meet.

Wednesday, October 2 (Moon in Cancer to Leo 9:59 A.M.). An inability to make up your mind is a rare occasion for you. Today, however, you might hem and haw a bit while trying to make a decision about a financial or personal matter (which might be interrelated). Regardless of your choice, strings seem to be attached.

Thursday, October 3 (Moon in Leo). However well you think you have the morning organized, all it will take is one arbitrary word or gesture to send the best-made plans down the tubes—and with a suddenness you wouldn't think possible. With that in mind, don't buck the boss or even imply a take-it-or-leave-it attitude!

Friday, October 4 (Moon in Leo to Virgo 12:46 P.M.).
You won't be at a loss for words today, especially when
talking to top people, which should enable you to feather
your nest where a career or business ambition is concerned. Whether it's today or in the near future, the time
is ripe for substantial progress.

Saturday, October 5 (Moon in Virgo). Travel may be on
your calendar this weekend, and for some, it could be
motivated by a very special social invitation. A happy
surprise is likely to brighten the day, such as an introduction to someone you've long wanted to meet. Your heightened personal magnetism attracts favors.

Sunday, October 6 (Moon in Virgo to Libra 4:01 P.M.).
You will surely benefit from weekend socializing with
successful friends and knowledgeable types today. Although your input is estimable, however, it may be better
to listen. High on the list of topics is money, career, and
business, information about which will be profitable.

Monday, October 7 (NEW MOON in Libra 4:40 P.M.). The
New Moon phase today shows that it will probably take
most of the business day for you to get your bearings.
Perhaps because of doubts about a personal decision, you
don't seem able to focus on essentials. By late afternoon,
however, your route to success will be clearer.

**Tuesday, October 8 (Moon in Libra to Scorpio 9:01
P.M.).** You're ready to put your foot down this morning
about someone who has been dragging their heels in a job
or business situation. The rest of the day is routine, but
tonight, you have to iron out a money snag with a friend
before you can enjoy the evening.

Wednesday, October 9 (Moon in Scorpio). After a stroke
of luck this morning, perhaps provided by a friend, you'll
be ready to welcome the remainder of the day with open

arms. And well you might, considering the impromptu social gatherings, delightful chance encounters, and other events that lift your spirits.

Thursday, October 10 (Moon in Scorpio). This won't be as carefree a day as yesterday as far as circulating on the social scene is concerned. However, people you meet now or in the near future are somehow connected with opportunities to get ahead in the world or are useful in widening the scope of your activities.

Friday, October 11 (Moon in Scorpio to Sagittarius 4:59 A.M.). You may feel a lot of tension and pressure as the day goes along and be tempted to do something rash as a quick and easy solution—such as making a confidential promise you can't keep. But you don't have to resort to that; stick to practical guidelines.

Saturday, October 12 (Moon in Sagittarius). As the weekend gets under way, you're likely to feel hampered by a variety of pesky obligations and private aggravations that seem to multiply as the day unfolds. You can certainly think of better ways to start the weekend, and the evening should promise an opportunity.

Sunday, October 13 (Moon in Sagittarius to Capricorn 4:11 P.M.). The spirit of adventure inspires you this morning to explore new job or business interests and commitments, as you eagerly seek expanded horizons. But don't extend yourself too far; since opportunities to follow up are limited, use today to test the waters.

Monday, October 14 (Moon in Capricorn). By midday, the beginning of various upsetting signals may throw you off course, even discourage you, but your well-planned business arrangements this morning and your perseverance contribute to the day's uneven success. Don't jeopardize your progress with ill-advised comments.

Tuesday, October 15 (Moon in Capricorn). Your inborn desire to enhance your personal credibility comes to the fore today. If you're in the mood to push through a favorite idea or plan, however, don't expect others to play follow the leader without a struggle, especially concerning a financial objective.

Wednesday, October 16 (Moon in Capricorn to Aquarius 5:05 A.M.). Something or somebody will ruffle your feathers early this morning, and two prime possibilities are a friend and/or a group tie somehow related to a financial problem. You're not in the mood to mince words, which the object of your comments soon finds out.

Thursday, October 17 (Moon in Aquarius). The tension that's been brewing between you and someone close to you may culminate today, with a few repercussions clouding the air after the shakeout. It's possible that personal friendships and social activity are the source of dissension; try to work out a compromise.

Friday, October 18 (Moon in Aquarius to Pisces 4:54 P.M.). Though in some ways this can be a more peaceful day for you and your associates, the main part of the problem—tempers and recriminations—may still run high. By midevening, someone who won't take no for an answer may be responsible for a cease-fire.

Saturday, October 19 (Moon in Pisces). An invitation to go on a short trip will find you feeling responsive, enthusiastic, and ready to go at the drop of a hat. However, be prepared for some mix-ups or delays and/or extra expenses. The day brings delightful chance encounters, one of which can stir up romantic interest.

Sunday, October 20 (Moon in Pisces). Your weekend involvement in a neighborhood project can lead to a stimulating new affiliation, one in which lively mental rapport and shared values are big attractions. You seem to be busy all day, running errands, returning phone calls, visiting, and generally enjoying yourself.

Monday, October 21 (Moon in Pisces to Aries 1:34 A.M.). If you try to get something accomplished around the home front, today's trends indicate that it will be more like "the mouse that roared." Between a variety of petty aggravations and an impromptu social diversion, you'll complain—but not too seriously.

Tuesday, October 22 (Moon in Aries). Problems concerning a parent may be at the heart of domestic worries you have to deal with today. Since this occurs first thing this morning, it won't put you into the best mood to face your workaday responsibilities. It won't take much to foster a "what's the use" attitude, either.

Wednesday, October 23 (FULL MOON in Aries 6:09 A.M.—Moon to Taurus 6:56 A.M.). You'll probably be mad as a hornet about a home or family upset this morning. In fact, feelings that are careening out of control can spill over and play havoc with your dating or other social plans tonight, but luck saves you.

Thursday, October 24 (Moon in Taurus). During this day of mixed emotions, your love life, creative pursuits, or delight through a child could be a source of fulfillment, at the same time that a money crunch affects your relationship with a friend or a group. Use your imagination to jump on the bandwagon of happiness.

Friday, October 25 (Moon in Taurus to Gemini 10:10 A.M.). Be alert to an opportunity just after midnight to capitalize on your powers of persuasion. You might want to sell a friend an idea. As the day unfolds, however, don't waste your time trying to line up a date. Fortunately, your work efforts go into high gear.

Saturday, October 26 (Moon in Gemini). Although you're in the mood to goof off, you'll probably have to devote at least part of the day to some sort of chore, perhaps some weekend job overtime or a weekend project that will garner precious little, if any, teamwork. You'll probably be very glad when the day ends.

Sunday, October 27 (Moon in Gemini to Cancer 12:38 P.M.). You start the day filled with self-confidence and positive expectations, possibly because you have a combined social occasion and business meeting scheduled as the weekend draws to a conclusion. A VIP you meet tonight could turn into a worthwhile friend.

Monday, October 28 (Moon in Cancer). A heart-to-heart talk with a friend could be about a developing relationship, or it might be that a platonic alliance is showing signs of turning into something that is stirring a different kind of feeling. Needless to add, you and/or the other person can be quite perplexed.

Tuesday, October 29 (Moon in Cancer to Leo 3:21 P.M.). A meeting of the minds with a stimulating companion this morning enables you to enjoy a livelier social whirl as the day goes along. The afternoon points to financial pressure; if you shop, be extra cautious. You could get good news from a faraway friend tonight.

Wednesday, October 30 (Moon in Leo). An undercurrent of buoyancy helps you to snap out of the touchy mood that mars the start of the day for you. You might be having trouble with someone with the power of the purse, who is in the mood to throw his or her weight around. It's best not to rise to the bait.

Thursday, October 31 (Moon in Leo to Virgo 6:48 P.M.). If differences with your mate or business partner about money seem at first to be a tempest in a teacup, the

situation could escalate if verbal sniping intensifies. Fortunately, once the morning is past, there's less need for
anyone to overreact defensively.

November 1991

Friday, November 1 (Moon in Virgo). Exceptionally fortunate influences sound the travel theme now and in the
weeks ahead, which can find you arranging a holiday (or
winter vacation) trip, or taking off on one already planned.
This lucky trend also accents academic goals, in-law relationships, social opportunities.

**Saturday, November 2 (Moon in Virgo to Libra 11:13
P.M.).** If you didn't do it yesterday, the preparations are
certainly in place today for you to step up in the world.
Whether it's the business, social, career, or ladder of
public prestige, you'll move up a few rungs now and will
thoroughly enjoy yourself doing it.

Sunday, November 3 (Moon in Libra). Another exciting
breakthrough is in store for you today, but it's more likely
to be in the social vein or pertain to the sudden enhancement of your personal credibility. In any case, be prepared
for a spur-of-the-moment invitation this morning that
promises contact with a VIP.

Monday, November 4 (Moon in Libra). If you are in a
postmidnight situation where you should be attentive to
the voice of authority, listen! (This is not the time to
challenge a traffic cop or whomever.) Later, the day produces so-so results for your job efforts, but a confidential
tip tonight could be profitable.

Tuesday, November 5 (Moon in Libra to Scorpio 5:10 A.M.). It may be necessary today to handle difficult friends with kid gloves. If you take a fresh look at an old money problem, it could help to resolve a bottleneck that stands in the way of your buying or selling or engaging in other financial activities.

Wednesday, November 6 (NEW MOON in Scorpio 6:12 A.M.). This could be a particularly exhilarating day in your social life, when you could be taken completely by surprise by events that put an exciting new slant on your friendships and organizational ties. Be ready to move quickly with fast-paced developments.

Thursday, November 7 (Moon in Scorpio to Sagittarius 1:22 P.M.). Research, investigation, and critical examination of all the angles of your current dream-in-progress can shed light on vulnerable points and weak arguments. You want to be very ready to go when the upcoming green light flashes its signal in a few days.

Friday, November 8 (Moon in Sagittarius). Someone close to you, perhaps a friend (or an incident involving a friend of a family member), could generate plenty of tension during the early hours this morning. Possibly because of this, you'll need to focus on your main intentions today instead of scattering your energies.

Saturday, November 9 (Moon in Sagittarius). Paste a note on your mirror about an important career or business advantage to remember in the weeks ahead, to wit: Socialize whenever possible with job colleagues, professional associates, etc., and it will seem like the promotion of your ambitions is on automatic pilot.

Sunday, November 10 (Moon in Sagittarius to Capricorn 12:17 A.M.). You might have to calculate carefully your approach or lessen your demands on an associate today in order to keep the peace. Joining with convivial companions in the evening is one sure way to conclude the weekend in a flurry of social excitement.

Monday, November 11 (Moon in Capricorn). An original, creative line of thinking enhances the potential of a near-future plan, perhaps an unusual itinerary for a trip you're arranging for the holidays ahead. Moreover, dynamic new influences in your social life practically guarantee fresh excitement on the party circuit.

Tuesday, November 12 (Moon in Capricorn to Aquarius 1:07 P.M.). Someone close to you may be wavering about a previously agreed-to confidential arrangement; continue to keep the plan under wraps until prospects are clearer. Meanwhile, this is one of those days to promote your ambitions by mixing business and pleasure.

Wednesday, November 13 (Moon in Aquarius). Excellent news concerning money is due in the early afternoon. You might also receive a tip about a place off the beaten path that's great for bargains or hard-to-find times. Or a talk with a financial adviser can put you onto more profitable ways to deploy your surplus funds.

Thursday, November 14 (Moon in Aquarius). Your urge to speculate or take other financial risks is not in tune with the day's stellar potential for Capricornians. Investigate, make your plans, but wait for a more propitious time to commit funds. This is also not a good time to dabble in romantic adventure.

Friday, November 15 (Moon in Aquarius to Pisces 1:34 A.M.). If a friend causes you worry this morning, his or her actions and gestures may reveal more than is realized (or intended). A question of loyalty could be an underlying concern. Your self-confidence can get a sudden boost tonight when you will least expect it.

Saturday, November 16 (Moon in Pisces). Your morale will be lifted if you keep your eyes on current events and bypass a too-rosy view of future or distant goals. Meanwhile, a legal or contractual matter may be proceeding favorably, if slowly, and a good friend may impart just the information you need for a special project.

Sunday, November 17 (Moon in Pisces to Aries 11:09 A.M.). The postmidnight hours could be particularly glamorous and romantic, though there is an undercurrent of practical reality to be faced. As the day unfolds, it will be a good time to take on a new domestic project that gains from your ability to bargain.

Monday, November 18 (Moon in Aries). If you didn't know it before, you could learn today that there is a price tag on leadership. You'll seem to be in a no-win situation concerning a conflict between home or family interests and business or career necessities. You're able to talk your way out of this, but it won't be easy.

Tuesday, November 19 (Moon in Aries to Taurus 4:50 P.M.). Emotional tension that seems to stem from business problems or relationship difficulties with a professional colleague is likely to be your big problem today. Soft-pedal this or it will suddenly escalate. A financial worry tonight is more easily managed.

Wednesday, November 20 (Moon in Taurus). After a sluggish morning, a midday surprise marks the beginning of favorable trends that bring a romantic aspiration, personal aim, and social activity to a peak of excitement. If you're unattached, there's an opportunity to meet a new attraction via a chance encounter.

Thursday, November 21 (FULL MOON in Taurus 5:57 P.M.—Moon to Gemini 7:23 P.M.). If you've been feuding with a friend and allow feelings to run amok today, it could be the end of the relationship (or the beginning of the end). By tonight, you'll shift your attention to practical matters, like your income prospects.

Friday, November 22 (Moon in Gemini). After a day that seems to be under a cloud of impaired judgment, don't compound problems by misgauging the meaning of an incident involving an authority figure or business associate. An invitation this P.M. may mean entirely different things to you than to the person who extended it.

Saturday, November 23 (Moon in Gemini to Cancer 8:26 P.M.). If you push too hard to get your own way today, you may find that your mate or partner could react with a barrage of verbal invective. You'll be smarter to keep channels of communication nicely open and to turn the charm knob up to high to promote accord.

Sunday, November 24 (Moon in Cancer). You'll get along better with friends or in groups today than with your mate or live-in companion. The latter may seem to be in an arbitrary mood, ready to challenge your every word or gesture. On the other hand, old friends or social interests are reassuringly dependable.

Monday, November 25 (Moon in Cancer to Leo 9:38 P.M.). This can be a really meaningful day for sharing, caring, making (or receiving) a marriage proposal, or joining a coveted, upscale social group. Your power of suggestion is in high gear, which will enable you to get your spouse to agree on all practical measures.

Tuesday, November 26 (Moon in Leo). Your plans for today proceed smoothly, and if there's a hint of a money problem, you'll know what to do or whom to ask. Prospects are somewhat clouded once the morning is past, however, as it appears your expectations are rather exaggerated, particularly concerning your own abilities.

Wednesday, November 27 (Moon in Leo). Financial conditions involving other people today are likely to seesaw back and forth considerably. Dealings with a friend or concerning a group's expenditures are apt to generate the most tension. On the other hand, a confidential business deal points to healthy profits.

Thursday, November 28 (Moon in Leo to Virgo 12:15 A.M.). Most of the day is likely to seem like a month in Murmansk, but at least the evening will be less boring and a lot livelier, either due to glad tidings from a distance (perhaps about an upcoming holiday trip or visitor) or similar incident that lifts your spirits.

Friday, November 29 (Moon in Virgo). Additional favorable trends today reveal happy prospects for near-future travel, scholastic achievement, a legal victory, or a new lease on life for one of your favorite goals. Don't undermine today's accomplishments by allowing a put-down to get under your skin.

Saturday, November 30 (Moon in Virgo to Libra 4:46 A.M.). If getting ahead with your worldly ambitions is all about pushing the right buttons, your aim will be exceptional today. With your powers of persuasion now, you'd be able to sell ice to an Eskimo. Your personal credibility and social popularity soar tonight.

December 1991

Sunday, December 1 (Moon in Libra). Weekend socializing could offer more than a good time; it looks as though you could also attract a career opportunity if you're mixing with business types, but perhaps you'd do better if you toned down your independence. A confidential message tonight may boost your expectations.

Monday, December 2 (Moon in Libra to Scorpio 11:34 A.M.). Social pleasures dominate this day, with a touch of romance thrown in for good measure. The best advice, however, is to keep a new attraction lighthearted until you know more about the person. You may be disappointed if you go shopping after work.

Tuesday, December 3 (Moon in Scorpio). Informal entertaining or a spur-of-the-moment get-together with special friends can turn this into a surprisingly pleasant day. Your self-esteem is high, and there's a dependable undercurrent of good, practical judgment to guide your financial decisions to best advantage.

Wednesday, December 4 (Moon in Scorpio to Sagittarius 8:33 P.M.). Don't hesitate to use an influential contact to promote a favorite objective. Perhaps a friend is in a position to be your entre into a special group or exclusive organization. By tonight, tired of the hustle and bustle, you'll seek a quiet haven.

Thursday, December 5 (NEW MOON in Sagittarius 10:57 P.M.). You may have a confidential financial scheme that you're itching to launch today, but it would be better to keep the lid on it for a while longer. There's every indication that it would convey the wrong impression now and spoil later chances for success.

Friday, December 6 (Moon in Sagittarius). Today is ripe for a misadventure, especially if you're around someone with a genius for self-puffery and/or exaggerations and inflated expectations from what is the usual "something-for-nothing" gambit. The lure may be a ridiculously cheap charter trip that is very iffy.

Saturday, December 7 (Moon in Sagittarius to Capricorn 7:42 A.M.). Your personal charisma is potent today, which may account for the increase in your social and romantic popularity. Invitations could start coming in for the various functions, glamorous and otherwise, now being planned for the holidays ahead.

Sunday, December 8 (Moon in Capricorn). The upsurge of energy and magnetism can continue to make you very popular, but possibly also a bit impulsive. If you feel like you're in a position to pick and choose, be discreet about it. Meanwhile, a confidant may bring some very good news that is job- or income-related.

Monday, December 9 (Moon in Capricorn to Aquarius 8:28 P.M.). You might alienate a friend today when you have to draw the line about a money matter that shapes up as a losing proposition for you. If not an outright loss, it may look to you as though you'll wait a long time before seeing your money (or a belonging) again.

Tuesday, December 10 (Moon in Aquarius). Although you're not entirely in the mood for it when the day starts, it will be a good time to get the jump on the thundering herd as far as Christmas shopping is concerned. Anyway, practical you would rather not wait until everything is picked over or items are out of stock.

Wednesday, December 11 (Moon in Aquarius). Today is similar to yesterday, and you'll probably operate under pretty much the same philosophy. It wouldn't hurt now, however, to team up with a companion who has the inside track on those out-of-the-way places where bargains as well as hard-to-find items can be located.

Thursday, December 12 (Moon in Aquarius to Pisces 9:20 A.M.). Although there are a lot of things on your must-do list, you don't seem able to get well-enough organized to accomplish any of them today. Instructions are liable to be garbled, messages go undelivered, and you may have misplaced your address book.

Friday, December 13 (Moon in Pisces). Be careful of your remarks this morning to someone who is starting the day with a chip on their shoulder. One wrong word could trigger a verbal blitz you hadn't bargained for on this day of ill-repute. Meanwhile, you might get some cards addressed or accomplish other chores.

Saturday, December 14 (Moon in Pisces to Aries 8:07 P.M.). You might not get all the errands done that are beginning to crowd your list now, principally because you may be having a problem with a VIP who is the key to the success of a secret holiday plan. You might have to coast along with things as they occur.

Sunday, December 15 (Moon in Aries). Property, home, and family interests come to the fore now in a productive way, with plenty of agreement as to holiday decorating and entertainment plans. You may also be cooking up a secret plan for the celebration of a family milestone to be a highlight of the seasonal festivities.

Monday, December 16 (Moon in Aries). An early morning family misunderstanding could be over a very minor matter. Try to nip it in the bud before it spawns an array of other irksome home developments. Otherwise, this is a pleasantly productive day, when you might spruce up the guest room for a holiday visitor.

Tuesday, December 17 (Moon in Aries to Taurus 3:11 A.M.). If you can manage to keep your frustrations under control and your noted practicality in top form, you can escape a morning financial hassle. Your underlying mood is restless and adventurous, with an unsatisfied longing for glamour and mobility.

Wednesday, December 18 (Moon in Taurus). This would be a good time to plan a near-future travel itinerary that is a highlight of your holiday scenario. You'll enjoy perusing the colorful brochures, checking the timetables and reservation availabilities, and deciding on a travel companion who shares your interests.

Thursday, December 19 (Moon in Taurus to Gemini 6:22 A.M.). Call on your prior experience or training to resolve a series of minor complications on the job. Troubles may be due to the holiday rush and consequent logjam. As the day rolls along, you'll be thinking of social-romantic activity in the midst of career aims.

Friday, December 20 (Moon in Gemini). Work pressures mount, and you need to be careful not to go for the most expedient solution to relieve the tension. Problems with schedules, production, or a co-worker are building to a climax today or tomorrow. It's essential now to be realistic and observe the most practical guidelines.

Saturday, December 21 (FULL MOON LUNAR ECLIPSE in Gemini 5:24 A.M.—Moon to Cancer 6:55 A.M.). Once the day starts, you'll be able to think of something else besides your working environment or daily routine. However, it won't be smooth sailing for relationships, which will present a new set of problems.

Sunday, December 22 (Moon in Cancer). The Sun's return to Capricorn today ignites your charisma and enhances your love life and social popularity. If you've found your one and only, some of you will exchange those bands of gold during the holidays, while others now meet a new attraction and begin a new romance.

Monday, December 23 (Moon in Cancer to Leo 6:39 A.M.). You might as well get financial differences with your mate or steady date settled before you start out on a last-minute shopping trip; then you'll be able to select what you want with less fuss and bother, or that's at least mutually agreeable to both of you.

Tuesday, December 24 (Moon in Leo). You may as well be alerted early that you may have to bow out of a social occasion tonight because of other demands on your time, like some final preparations for tomorrow's festivities that had somehow been overlooked. Meanwhile, a lunch date today will be stimulating.

Wednesday, December 25 (Moon in Leo to Virgo 7:24 A.M.). A trip may be on your agenda today or a visitor from another locale may arrive, providing a heartwarming opportunity to reaffirm harmonious relationships in the farthest reaches of the family network. Your cup should be running over with happiness today.

Thursday, December 26 (Moon in Virgo). This is not the best day to travel, but if you and yours have no choice, be prepared for delays or detours. In particular, be careful in unfamiliar locales and be wary of strangers. Guard your luggage and/or other belongings. By being careful, you safeguard the day's enjoyments.

Friday, December 27 (Moon in Virgo to Libra 10:38 A.M.). The focus is on career essentials and your earnings potential, but the day may be lacking in opportunities to do anything about your objectives. Tonight, however, it's another story, when you'll know how to talk money and can come up with some convincing ideas.

Saturday, December 28 (Moon in Libra). Be careful that you're not too quick to say what you think this morning in connection with a job or career snag; you could be wrong. An ultimatum would be ill-timed, to say the least. And try to make level-headed decisions about near-future travel arrangements or other plans.

Sunday, December 29 (Moon in Libra to Scorpio 5:04 P.M.). Now that the stepped-up seasonal pace has slackened, you'll have more time for outside activities other than overtime on the job as the weekend gets under way. Even if you don't get a lot accomplished, it's a good feeling to know it's your choice.

Monday, December 30 (Moon in Scorpio). The holiday social bandwagon rolls merrily along, and you're as ready as ever to hop aboard and spread the good cheer. The mix at gatherings now is particularly bubbly, with out-of-towners and VIPs as extra-added attractions. In fact, you might have more fun today than tomorrow night.

Tuesday, December 31 (Moon in Scorpio). The social theme continues, but with a lot less intensity than yesterday. It might be wise, therefore, to opt for a low-key celebration instead of imbibing all that bubbly in a sea of paper hats and popping all those balloons in a noisy setting to celebrate the start of 1992!

January 1992

Wednesday, January 1 (Moon in Scorpio to Sagittarius 2:31 A.M.). As the New Year begins and the holiday festivities and flurry of seasonal activities fade once more into history, your yen for socializing or companionship is much more subdued. As it happens, a quiet rendezvous might also yield financial benefits.

Thursday, January 2 (Moon in Sagittarius). Don't become too enthused about what a confidant tells you today; the implications of a secret aren't as rosy as you're likely to assume or are led to believe. For your part, try to keep private matters private—or you could innocently create an awkward situation.

Friday, January 3 (Moon in Sagittarius to Capricorn 2:10 P.M.). A flurry of activity behind closed doors may pertain to plans you have for the family or home front interests in general. A property purchase or sale or a parental change may be in the works—one that you're not ready to let the world know about yet.

Saturday, January 4 (NEW MOON Solar Eclipse in Capricorn). You're in the mood to pursue personal goals in a far-sighted way, which coincides with a spur-of-the-moment opportunity that points to a totally different future. Now is the time to seize the bull by the horns and capitalize on the luck that surrounds you.

Sunday, January 5 (Moon in Capricorn). This is another day that's brimming with luck and opportunity; take full advantage to mix and mingle with any VIPs who might be brightening the weekend social whirl. Someone could take a shine to you who has valuable privileged information that is ringed with dollar signs.

Monday, January 6 (Moon in Capricorn to Aquarius 3:00 A.M.). You are able to get your no-nonsense money-making or other financial ideas across with flying colors, as you take one or two associates into your confidence concerning a long-range scheme. A quiet walk with someone you love completes the picture.

Tuesday, January 7 (Moon in Aquarius). Personal doubts or uncertainties could keep you preoccupied most of the day, which makes it difficult for you to make decisions about money—or anything else for that matter. With your emphatic, down-to-earth mind, evasive answers to your questions make you anxious.

Wednesday, January 8 (Moon in Aquarius to Pisces 3:53 P.M.). As things become clearer and the tempo picks up encouragingly, you'll no longer feel as though you're trapped in the twilight zone. A midday meeting will yield the kind of information you want, and you'll act on it during the afternoon.

Thursday, January 9 (Moon in Pisces). In the weeks ahead, you'll have more of the enterprising spirit and plenty of energy and drive to back it up as you strive to attain one or more of your top priority personal goals. And if one way doesn't work quickly, you'll be ready with another to blaze new trails.

Friday, January 10 (Moon in Pisces). Your results-oriented mentality will get a productive workout in the weeks ahead. This afternoon, in fact you're likely to voice some ideas that pertain to achieving a personal ambition. Articulate and voluble, you'll nevertheless be interested in your listener's input.

Saturday, January 11 (Moon in Pisces to Aries 3:23 A.M.). Your eagerness to express your views could get you into hot water around the home front; the day is apt to get off to a thorny start via a verbal clash with a family member. A later beneficial financial development helps to restore domestic harmony.

Sunday, January 12 (Moon in Aries). The domestic theme continues and at various times between morning and night could be pretty aggravating. This is offset, however, by a pleasant surprise that may pertain to weekend travel or entertaining a visitor who may play a role in your expanding personal horizons.

Monday, January 13 (Moon in Aries to Taurus 12:01 P.M.). Friends and social life as well as group affiliations keep you on the go today and you're able to organize your schedule to gain the most from your activities. A date tonight with someone who is very mentally stimulating will be the icing on the cake.

Tuesday, January 14 (Moon in Taurus). Beginning with a midday lunch date or other meeting, your love life can take off like a rocket, which is just the thing to keep your spirits buoyant. Today's fortunate influences also benefit your creative endeavors, which could be highly imaginative and original now.

Wednesday, January 15 (Moon in Taurus to Gemini 4:56 P.M.). This is no time to play games if you've come under the spell of a new admirer. And it's certainly not smart to talk about former conquests, even in a self-mocking way. Be conventional and practical to guide love into the direction you prefer.

Thursday, January 16 (Moon in Gemini). Mixed trends today denote job and/or physical welfare benefits, but don't let early-morning success go to your head and make you careless. In your eagerness to get away this afternoon, you could leave something undone or take a chance on some other ill-advised gamble.

Friday, January 17 (Moon in Gemini to Cancer 6:27 P.M.). Collect more information before beginning a program or project behind closed doors today. There's a possibility of being sidetracked by insufficient data or by slighting the feelings of a nitpicky co-worker. Tread lightly or you'll step on somebody's toes.

Saturday, January 18 (Moon in Cancer). About the only thing you and your mate or other close associate will agree on today is when to take a journey and where to go and what or whom to see. Otherwise, your views on most things will be 180 degrees apart. Don't fuel the fire by bringing up controversial topics.

Sunday, January 19 (FULL MOON in Cancer—Moon to Leo 5:58 P.M.). The Full Moon could leave you in a quandary in connection with yesterday's unpredictable relationship developments, but your ample supply of ideas and enhanced ability to express yourself enables you to talk your way out of almost any predicament.

Monday, January 20 (Moon in Leo). The lingering effect of a financial mistake or the loss of a possession continues to cause feelings of disappointment and frustration. Steer clear of all money involvements with people you care about until the situation makes sense. Your personal credibility is at a low ebb.

Tuesday, January 21 (Moon in Leo to Virgo 5:23 P.M.). The highly inspirational ideas or concepts you express today may cause your hearers to react as though you've turned the knob to high on the dream machine—without any thought as to the consequences. If others don't get your message, that's their problem.

Wednesday, January 22 (Moon in Virgo). Today's accent on a fresh perspective, broader interests, and a possible travel opportunity fits in with your current progress report—which is onward and upward! You could receive help from an unexpected quarter today, and there might even be a love-at-first sight encounter.

Thursday, January 23 (Moon in Virgo to Libra 6:43 P.M.). In case you're up and about during the postmidnight hours, you could hear good news or receive information that you can put to good use when the day gets under way. As the afternoon unfolds, however, a peculiar job or career matter may befuddle you.

Friday, January 24 (Moon in Libra). The morning is a lot better than the afternoon, particularly from the standpoint of solid career progress (possibly stemming from the preferential treatment of a VIP), as well as a nice upsurge in your earnings potential. Don't get your dander up on the job this afternoon.

Saturday, January 25 (Moon in Libra to Scorpio 11:33 P.M.). Verbal give-and-take with a friend results in both of you being better informed on one or more subjects. Just be sure that you put your newfound knowledge (or expertise) to proper use as the day unfolds; there's a chance you'll use it inappropriately.

Sunday, January 26 (Moon in Scorpio). Any way you look at it, today is not likely to make your list of favorites. In fact, quite the reverse; from the word "go" this morning, it will seem to roll along on flat wheels. Possible areas of trouble probably include friends and money, also probably interrelated.

Monday, January 27 (Moon in Scorpio). Social contacts could be the magic link with success today, whether this applies to business, personal, or distant interests. In fact, you're now somewhat of a wizard in your approach to life and can be mightily persuasive in your dealings with others. Group interests flourish tonight.

Tuesday, January 28 (Moon in Scorpio to Sagittarius 8:21 A.M.). Moments of solitude on this generally irksome day will enable you to realign your thoughts and focus on important plans for the immediate future. There's a chance of misunderstandings or misinterpretation of what you're up to now behind the scenes.

Wednesday, January 29 (Moon in Sagittarius). You could seem pretty distant today as you thoroughly weigh all the pros and cons of a tricky financial situation. Split-second decisions are not your style, and you may stall about one involving a financial shortcut beyond the time that it is worthwhile.

Thursday, January 30 (Moon in Sagittarius to Capricorn 8:08 P.M.). After yesterday's pressures, you won't be averse to a breather today. Minor aggravations aren't too important unless you dwell on them and they wind up getting on your nerves. Keep everything in proper perspective and just relax when you can.

Friday, January 31 (Moon in Capricorn). A chance to shine in a glamorous social situation (a theater opening night or some other glittering event) brings you flattering attention. Another upscale development might be career-related. And for some, potent eye contact could spell a new romantic beginning.

February 1992

Saturday, February 1 (Moon in Capricorn). If you have to prove something today in order to advance a personal ambition, an intuitive flash will tell you how to handle tests of your capabilities and disposition. If you have a dream of success you'd like to promote, this is the day to put out some feelers.

Sunday, February 2 (Moon in Capricorn to Aquarius 9:10 A.M.). The management of money—both personal finances and security as well as current job earnings—will require intelligent handling today, and you'd be smart to put off making any decisions until tonight, when expert advice will be available.

Monday, February 3 (NEW MOON in Aquarius). After some serious thought, you'll have a ready-to-go attitude about fresh financial prospects and developments, but opportunity seems to be lacking. Just keep your plans on the middle burner for the time being; perhaps they need more polishing or revision.

Tuesday, February 4 (Moon in Aquarius to Pisces 9:52 P.M.). Someone you love may have an attractive blueprint for entertainment today, although you may be somewhat preoccupied with a money worry. Nevertheless, time spent together will be very enjoyable, as shared enthusiasms and views mesh rewardingly.

Wednesday, February 5 (Moon in Pisces). This can be a day for spontaneity and could result in your taking an unscheduled trip or changing directions once you have embarked on an errand or an out-of-town visit. However, unplanned events may not be so successful if you give in to runaway, unwarranted enthusiasm.

Thursday, February 6 (Moon in Pisces). An exciting day can segue into an enchanted evening; romance and glamorous, spur-of-the-moment socializing will be especially enjoyable because of your cheerful, anything-goes attitude. If you haven't as yet found your true love, the evening may bring a happy surprise.

Friday, February 7 (Moon in Pisces to Aries 9:16 A.M.). Use today to tie up loose ends, finish minor projects, and resolve family snags. As for the latter, let folks around the home front believe they have won a battle and are entitled to some sort of settlement—but only you know how insignificant it really is.

Saturday, February 8 (Moon in Aries). Just when you might feel like your energy is running out, you get your second wind. This is none too soon, as you come to grips with an outside source of domestic upsets. Try to steer clear of an unpromising emotional situation developing between you and a family member.

Sunday, February 9 (Moon in Aries to Taurus 6:37 P.M.).
You might be going great guns today in the promotion of a personal aim, but be careful that you don't come off to others around you (especially anyone who you think is in your way) as brash, too self-centered, too ambitious, or just plain pushy.

Monday, February 10 (Moon in Taurus). If the thought of starting another week on the job (or daily routine) doesn't exactly put a big smile on your face this morning, the day will in fact turn out better than your apprehensions would indicate. Perhaps the enterprising spirit takes over and sparks enthusiasm.

Tuesday, February 11 (Moon in Taurus). You'll be on the go from morning till night, and if you can bypass a distraction or two, you will accomplish a lot. If not, you might find yourself getting involved in a tangled financial discussion that dredges up an old complaint you have about a friend and money.

Wednesday, February 12 (Moon in Taurus to Gemini 1:09 P.M.). If you didn't resolve yesterday's verbal squabble, you'll have another go at it today—which will be more intense and hopefully final. That takes care of the morning; the rest of the day is much more sociable and possibly very romantic.

Thursday, February 13 (Moon in Gemini). From the sound of the starting bell, most of the day will be taken up with an array of petty aggravations that are as varied as they are irksome. By the time the evening rolls around, however, the picture brightens, as you make progress with an interesting (and profitable) project.

Friday, February 14 (Moon in Gemini to Cancer 4:32 A.M.). Although a lot less active, this can be a trying day for marital interests and other important relationships.

News from a distance tonight, or about a legal matter, ends the day on an upbeat note. Perhaps someone you like plans a near-future visit.

Saturday, February 15 (Moon in Cancer). If you allow your hunches or imagination to work overtime where key relationships are concerned, your emotional elevator can zoom upward too quickly and then crash back to the basement, all before the day is half over. However, the evening promises to be enjoyable.

Sunday, February 16 (Moon in Cancer to Leo 5:16 A.M.). If you stay too long at a party that began last night, as it goes into the wee hours this morning, your final assessment will be that you wish you had called it a night earlier. That way, you could have avoided getting into a money hassle—perhaps with a family member.

Monday, February 17 (Moon in Leo). Today may be upsetting where financial matters and social affairs are concerned. Particularly accented are those dealings or transactions that involve or depend on the cooperation, expertise, or approval of other people—who today are inclined to dwell on past grievances.

Tuesday, February 18 (FULL MOON in Leo—Moon to Virgo 4:48 A.M.). The Full Moon may reflect adversely on your in-law relationships. An important scholastic goal may undergo a change in direction or emphasis, prompted by a sudden change in your attitude. After a talk, everything works out advantageously.

Wednesday, February 19 (Moon in Virgo). A surprise or a secret may make today exciting, especially in the area of faraway places, love (a long-distance romance), or a creative inspiration. There may even be a "mystery person" in the wings. Whatever the specifics, your magnetism and social popularity soar.

Thursday, February 20 (Moon in Virgo to Libra 5:05 A.M.). There's a splendid opportunity today to aim for very high stakes in the business, job, or career realm, and the morning finds you ready, willing, and able. Turn on the charm to maximize your advantage, because the rest of the day isn't as great.

Friday, February 21 (Moon in Libra). As far as you are concerned, there's always room at the top, but you're apt to go about getting there the wrong way this morning. What you may think of as an original ploy is apt to backfire. Don't overcompensate tonight with flighty ideas that are highly impractical.

Saturday, February 22 (Moon in Libra to Scorpio 8:12 A.M.). A call from a friend may extend to you a glamorous social invitation, and an emphasis on the first half of the day may also include news about a former friend or lover. Be careful of making a late lunch date; it could be aggravating as well as expensive.

Sunday, February 23 (Moon in Scorpio). The weekend social whirl rolls along its merry way, much to your and a friend's delight. However, an echo of yesterday's annoyance could creep into the picture—another unsettling incident about money. If you keep it in perspective, though, it won't mar the day.

Monday, February 24 (Moon in Scorpio to Sagittarius 3:27 A.M.). You're still in tune with the social theme, but it's not likely to sound much today. If by some remote chance it does, the most you can look forward to is a few sour notes. If little differences come up, settle them in your best no-nonsense manner.

Tuesday, February 25 (Moon in Sagittarius). The day gets off to a lively start, and it should be a breeze to maintain the brisk momentum, in which case you'll get a lot more accomplished than you did yesterday. However, don't be swept away by any pie-in-the-sky ideas or plans, particularly about travel or education.

Wednesday, February 26 (Moon in Sagittarius). Today's influences cast their rays on past experiences. Since nostalgic reflection is not one of your favorite pastimes (you're too practical or present-oriented for that), there are lessons to be learned from past mistakes—before they become private problems.

Thursday, February 27 (Moon in Sagittarius to Capricorn 2:34 A.M.). Today finds you back in stride and confident—your typical "strictly business" self. News and exchange of views with VIPs, possibly at a distance, can be instructive and valuable. Creativity flows too, so take advantage of it.

Friday, February 28 (Moon in Capricorn). You start the day with some good ideas, perhaps inspired by a friend, and then you can give in to erratic urges that cause you to stray far from your intended course. You could become even more adventurous as the day unfolds (not to say careless), which you have to answer for tonight.

Saturday, February 29 (Moon in Capricorn to Aquarius 3:35 P.M.). Finances require your attention today; follow up on good ideas that may have come to you during the night. Conduct all business with security and economy uppermost in your mind. However, if a new venture won't budge, your timing may be off.

March 1992

Sunday, March 1 (Moon in Aquarius). You may start the day with a sure-fire money plan, but practical you will slow down and test it in numerous ways before you risk any of your hard-earned dollars on it. You know that if you rush ahead to the pot of gold, the rainbow may be a mirage, which won't pay the rent.

Monday, March 2 (Moon in Aquarius). Try to keep private financial matters confidential, since you might reveal the wrong things to the wrong people today. Be careful of your dealings with a friend or a group you belong to, particularly if the subject is money. Advice about finances may stem from ulterior motives.

Tuesday, March 3 (Moon in Aquarius to Pisces 4:12 A.M.). Be very skeptical today around a boastful type, someone determined to make a big impression and willing to embroider the facts to do it. Stay within practical guidelines when making any important decisions—about travel, education, or a legal matter.

Wednesday, March 4 (NEW MOON in Pisces). The New Moon shows that you're able to capitalize on unexpected opportunities to promote a personal plan (or yourself). An innovative approach will stir the imagination of people targeted for response. Your success paves the way for an exciting, near-future breakthrough.

Thursday, March 5 (Moon in Pisces to Aries 3:08 P.M.). A fortunate follow-up is in the wind this morning in regard to yesterday's trail-blazing developments. Words are lively and stimulating in various contexts, which may give a promotional project a welcome push. Tonight, a domestic project benefits.

Friday, March 6 (Moon in Aries). You may feel a bit under the weather today, as a financial matter is taking more of your time and energy than you anticipated. This is likely to be family or property related, with a lot of onerous details to take care of. In the end, though, you'll be glad you went to so much trouble.

Saturday, March 7 (Moon in Aries). As noted at the New Moon, today you may have reason to celebrate, perhaps due to an exhilarating (or impending) change in your lifestyle. This may come about through an out-of-the-blue personal opportunity, a romantic meeting when least expected, or a sudden financial windfall.

Sunday, March 8 (Moon in Aries to Taurus 12:06 A.M.). Though somewhat milder than yesterday, this is another memorable day for personal success. You were probably more on the go the past few days, but the theme and your favorable prospects remain the same. The mesmerizing effect you now have on others is lucky.

Monday, March 9 (Moon in Taurus). If it weren't for various financial hassles, your streak of good fortune would continue today. As it is, the late-morning provides a chance to capitalize on yesterday's favorable events. But the early morning and evening can bring money problems with your mate or a friend.

Tuesday, March 10 (Moon in Taurus to Gemini 7:04 A.M.). This is a practical, down-to-earth day, when a procedural misunderstanding (job- or health-related) must be cleared up or some other misconception clarified. After you've made the effort to straighten out other's thinking, the P.M. improves considerably.

Wednesday, March 11 (Moon in Gemini). This is a stimulating, go-ahead day on the job, which will pay off in more substantial earnings over the longer term—if not immediately. Physical fitness efforts also yield commendable results as you feel better and are more organized and efficient with daily routine.

Thursday, March 12 (Moon in Gemini to Cancer 11:51 A.M.). The best (and probably most active) part of the day is the morning, when congeniality on the job could translate into some sort of financial benefits. If you're looking for a change, a co-worker might put you on to a better-paying position.

Friday, March 13 (Moon in Cancer). It's that day again, and although you're not typically superstitious, relationship upsets today might lead you to conclude that there are indeed some ill winds blowing in your direction. Oddly enough, there might not be any rational explanation for your troubles.

Saturday, March 14 (Moon in Cancer to Leo 2:21 P.M.). The early morning hours support marital and partnership interests or might produce a marital opportunity if you are unattached. There might also be a chance to move into a more upscale social milieu through a close associate or a resourceful friend.

Sunday, March 15 (Moon in Leo). A successful negotiation concerning property, a money-related family matter, or a joint financial enterprise can be wrapped up early in the day. At least aim for that, because as the afternoon gets under way, you're apt to run into a variety of financial roadblocks.

Monday, March 16 (Moon in Leo to Virgo 3:14 P.M.). It would be unwise to take certain friends into your confidence today, but keep your ears open for tidbits of information others let slip into the conversation. Don't depend too much on evening plans; a date or other get-together is apt to be canceled.

Tuesday, March 17 (Moon in Virgo). Always happy when you are being mentally stimulated, you'll enjoy portions of today as you proceed smoothly with an educational project or make a detailed itinerary for a trip in the not-too-distant future. Your intuition and hunches are well worth a follow up tonight.

Wednesday, March 18 (FULL MOON in Virgo—Moon to Libra 3:56 P.M.). The Full Moon today could intensify, however briefly, recent travel or communications snafus. As the day unfolds, the accent will gradually shift to business affairs or worldly progress, the course of which won't be entirely smooth.

Thursday, March 19 (Moon in Libra). Mixed trends suggest some stress or conflict between your domestic and career responsibilities. You're not easily deterred, however; by pointing out financial advantages, you're able to convince a key family member of the enduring value of your out-of-home efforts (or priorities).

Friday, March 20 (Moon in Libra to Scorpio 6:21 P.M.). Today's dualistic theme includes a clear road ahead (probably in the fast lane) in the area of financial gain, security, earnings, and career enhancement, but also strain in certain relationships. You may overreact when your patience runs thin.

Saturday, March 21 (Moon in Scorpio). If you have an out-of-town plan for the weekend, an early start today should get you happily en route. Plans currently on tap will bring you into contact with charming and interesting people, among whom might be a new romance prospect. Be alert to money snags tonight.

Sunday, March 22 (Moon in Scorpio). Perhaps more exciting than convivial, today's blueprint is very similar to yesterday's as far as the social theme is concerned. The difference is to be ready to take off on a new adventure at a moment's notice. Meanwhile, the P.M. again can bring a financial hassle.

Monday, March 23 (Moon in Scorpio to Sagittarius 12:14 A.M.). An idea proposed to you in confidence may be linked with a scholastic or travel plan (possibly interrelated), but if it sounds too good to be true, check it out before you commit yourself. You can count on the private support of a family VIP.

Tuesday, March 24 (Moon in Sagittarius). A secret ally or your own on-target intuition can help you to attain goals today. Be on the lookout, too, for subtle opportunities and ways in which you can use your background knowledge and experience to advance covert aims. The less others know now, the better.

Wednesday, March 25 (Moon in Sagittarius to Capricorn 10:09 A.M.). You might change your mind about a domestic decision today, particularly after you've had a glimpse of the alternatives. Acquire facts and don't let a bossy family member rush you into any commitments before you've had time to think.

Thursday, March 26 (Moon in Capricorn). This can mark the beginning of a new personal venture, which might be part of a financial development, or some particular way in which you intend to express your inner uniqueness. Someone around the home front helps you along by feeding you interesting ideas.

Friday, March 27 (Moon in Capricorn to Aquarius 10:45 P.M.). Today will be supportive to subtle networking, whether in a business context or in connection with your social aspirations. Calling on assorted others, who will in turn call on assorted others, will divide the labor and achieve your aims.

Saturday, March 28 (Moon in Aquarius). A love-at-first-sight encounter may be the reason you stayed longer than expected at a party that began last night—and which you didn't depart until the wee hours this morning. Nevertheless, you start the day in a chipper mood, ready early for household shopping.

Sunday, March 29 (Moon in Aquarius). On a weekend financial note, you can obtain financial leverage if you practice a double whammy on mounting expenses; cut down social and entertainment expenses to the bone, and pay off all the bills you can. On a happier note, the romance theme continues to be rewarding.

Monday, March 30 (Moon in Aquarius to Pisces 11:24 A.M.). Communications appear to be under siege today, so be sure to check all details and instructions carefully—and don't take it for granted that those around you can read your mind; be explicit. In particular, be careful about all transportation or driving.

Tuesday, March 31 (Moon in Pisces). Most of the day is apt to drift by in an uneventful way. By tonight, though, your articulate presentation of a subject with which you are familiar can have a galvanizing effect on listeners. You'll certainly surprise one or more in a way that boosts your personal credibility.

April 1992

Wednesday, April 1 (Moon in Pisces to Aries 10:05 P.M.). Your charisma soars today, and you attract favorable social, business, and romantic attention. You might feel propelled toward a special goal and move as though you really do have the "wind at your back." You could meet fascinating new people now.

Thursday, April 2 (Moon in Aries). Everything about your domestic situation seems to be low key today. Problems with family members or a conflict with your mate all appear to be things of the past. This will be a good time to make preparations for dinners, parties, or celebrations to come at a later date.

Friday, April 3 (NEW MOON in Aries). The New Moon can find you busy with plans or activities for freshening up (or refurbishing) your home environment. For some, this may simply mean a spring cleaning project, whereas others will have something more extensive in mind, such as a more luxurious decor.

Saturday, April 4 (Moon in Aries to Taurus 6:19 A.M.). You start the day in an adventurous (not to say careless mood), ready to tackle anything and everything—which won't be wise in all situations. After finding that you can't possibly cram everything you can think of into the day's agenda, you'll do what you can.

Sunday, April 5 (Moon in Taurus). The focus is on home, property, or family interests, all of which will be fortunate in some money-related way. If a real estate deal is pending, it could go through now, perhaps due to the support of a key individual. A residential move will be to a more prestigious address.

Monday, April 6 (Moon in Taurus to Gemini 12:34 P.M.). The morning is the best time to voice your ideas, to sell something, or to obtain agreements or sign contracts or other documents. A billet-doux or other welcome communique might also arrive. Someone around you tonight gushes at the slightest provocation.

Tuesday, April 7 (Moon in Gemini). Your feisty, take-it-or-leave-it attitude this morning is not the best way to start the day—and doesn't bode well for most of it. No doubt someone will trigger your urge to get out of a real or imagined rut, but there are better ways to go about it—as you learn this afternoon.

Wednesday, April 8 (Moon in Gemini to Cancer 5:19 P.M.). Perhaps more on the verbal level, today in its way is just as disjointed as yesterday. It's not your style to miscalculate in any major way, but you're apt to thoroughly misjudge a home or family matter—and argue your position on into the night.

Thursday, April 9 (Moon in Cancer). Today brings welcome relief from the tempests of the past few days. Make a phone call to let someone know he or she is in your thoughts. If a love (or other relationship) has reached the commitment stage, you might make or receive a proposal to make it permanent.

Friday, April 10 (Moon in Cancer to Leo 8:47 P.M.). From the wee hours till the start of day, there seems to be a persistent theme of unrest, whether it's you, your mate, or a family member who keeps alive a noncooperative attitude. As the day gradually unfolds, however, more harmonious notes are sounded.

Saturday, April 11 (Moon in Leo). This is a good day to go weekend shopping for home items, which can be even more fun if a companion tags along with you—perhaps a family member as interested as you are in improving home appearances or creature comforts. The earlier you start this morning, the better.

Sunday, April 12 (Moon in Leo to Virgo 11:10 P.M.). Due to an early-morning financial fracas, the day starts off on the wrong foot, but cooler heads soon prevail and the day gets back on course. There are productive echoes of yesterday's money-related home or family theme—with some profitable results.

Monday, April 13 (Moon in Virgo). The way it begins early this morning, you might think this is going to be your lucky day, but it could turn out to be an enticing invitation to misadventure. Avoid hazards in travel or other transportation matters. Be sure to obtain written confirmation of any reservations.

Tuesday, April 14 (Moon in Virgo). Family or friends at a distance may be in touch today, or perhaps you are planning to visit someone in another region in the near future. During this period, you should be getting your act together, as planetary patterns support your newly emerging interests and views.

Wednesday, April 15 (Moon in Virgo to Libra 1:11 A.M.). This is a day when information, messages, mail, or agreements can somehow go haywire. People seem to be more interested in making a nice impression than in emphasizing accuracy—but, being a Capricorn—facts are mainly what you're interested in.

Thursday, April 16 (FULL MOON in Libra). Don't realign any of your basic career or business values or priorities on the basis of today's misleading activities; the grass always looks greener on the other side. If the advice of someone helping you with a work project seems impractical, just don't follow it.

Friday, April 17 (Moon in Libra to Scorpio 4:11 A.M.). After a morning that just ambles along, the tempo picks up nicely around midday—possibly due to a gregarious friend who proposes social activities that get your adrenaline going. Whether or not this applies to today, at least your enthusiasm is aroused.

Saturday, April 18 (Moon in Scorpio). You could be gung-ho about a social invitation or proposal this morning and then realize how big a dent it will put in your purse. As the day goes along, however, it won't take much persuasion to get you to overlook that fact and go ahead with the plans.

Sunday, April 19 (Moon in Scorpio to Sagittarius 9:41 A.M.). Most of the day will just seem to plod along and go nowhere in particular until the afternoon, when a home development proves to be interesting in a quiet sort of way. If titillating gossip reaches your ears tonight, take it with a grain of salt.

Monday, April 20 (Moon in Sagittarius). Use originality to streamline your workday; retain solid values but be flexible in adding the best of current innovations. Relax tonight, preferably with a loved one or other very compatible companion who will understand when you want to bypass controversial topics.

Tuesday, April 21 (Moon in Sagittarius to Capricorn 6:41 P.M.). A family member or older friend may advise against one of your current plans or intentions, but this person may not have all the facts or be motivated by self-interest. Tonight, however, you'll attract the respect and admiration befitting a VIP.

Wednesday, April 22 (Moon in Capricorn). Today's adverse emphasis on home, family, and midweek activities in general will surely involve a repair project or an entertainment agenda that's more of a duty (and a dreary one) than a pleasure. Don't look to family members for help; you're on your own now.

Thursday, April 23 (Moon in Capricorn). Be flexible in your plans and attitude; a peculiar setback that is totally unexpected may require on-the-spot adjustment if you're not to hurt the feelings of a touchy family member. By midday, the picture is much brighter, with social activities that stir your interest.

Friday, April 24 (Moon in Capricorn to Aquarius 6:39 P.M.). Lucky influences may bring a new love into your life or give you a fresh slant on an on-going twosome, assuring you that it has a long-range future. You might set the date for a trip to the altar. Set your sights high now and aim for the stars.

Saturday, April 25 (Moon in Aquarius). An upsurge in social activity may include a coveted social invitation for which you may have been subtly angling for a long time. A chance for productive networking may come about through a family connection. Tonight, though, you may feel the effects of a money pinch.

Sunday, April 26 (Moon in Aquarius to Pisces 7:21 P.M.). This can turn out to be a so-so day when everything you begin encounters a delay or thinly veiled mistrust; yet you have enough presence of mind to somehow muddle through. An afterwork date, however, may bring news of a good job or career development.

Monday, April 27 (Moon in Pisces). Don't try too hard to please people at the start of the day—and certainly don't bend the truth or exaggerate the scope of benefits promised from an agreement. Before the morning is over, and if you're still unattached, a meeting can mark a turning point in your relationship status.

Tuesday, April 28 (Moon in Pisces). The power of suggestion can be a powerful weapon today if you're trying to convince others of your point of view about an important issue. If the answer isn't immediate this morning, just bide your time. When the facts finally sink in, you'll get the answer you want.

Wednesday, April 29 (Moon in Pisces to Aries 6:14 A.M.). You'd probably like to get something done around the home front or concerning a family matter, but you'll probably feel like you're adrift in the middle of the Sargasso Sea. Try as you might, you probably won't stir up any interest in your ideas.

Thursday, April 30 (Moon in Aries). You might discover that something in connection with your home life needs updating. You could be considering a computer to make your household accounts and related financial tasks—or work you do at home—easier. Expect some changes in domestic plans after work.

May 1992

Friday, May 1 (Moon in Aries to Taurus 2:10 P.M.). The day builds to an exhilarating evening, when you could make a dynamic impact on a new romantic prospect. If you're already involved, news from a distance from a special someone lifts your spirits. An opportunity may come concerning a creative project.

Saturday, May 2 (NEW MOON in Taurus). Lucky events either yesterday or today could mark the beginning of an exciting new chapter in your love life. It is also a very fruitful period for artistic inspiration and could greatly benefit a work in progress or get a new creative project off to a marvelous start.

Sunday, May 3 (Moon in Taurus to Gemini 7:29 P.M.). You'll have your ups and downs today in regard to home interests, with the probability of a personality clash with a family member over your ideas—which may seem a bit far out coming from you. On the other hand, there is accord over household money management.

Monday, May 4 (Moon in Gemini). Don't try to take on more than you can handle at work or in connection with daily routine; don't let pressures swamp you; don't make promises you can't fulfill; you're only one person. Your temptation to overdo could adversely affect your health; take your time when dining.

Tuesday, May 5 (Moon in Gemini to Cancer 11:10 P.M.). The happy start to this day leads you to conclude that it is made for love. In any event, you'll have no trouble rustling up a date that fills you with pleasurable anticipation. Meanwhile, though the money outlook is good, the home front spells trouble.

Wednesday, May 6 (Moon in Cancer). Romantic and other key relationships continue to sail smoothly along, providing you with a chance to apply any needed finishing touches to yesterday's fruitful developments. Some who have met their one and only could now set the date for a traditional June wedding.

Thursday, May 7 (Moon in Cancer). Between one thing and another, it may be difficult to pin down your mate or other close associate to saying exactly what he or she means or to express a definite opinion or make a decision. Dealings with friends may be a lot more enjoyable, particularly if you have a lunch date.

Friday, May 8 (Moon in Cancer to Leo 2:08 A.M.). You're in a take-charge mood and would like to experiment as the day gets going, but this is not your day. Your hopes are high, but those around you are disapproving or uncooperative, especially about money—which may put a big crimp in your plans.

Saturday, May 9 (Moon in Leo). Yesterday's pattern continues; you're full of inspiration as the day gets under way, but you'll have to be a lot more earth-bound about finances if you expect others to go along with any of your plans or ideas. It's definitely not the day for weekend shopping with a companion.

Sunday, May 10 (Moon in Leo to Virgo 4:57 A.M.). If most of the outlook is humdrum, with the possible exception of a middle-of-the-night idea, the ensuing afternoon will offer some compensations that should please you as well as inform you. Distant happenings could provide a fresh viewpoint on private yearnings.

Monday, May 11 (Moon in Virgo). Spontaneous dealings with people at or from a distance may stem from your efforts to broaden your knowledge, strengthen an important relationship, or create exciting travel opportunities during the upcoming summer vacation season. You're able to defuse some tension tonight.

Tuesday, May 12 (Moon in Virgo to Libra 8:06 A.M.). A domestic issue may seem to be on the brink of being resolved, but job or career demands may keep interfering with your best intentions. You (or someone around the home front) could be pretty exasperated by the time the workday ends, resulting in a flare-up.

Wednesday, May 13 (Moon in Libra). Someone in your environment will support your plans for a trip or an academic project, even if there is an unexpected disapproving note (or some sort of strings attached). Be wary of afternoon tension about a business matter; it's not a good time for you to buck the boss.

Thursday, May 14 (Moon in Libra to Scorpio 12:16 P.M.). A new page turns today, but it's mostly blank, especially where your social life is concerned. This could be an advantage, however, because it means that you can write your own scenario, one that may include summer visits to friends in faraway places.

Friday, May 15 (Moon in Scorpio). Most of the day is likely to roll along its modestly bumpy way without arousing much interest. The evening, though, is another story, with a mix of social and/or romantic excitement and financial frustrations. If a date is broken, the alternative will be enjoyable.

Saturday, May 16 (FULL MOON in Scorpio—Moon to Sagittarius 6:23 P.M.). A decision regarding a child, or a romantic dream that becomes a serious reality, can be today's overriding themes. However, there may be some heavy insecurities about money. Love plus responsibility could be a tough challenge.

Sunday, May 17 (Moon in Sagittarius). After a rather unfocused, carefree start, the day proceeds nicely with you in the mood to clear the decks of neglected tasks. Evening social-romantic plans are pleasurable. Sports or some form of competition could stimulate you. Home may be the setting for lively activities.

Monday, May 18 (Moon in Sagittarius). While this is a generally fortunate day, particularly for finances, you may feel somewhat hampered regardless of upbeat money signals. Staying in the background enables you to cash in on some privileged information that's more reliable than tonight's dating plans.

Tuesday, May 19 (Moon in Sagittarius to Capricorn 3:14 A.M.). A stroke of luck may open the way to turning everything around on a less-than-satisfactory personal matter. A new approach to this situation can make all the difference. Your persuasiveness and magnetism are heightened, attracting new admirers.

Wednesday, May 20 (Moon in Capricorn). Today you could find out where you stand in a key situation. Added to this, an energy high sends you up the scale of accomplishment in some significant personal way. Even though it will at times be a bit choppy, you'll be satisfied tonight by the way the day turns out.

Thursday, May 21 (Moon in Capricorn to Aquarius 2:44 P.M.). You're able to use your imagination and keen mind to clear away the aftertaste of a nocturnal worry. The day in its way, is as satisfactory as yesterday, except that a similar number of activities will be compressed into a shorter amount of time.

Friday, May 22 (Moon in Aquarius). Though it may not be immediately apparent, today's happenings could mark the beginning of a new trend in your social life and/or love life, as well. Perhaps a parting of the ways with a friend will pave the way to increased rapport with your mate or other close companion.

Saturday, May 23 (Moon in Aquarius). This is a day ringed with dollar signs—only the dollar signs aren't facing in your direction, or they're upside down or backwards. Take this as a warning that your expenditures—to say nothing of bills—are catching up with you. Think about overhauling your money habits.

Sunday, May 24 (Moon in Aquarius to Pisces 3:26 A.M.). If you didn't learn anything from yesterday's developments, you'll probably give in to today's sky's-the-limit attitude about money—and you'll spend, spend, spend. It will all be much fun in terms of distant interests, but sooner or later you'll pay the piper.

Monday, May 25 (Moon in Pisces). Someone else will be right in tune with your long-range perspective and vision concerning business, politics, relationships (especially sibling), and other subjects of mutual interest. A surprise twist in your social life may have brought this person into your sphere and thoughts.

Tuesday, May 26 (Moon in Pisces to Aries 2:53 P.M.). You'll start the day in a sort of shoot-the-works mood about romance, travel (a summer vacation plan), a job matter, or your physical welfare. Don't try to break any speed or endurance records while running. As the day unfolds, you become more practical.

Wednesday, May 27 (Moon in Aries). You'll enjoy increased rapport with coworkers now, and you'll have a lot of productive ideas about job efficiency and health matters in the weeks ahead. Afterwork socializing with colleagues will be very enjoyable—and it might also increase your success potential.

Thursday, May 28 (Moon in Aries to Taurus 11:17 P.M.). Home-related interests should proceed smoothly enough today, though there is an ever-present likelihood of a favorite relative popping in at unexpected times and totally upsetting the domestic schedule. So be prepared to make spur-of-the-moment adjustments.

Friday, May 29 (Moon in Taurus). Mixed trends make this a day to air your views in the most practical way possible, or perhaps to finalize a legal matter. But it is not the appropriate day on which to challenge an adversary or try to convince someone to change an opinion—especially if your facts aren't convincing.

Saturday, May 30 (Moon in Taurus). Today you have a chance to coast along on a wave of job or business success—the Big Wave! But coasting along is not exactly the same as acquiring large chunks of your favorite-color metal: gold. But you can probably enjoy a modest little shopping spree, anyway.

Sunday, May 31 (Moon in Taurus to Gemini 4:20 A.M.—NEW MOON in Gemini). The New Moon could herald the auspicious beginning of a new chapter in your job or career fortunes. Capitalize on excellent new ideas, but don't fritter away opportunity having a good time. Concentrate on maximizing results from your endeavors.

June 1992

Monday, June 1 (Moon in Gemini). You're in the driver's seat on the work scene as well as around the home front. More work is on your platter, and today it's more routine; business as usual, but the rewarding kind from the financial point of view. Everything works out now, as various jobs get done.

Tuesday, June 2 (Moon in Gemini to Cancer 6:59 A.M.). Don't take differing views too seriously; actually, you will probably change your mind later and may be surprised to find that the other person has done the same. In the meantime, higher mind interests are favored and will flourish in today's stellar climate.

Wednesday, June 3 (Moon in Cancer). Forcing an issue with your mate or steady date will have its drawbacks, such as alienating them for the remainder of the day. Your best bet is to compromise, especially if you're planning to socialize together tonight—which will be a lot more pleasant without tension.

Thursday, June 4 (Moon in Cancer to Leo 8:36 A.M.). The postmidnight hours can find you winding up some work you brought home last night. Later trends as the day unfolds denote some troublesome crosscurrents where money, especially dealings with other people, is concerned. Don't try to make final decisions now.

Friday, June 5 (Moon in Leo). You might be involved, or perhaps playing a leading role, in some sort of community affair or summertime outing, possibly job-connected. In any case, activities begin early and then run afoul of a money snag. Later on, you'll be needed at home for one reason or another.

Saturday, June 6 (Moon in Leo to Virgo 10:29 A.M.). Quick-wittedness will come in handy this afternoon, particularly if you're en route to a destination or already enjoying a weekend away. If you have to adapt to altered plans on short notice, you'll know what to say to turn a change around to your advantage.

Sunday, June 7 (Moon in Virgo). This is another day that favors a sojourn in a different, perhaps quite faraway locale. If you're traveling, however, you might not care for the attitude of a functionary—perhaps a ticket clerk or other attendant. Consider the source, however, and go ahead and enjoy the day.

Monday, June 8 (Moon in Virgo to Libra 1:34 P.M.). The day starts off on a familiar note of message mix-ups or other misunderstandings—probably about money or a job matter, but improves considerably as evening approaches. Interesting job developments involving a VIP bode well for your earnings prospects.

Tuesday, June 9 (Moon in Libra). Shop talk tonight initially will not seem to be a good idea, especially if your attitude or ideas are a bit avant-garde. Wait a while, however, and you'll find others gradually coming around to your way of thinking and turning out to be friendlier than expected in the process.

Wednesday, June 10 (Moon in Libra to Scorpio 6:28 P.M.). Aside from a sluggish morning and an early-afternoon altercation around the home front, your plans are due to proceed exactly as you wish today. Little or no interference will come between you and your heart's desires, whether romantic, social, or financial.

Thursday, June 11 (Moon in Scorpio). An uneventful day is followed by a fruitful evening. You might go over a community project, perhaps a social occasion to raise funds, with a congenial friend. Contact with people at a distance is also productive, as you might make final plans for an upcoming trip.

Friday, June 12 (Moon in Scorpio). Social and group interests are accented today, and it seems that whatever activities you get involved with along those lines is bound to be a success. Others listen to your words of wisdom, and your innovative ideas get a warm reception. You could be the life of the party.

Saturday, June 13 (Moon in Scorpio to Sagittarius 1:30 A.M.). If vacation travel is on your agenda (or it's simply a summer weekend away), you couldn't have picked a more ideal time for it. You're stimulated this morning, and you'll radiate charm in all directions. You won't even mind a chore that needs doing.

Sunday, June 14 (FULL MOON Lunar Eclipse in Sagittarius). The Full Moon shows one thing that you can be sure of; your love life certainly won't be dull in the weeks ahead. And if you're creative, you'll have more energy than usual for your projects. Heed an insider financial tip that comes your way today.

Monday, June 15 (Moon in Sagittarius to Capricorn 10:51 A.M.). You may be eager to step out in a new entertainment direction this evening. Meanwhile, your initiative, enterprising spirit, and abundant energy are the keys to today's successful ventures. You can head straight for the mark to attain a goal.

Tuesday, June 16 (Moon in Capricorn). Mixed trends may impel you to be rather arbitrary or noncooperative with those in authority, at the same time that you desire to push your favorite project to these same people. If this applies to a situation in the social milieu, it won't help your upward climb.

Wednesday, June 17 (Moon in Capricorn to Aquarius 10:20 P.M.). The day will drift along in no particular direction. After a while, you'll get the hint that it's not the best day to get your ideas across to others. You'd like to stir up some sort of financial activity, even shopping, but it isn't the time.

Thursday, June 18 (Moon in Aquarius). Circle this date as a warning to steer clear of financial disputes or other relationship hazards. You either won't have the right answers, or will have the wrong attitude, possibly stemming from a restless night. Don't be so ready with a quick retort this morning.

Friday, June 19 (Moon in Aquarius). Today is in the same vein as yesterday; the subject is money and other assorted differences; back talk continues to be a hazard, but there may be more aggravation to deal with. Friends and money will be a discordant combination; you may have to trim social expenditures.

Saturday, June 20 (Moon in Aquarius to Pisces 11:01 A.M.). Do you feel like heading for a summer weekend change of scene or a romantic adventure? Perhaps a summertime fling? Your mood is right on target, so pack your bags and try your luck—and the earlier you start the better; no point keeping Cupid waiting.

Sunday, June 21 (Moon in Pisces). Good news travels fast and you're likely to get some this morning (or earlier—during the nocturnal hours—if you're a night person). The key word tonight is "surprise," and you'll be in the right place at the right time for a development that sends your spirits soaring.

Monday, June 22 (Moon in Pisces to Aries 11:04 P.M.). An agreement or rapprochement with someone who was formerly difficult to convince paves the way for some favorable publicity. The right solution is at hand if you have an issue to resolve with a relative or neighbor. Read between the lines of incoming mail.

Tuesday, June 23 (Moon in Aries). There seems to be a strong difference in your respective values, as you and a family member strive to reach agreement about a domestic matter. Try being more objective than emotional. Restating mutual aims, methods, and hoped-for results keeps channels of communication open.

Wednesday, June 24 (Moon in Aries). Mixed trends today show that if you were able to reach a compromise yesterday, you will have settled a home- or family-related financial matter to everyone's satisfaction. If you didn't, you can use that possibility as a wedge to restore harmony around the home front.

Thursday, June 25 (Moon in Aries to Taurus 8:29 A.M.). This should be a thoroughly rewarding day, whether you are centered on work, play, romance, or family entertainment activities. A nice financial boost could be in the picture, too, as a result of your work efforts or ideas to improve job efficiency.

Friday, June 26 (Moon in Taurus). A "new you" will have an unforeseen opportunity today to go forth and test the waters of your new lifestyle. Although there may be new financial responsibilities as part of the package, you're ready to handle the risks and to move quickly with each twist and turn of events.

Saturday, June 27 (Moon in Taurus to Gemini 2:15 P.M.). If you're twiddling your thumbs the first part of the day, you'll probably focus on a weekend project or perhaps will put in some weekend job overtime by early afternoon. Your mind is in it's practical mode, so you'll do something that pays dividends.

Sunday, June 28 (Moon in Gemini). This should be a satisfying day when your agenda proceeds smoothly and delays are at a minimum unless you become careless. Expansive thinking adds an upbeat tone to your weekend work efforts, and the P.M. brings reassurance about your financial solvency for a long time to come.

Monday, June 29 (Moon in Gemini to Cancer 4:43 P.M.). Although you're not likely to take any particular action today, you might be thinking a lot about various work matters and/or your physical welfare—and how you might improve the future potential for either. You'll mull over key relationships tonight.

Tuesday, June 30 (NEW MOON Solar Eclipse in Cancer). If you missed out on a June wedding, you and your intended could make up for lost time now and schedule a near-future march down the aisle. If you're single and looking, your quest might suddenly end. Try to handle abrupt opposition tonight with tact and patience.

July 1992

Wednesday, July 1 (Moon in Cancer to Leo 5:16 P.M.). Fortunate developments brighten the day, which may be the reason that your energy level is high and your enthusiasm knows no bounds. Travel or visiting plans, either for a vacation trip or the upcoming holiday are adventurous and sail along productively.

Thursday, July 2 (Moon in Leo). Dark clouds seem to be gathering in the wake of yesterday's upbeat developments, perhaps in the form of discord with a loved one about upcoming holiday expenditures. There's a conflict between an urge to splurge and a need to economize which threatens to strain an important alliance.

Friday, July 3 (Moon in Leo to Virgo 5:38 P.M.). Except for minor details, today is practically a carbon copy of yesterday. The difference is that you and others on opposite sides of a financial issue will express disapproval with the silent treatment instead of a verbal flare-up or other abrupt gesture.

Saturday, July 4 (Moon in Virgo). Travel signs predominate, there's an exceptional line-up of favorable stellar influences, and all indications point to a terrific day to celebrate the nation's birthday—so all that remains is for you to take full advantage of opportunities to get the weekend off to a fabulous start!

Sunday, July 5 (Moon in Virgo to Libra 7:28 P.M.). It will be easy for a new romance to begin or love to bloom in the happy wake of yesterday's exhilarating developments. A dynamic new romantic attraction could cross your path at a beach outing or patio party—and it's apt to be more than a summertime fling.

Monday, July 6 (Moon in Libra). It's back to the workaday world of daily routine and/or job and career strivings, which you'll take to better during the day than tonight—when shoptalk or other business-related efforts can find you in a decidedly unreceptive mood. A creative project could benefit from a shortcut.

Tuesday, July 7 (Moon in Libra to Scorpio 11:54 P.M.). If an important relationship has been wavering, today's upsetting developments bring it to the brink of a split—if not over the edge to abrupt and permanent separation. The final outcome will be up to both parties involved, and a willingness to compromise.

Wednesday, July 8 (Moon in Scorpio). The way things go today, if you've been mulling over some summer social or weekend travel plans, you'll have to weigh all the pros and cons a lot more before coming up with a satisfactory solution. However, with a bit of imagination, you'll enthuse about an answer tonight.

Thursday, July 9 (Moon in Scorpio). This is an action-packed day, the fortunate outcome of which is threatened by your tendency to daydream, get lost in wishful thinking, or wander up meaningless alleys under the peculiar influence of unfamiliar people. Stick strictly to essentials and shun strange newcomers.

Friday, July 10 (Moon in Scorpio to Sagittarius 7:18 A.M.). Whether you need to catch your breath or recover from the recent stumbling blocks that cluttered your path, the pace slows down considerably today. Perhaps you'll have to stop and brush up a bit on the details of recent events before all the pieces fit.

Saturday, July 11 (Moon in Sagittarius). You're back in the groove and rarin' to go as the weekend gets under way. Whether it's joining forces with another to achieve a home front objective or attain some sort of financial goal, you'll go about it quietly and efficiently—the better to enjoy your efforts.

Sunday, July 12 (Moon in Sagittarius to Capricorn 5:17 P.M.). From the wee hours of the morning on, the day is likely to be under a cloud of uncertainty. You're in your stop-and-go mode, especially regarding affectional ties and their effect on your social prospects. Don't try to make up your mind now; wait.

Monday, July 13 (Moon in Capricorn). There's not much worth doing today, as cooperation from others continues to be scant and your own judgment is not exactly on target.

Nevertheless, you're able to put discord behind you tonight and enjoy a date with a favorite admirer with whom you share great mental rapport.

Tuesday, July 14 (FULL MOON in Capricorn). The Full Moon warns you to quell feelings of independence today and instead concentrate on your own personal ambitions and aspirations—which could be rather lofty and not immediately understandable to those closest to you. Everyone doesn't share your vision.

Wednesday, July 15 (Moon in Capricorn to Aquarius 5:04 A.M.). Be sure you're not touching a nerve, in terms of a money gripe, when you try to push through a new financial suggestion or plan. Don't expect a partner to agree without questioning your motives. Your confidence may be more irritating than persuasive.

Thursday, July 16 (Moon in Aquarius). Financial hassles make it difficult to get along with other people and to get through the day without a spat (or worse). Problems can run the gamut from arguing about the change you receive in a store to a checking account mistake—to opposing ideas about partnership funds.

Friday, July 17 (Moon in Aquarius to Pisces 5:45 P.M.). Adverse influences denote that emotional anxieties can get the best of you when dealing with loved ones or friends. Your temper has a short fuse now; don't become irritable if someone teases you. You can get your way if you go about it diplomatically.

Saturday, July 18 (Moon in Pisces). The weekend gets off to a slow start today, but you'll make up for that tomorrow with a superactive (and enjoyable) day. Meanwhile, be specific when making plans for tonight, particularly travel or transportation arrangements; don't leave any details up to chance.

Sunday, July 19 (Moon in Pisces). This is a super day, especially for a summer weekend away or if you happen to be on vacation. There will be lots to do and see, and getting there (whatever your destination) will be loads of fun. A sightseeing side trip, which you had not originally scheduled, is also informative.

Monday, July 20 (Moon in Pisces to Aries 6:08 A.M.). After a moderately aggravating day, take advantage tonight of opportunities to enjoy your home, entertain friends, make new acquaintances, and/or spruce up the decor (maybe get the guest room ready for a summer visitor). A property transaction is profitable.

Tuesday, July 21 (Moon in Aries). It isn't just wishful thinking if you see some light at the end of the tunnel regarding today's home or family upsets—which some edginess on your part may help to precipitate. However, by the time the day is over, everything is shipshape, especially re finances.

Wednesday, July 22 (Moon in Aries to Taurus 4:37 P.M.). Various minor setbacks make this a day to work on routine matters. Don't take anything for granted when dealing with a higher-up or a co-worker, particularly if money is an issue; wait for the practical follow-up of a recently made promise.

Thursday, July 23 (Moon in Taurus). Although there could be some differences about the financial particulars or long-term ramifications, someone with whom you have a close and understanding relationship will support your plans for a trip or academic project. You're ready to shake the dust from your heels now.

Friday, July 24 (Moon in Taurus to Gemini 11:45 P.M.). After a pleasant dream, tension-generating influences are enough to add up to a fitful awakening. Perhaps your mind is struggling to find an answer to job-related personal problems or a money dilemma that defies solution during waking hours.

Saturday, July 25 (Moon in Gemini). Your desire to please a VIP heads you in the direction of a weekend project—about which you will be very conscientious. Toward the end of the day, however, a hazard may arise in the guise of an invitation to go shopping with a companion; if you value the relationship, don't!

Sunday, July 26 (Moon in Gemini). Although there may still be an undercurrent of resentment or frustration remaining from your turndown of an invitation yesterday, this is a generally pleasant day with which to wind up the weekend. You're able to pour oil on troubled waters if someone continues to carp.

Monday, July 27 (Moon in Gemini to Cancer 3:09 A.M.). You probably wouldn't miss today if it were left off the calendar. You'd like to see some positive developments in a relationship or about a legal matter, but encounter one petty aggravation after another that delays or blocks your progress.

Tuesday, July 28 (Moon in Cancer). Don't expect your mate or others with whom you are closely involved to brim over with sunny smiles and good cheer all day. Instead, expect periods that are surprisingly rocky as the day goes along. However, if you stay on top of the situation, you can restore harmony.

Wednesday, July 29 (Moon in Cancer to Leo 3:40 A.M.— NEW MOON in Leo). The New Moon marks an opportunity to work out a promising financial arrangement with someone who is a real go-getter when it comes to money. Your activities start off early with necessary preparations and everything will be ready to go this afternoon.

Thursday, July 30 (Moon in Leo). In terms of yesterday's fast-paced developments, you may have to backtrack a bit today, perhaps fill in a few essential details you may have glossed over in your haste to get a new project airborne. Your efforts should culminate in a congenial and profitable lunch date.

Friday, July 31 (Moon in Leo to Virgo 3:02 A.M.). The eve of the weekend finds you in top form, as the entire pace of your life quickens and your energies are high—to match your spirit of derring-do and adventure. Whether or not you've planned on it, you will probably soon head for a faraway locale.

August 1992

Saturday, August 1 (Moon in Virgo). If you've been dreaming of the bucolic delights of a summer outing away from it all, moonlit nights on an exotic beach, or other such warm weather diversions, this should be your day for it all to come true. You'll be brimming over with enthusiasm as the weekend gets under way.

Sunday, August 2 (Moon in Virgo to Libra 3:18 A.M.). Another stimulating day now is centered on family activities and/or around your base of operations. If you are away in a distant locale, you probably won't stray far from your accommodations. There certainly won't be any lack of amusing ideas for fun and games.

Monday, August 3 (Moon in Libra). If the thought of starting another week on the job doesn't exactly put a smile on your face this morning, the thought of the financial rewards will help to keep you motivated. If you haven't

as yet gotten the okay on a home-related financial proposal, it may come tonight.

Tuesday, August 4 (Moon in Libra to Scorpio 6:17 A.M.).
Today doesn't bode well for monetary interests, or much
of anything else that might also involve a friend. Go on
shopping trips alone. Steer clear of people you know to
have views that clash with yours. Keep your mind on
security, your car keys, and wallet.

Wednesday, August 5 (Moon in Scorpio). The way the
morning unfolds, you won't be looking forward to the rest
of the day. However, it soon improves, and a fascinating
evening is in store. Among other things, you'll strike it rich
when a coveted invitation arrives, and through circumstances you'll least expect.

**Thursday, August 6 (Moon in Scorpio to Sagittarius
12:58 P.M.).** A journey to a faraway locale (or planning
one for a summer breakaway weekend) may be in the
works, but you may have to polish certain details, or get
someone's agreement, before you can finalize arrangements. Diplomacy is essential now.

Friday, August 7 (Moon in Sagittarius). This is probably
going to be one of those days when you've had your fill of
the world and its problems, but you'll find that you can't
distance yourself totally from aggravations—particularly in
the financial realm, where you're likely to encounter frustrating obstacles.

**Saturday, August 8 (Moon in Sagittarius to Capricorn
11:01 P.M.).** There's little or nothing going on today, but
what better way to spend a lazy summer weekend day than
by not having to bestir yourself for any reason? Take
advantage of the inactivity to give your nerves and energies
a much appreciated rest.

Sunday, August 9 (Moon in Capricorn). Today follows yesterday's path, more or less, as there continues to be little that will arouse your interest. If you're on vacation somewhere, you won't be in the mood to go traipsing off to another museum or cathedral, preferring just to laze around and let the day drift by.

Monday, August 10 (Moon in Capricorn). Be flexible in your plans and attitude; a change that is totally unexpected may require on-the-spot adjustment. A personal responsibility could be involved; you may have to come up with a convincing explanation for one of your actions. There's a price tag on leadership.

Tuesday, August 11 (Moon in Capricorn to Aquarius 11:07 A.M.). You may try to dodge a financial issue with your mate or other close associate by taking the line of least resistance. It probably won't work, however, because others already know that you're too practical to rely on flimsy rationales.

Wednesday, August 12 (Moon in Aquarius). If a financial dispute wasn't resolved yesterday to everyone's satisfaction, today could bring the grand finale in the form of a disruptive showdown. Don't let reactions get out of hand, however, especially if a third party (a friend?) also gets into the act.

Thursday, August 13 (FULL MOON in Aquarius—Moon to Pisces 11:52 P.M.). Feelings may continue to run high about financial issues, but the outcome may be more a tempest in a teacup than jarring reactions. All concerned may conclude there's nothing to be gained by keeping discord alive and flailing a dead horse.

Friday, August 14 (Moon in Pisces). Your heart may not be in your job or other daily routine today as the workweek draws to a close. The evening may bring further frustration, too, as plans for a weekend trip or other summertime diversion may be canceled. The other person may be just as disappointed as you are.

Saturday, August 15 (Moon in Pisces). Suddenly, weekend prospects look bright again, and you'll be ready to take off on a day trip (or for an overnight stay) at the drop of a hat. But don't get carried away in your haste to depart and forget your driver's license, credit cards, or sundry other items you might need.

Sunday, August 16 (Moon in Pisces to Aries 2:02 P.M.). This is another one of those balmy summer days that just seem to uneventfully drift by. If that's the way it shapes up, why fight it? What better way to draw the curtain on a generally pleasant weekend? Find a nice hammock or deck chair somewhere and settle in.

Monday, August 17 (Moon in Aries). After a nice respite, a fresh surge of the enterprising spirit is just the thing to enable you to achieve a few more of your ambitions, both personal and worldly. Coupled with your no-nonsense work habits, even a setback or two won't prevent you from making worthwhile progress.

Tuesday, August 18 (Moon in Aries to Taurus 11:11 P.M.). A love-at-first-sight encounter could be the highlight of the day (or more probably, the evening). This signals a lucky turning point in your love life, which may be due for (or already undergoing) a surprising transformation—along with your general outlook.

Wednesday, August 19 (Moon in Taurus). A verbal squabble about money could put an affectional tie to the test; whatever the rights or wrongs of differences, you should try to settle them this afternoon; at least you'll have a chance then. Meanwhile, curb any spending that might add fuel to the fire.

Thursday, August 20 (Moon in Taurus). Despite a tense situation here and there, this is overall a better day than yesterday, and a lot busier. The warm glow of romance enlivens everything you do, whether enjoying a lunch date with a special someone, or savoring a night on the town that enhances togetherness.

Friday, August 21 (Moon in Taurus to Gemini 7:37 A.M.). You could use some time alone today, to mull over job or health problems—which may be money-related at this point. Because it is a generally adverse day—in terms of solving or starting anything—better to delay action than to make the wrong move.

Saturday, August 22 (Moon in Gemini). If a weekend chore is on your calendar today, you'll get an early start and go at it tooth and nail—which means that you could finish up ahead of time by early afternoon. From then on, it looks as though it's "no holds barred" in the fun department—but try not to go overboard.

Sunday, August 23 (Moon in Gemini to Cancer 12:37 P.M.). Weekend social gatherings can be warmly rewarding today, and may include a reunion with someone from a distance—whether family, school chum, or a favorite teacher. If a community project or humanitarian goal is on tap, it gets a congenial reception.

Monday, August 24 (Moon in Cancer). You and your mate or live-in companion could be one hundred and eighty degrees apart on a controversial topic that brings out the worst in both of you (if you let it). Whether this involves broad issues such as liberty and justice, or something more personal, you patch it up tonight.

Tuesday, August 25 (Moon in Cancer to Leo 2:16 P.M.). This is mostly a ho-hum day. It's not like you to feel that you have any personal limitations, but it's possible that someone's remark today will set you to thinking about your lacks or flaws. This could also be a reminder of former feelings of inadequacy.

Wednesday, August 26 (Moon in Leo). You and a close associate could be in the mood to resolve a longtime impasse (probably minor) concerning joint money interests or a belonging. This can be done quietly but effectively. Also, a turn of events could shine the beckoning light on one of your social or travel plans.

Thursday, August 27 (Moon in Leo to Virgo 1:47 P.M.— NEW MOON in Virgo). The New Moon shows that you could be inspired a bit like Stephen Leacock's hero today—ready to gallop off in all directions—but with nothing particular in mind. Save your energy for tomorrow, when you have goals more firmly focused.

Friday, August 28 (Moon in Virgo). Fortunate influences show that a change of scene (and people) will brighten your outlook, especially if you can enjoy it in the company of a favorite companion. If you're unattached and marriage-minded, travel to a distant locale can bring an attractive newcomer into your orbit.

Saturday, August 29 (Moon in Virgo to Libra 12:51 P.M.). Whether love flickers or burns bright today may be up to you this morning. If you get busy early on and make a date, it's certainly a step in the right direction to assure a rewarding evening—especially with someone who shares your mental interests.

Sunday, August 30 (Moon in Libra). The best part of the day, especially for community activities (such as your involvement in a fund-raising campaign), will be the late morning—so schedule meetings around that time (perhaps after church) if you can. You won't be anybody's favorite person this afternoon.

Monday, August 31 (Moon in Libra). The weeks ahead will bring many opportunities to wine and dine with the right people, the kind who can ease your way into a better job or position—or perhaps into the executive suite. Today, however, is just a good time to plan strategies and come up with a workable game plan.

September 1992

Tuesday, September 1 (Moon in Scorpio). The month gets off to a bright start; your plans have an excellent chance of being realized enjoyably. And, in case you need a favor from a VIP or seek to promote a special objective, you ought to do very well. In any event, social and family entertainment is fun.

Wednesday, September 2 (Moon in Scorpio to Sagittarius 7:51 P.M.). A new romance prospect could be on today's calendar. Following up on a recent introduction can lead to enjoyable discoveries. But choose well in a social matter, inasmuch as the leisure pleasure of several friends may depend on your selection.

Thursday, September 3 (Moon in Sagittarius). The post-midnight hours seem made for romance. For unattached Capricornians, there could be a flurry of engagements and wedding plans developing from today's trends. Welcome news via a phone call tonight could concern a money matter with long-term implications.

Friday, September 4 (Moon in Sagittarius). Try to avoid arguing about how something should be done at work today, or about a health matter, since accurate facts will not be available—or used, if they are. Emotions could run high, especially in any partnership effort that would include a family member.

Saturday, September 5 (Moon in Sagittarius to Capricorn 5:07 A.M.). The weekend begins on a positive note, as stellar trends converge to surround you with favorable attention, good fortune, and no need to become assertive. You can drift happily through the day, but be ready with an alternative social plan tonight.

Sunday, September 6 (Moon in Capricorn). Even more so than yesterday, this can be your day all the way. You could be very elated by the new direction taken by your personal interests, which points to an exciting breakthrough for one of your long-range plans. Use your imagination to maximize current opportunities.

Monday, September 7 (Moon in Capricorn to Aquarius 5:09 P.M.). Someone else will be right in tune with your long-range perspective and vision concerning business, politics, relationships, and other subjects of mutual interest. A recent surprise twist may have brought this person into the social orbit you travel.

Tuesday, September 8 (Moon in Aquarius). Today's events may give you a chance to improve your knowledge of job matters or the general field of money, credit, and successful business methods. What you'll probably surmise is that there's no substitute for knuckling down and putting in plenty of time and effort.

Wednesday, September 9 (Moon in Aquarius). Social life and friends in general are much more likely to give you trouble today than staying with your regular down-to-earth practical interests. It's not a good day to lend or borrow money or belongings from acquaintances, especially for spurious reasons.

Thursday, September 10 (Moon in Aquarius to Pisces 5:57 A.M.). A strong emphasis on your career aims and a particular job you are doing today should translate into an invitation to hobnob with the upper echelon at work in recognition for your splendid accomplishment. This is a rewarding day in many unexpected ways.

Friday, September 11 (FULL MOON in Pisces). You could reap the ample benefits today of recent endeavors to promote yourself or your capabilities. There should be more than one admirer now only too happy to pass on the good word about you. Heed a strong hunch today about education or a travel matter.

Saturday, September 12 (Moon in Pisces to Aries 6:03 P.M.). Some barriers to your social or group involvements may arise today, such as a short trip you are planning, a community project, or perhaps a new romance that's pushing everything else to the back burner these days (and probably a few nights).

Sunday, September 13 (Moon in Aries). If you are playing a key role in a club or community function today, you will probably relish the feeling of increased status. Also on the schedule may be a meeting of the minds with a new acquaintance, as well as a chance to shop to improve creature comforts.

Monday, September 14 (Moon in Aries). You have the utmost confidence in yourself today, and while friends and influential contacts can be helpful now, you'd really prefer to provide all the assertiveness and get all the credit. In fact, you may be planning a near-future career move that hinges on distant developments.

Tuesday, September 15 (Moon in Aries to Taurus 4:48 A.M.). Increased togetherness with your mate or favorite companion may be the best part of a somewhat ho-hum day. For the rest of it, stay with original dating or social plans and don't allow a surprise message to divert you from recreational pleasures.

Wednesday, September 16 (Moon in Taurus). An extra rush of activity at work or a chance to follow up on a desired academic or travel opportunity makes today a winner. Even though you and a neighbor or relative disagree on a certain matter (probably money), there's a way for you to resolve it tonight.

Thursday, September 17 (Moon in Taurus to Gemini 1:41 P.M.). Sometimes you may feel as though you are on a merry-go-round, insofar as your social and group connections and romance are concerned, and this could be one of those days. Happily, you won't mind a bit, as this busy day gives your spirits a lift.

Friday, September 18 (Moon in Gemini). Today could be quite a change from yesterday, as now you seem to be all work and no play, which is actually more typical of you than the other way 'round. In any case, you rarely work without a goal in mind, and today you'll be focused on increasing your earnings.

Saturday, September 19 (Moon in Gemini to Cancer 8:00 P.M.). Carefully assess any news or rumors you hear today. Gross exaggeration is in the works, so be sure to check out all claims made, particularly the boastful or rosy ones. You can be sure that there is a lot less than meets the ear or eye today.

Sunday, September 20 (Moon in Cancer). There may be a basic flaw in your strategy concerning a legal, family, or domestic objective, which could lead to an argument with someone close to you, robbing you both of sleep. A quiet confab with someone who is an expert on this particular subject will be helpful.

Monday, September 21 (Moon in Cancer to Leo 11:20 P.M.). Romantic or marital sensitivities may be under fire today, beginning with postmidnight stress. Try to get an adequate diet, enough rest, and some exercise, despite a squeeze on your time. Don't thoughtlessly do anything to ruffle feathers at work.

Tuesday, September 22 (Moon in Leo). This is a day ringed with dollar signs, but after a profitable start to the morning, they may be pointing away from you by the end of the workday or tonight. If you're in the mood to spend, someone with the power of the purse may put a depressing damper on your proclivities.

Wednesday, September 23 (Moon in Leo). Today's agenda is the reverse of yesterday's, particularly in reference to the money theme and your involvement with (or dependence on) others for smooth-flowing activities. You're likely to run into trouble this morning, but as the day goes along, happily see it fade away.

Thursday, September 24 (Moon in Leo to Virgo 12:09 A.M.). Your self-assurance, dynamism, and abilities may make a great impression on someone who is in a position to help your future plans to come true. If this includes marriage, you're due for a happy surprise today—and might soon be setting the wedding date.

Friday, September 25 (Moon in Virgo to Libra 11:56 P.M.). Your charisma soars today, and you can attract favorable social, business, and romantic attention. Your reaction to being very much in demand everywhere you go is to prefer to be secretly in demand by that one special person, but the group scene takes priority.

Saturday, September 26 (NEW MOON in Libra). The New Moon is a mixed blessing. You could land a great new position if you've been job-hunting, and your earnings potential is substantially increased today, but there's also a chance that you'll lock horns with someone whom you can ill afford to have as an enemy.

Sunday, September 27 (Moon in Libra). This could turn out to be another unsettling day. Again, you should make every effort to avoid challenging an authority figure (even though you may be right, this could be a decidedly undiplomatic move). If the day seems to drift into a nonevent, don't fight it.

Monday, September 28 (Moon in Libra to Scorpio 12:45 A.M.). Use your imagination and wit to facilitate your successful handling of a touchy situation with a friend today. You may seem brusque to the supersensitive people around you now, so be prepared to soothe them without committing yourself financially.

Tuesday, September 29 (Moon in Scorpio). Yesterday's social theme continues, but with the decided advantage of fewer hazards and many more benefits. In fact, you can pretty much write your own scenario as far as friends and social activities are concerned. If the momentum dwindles this afternoon, just relax tonight.

Wednesday, September 30 (Moon in Scorpio to Sagittarius 4:34 A.M.). Privileged information you receive today could be the catalyst that starts you off in a new and most promising career or business direction. However, it may be to your advantage to keep contact with a VIP under your hat for now.

October 1992

Thursday, October 1 (Moon in Sagittarius). You know how to be adroit and low key in everything you do today; you will probably arrange an off-the-record meeting tonight with someone who can help you to achieve a job, career, or business goal. You might also be giving a lot of thought now to physical fitness.

Friday, October 2 (Moon in Sagittarius to Capricorn 12:30 P.M.). Try to complete unfinished odds and ends of work prior to the noon whistle, after which more personal interests take over. A social or organization function tonight may include an extra expense; a group fee may not be such a big bargain.

Saturday, October 3 (Moon in Capricorn). The morning starts off on a deceptively cheery note, and from then on, it's downhill all the way. Nobody seems to be in a cooperative mood, so no matter what diplomatic tactics you use, you're going to stir up animosity whether or not you're wrong or right.

Sunday, October 4 (Moon in Capricorn to Aquarius 11:54 P.M.). Mixed trends bring substantial good fortune in your career strivings and financial potential and rewarding developments in personal relationships, but lots of friction with people in the business or professional milieu, especially higher-ups.

Monday, October 5 (Moon in Aquarius). Your personal financial picture develops a healthy glow today, perhaps due to a bold, no-nonsense step you take that assures long-range benefits. Your activities not only enhance your income potential, they also deploy your surplus funds in more lucrative ways.

Tuesday, October 6 (Moon in Aquarius). This is another day when your personal affairs prosper, but your career or other outside interests run into obstacles, probably in a way that will take you completely by surprise. Handle authority figures with kid gloves; it's no time for independent posturing.

Wednesday, October 7 (Moon in Aquarius to Pisces 12:39 P.M.). Slowly the tide turns, and today you should notice a much more harmonious environment and many more receptive ears to listen to your ideas. For some, a previously stymied romance is also due to blossom nicely, along with social life in general.

Thursday, October 8 (Moon in Pisces). Your creativity is strong today, whether in a solo enterprise or a group project. Romance, too, may put stars in your eyes as you and a loved one see heart to heart on an important decision. For some, a platonic relationship may show signs of going in a more beguiling direction.

Friday, October 9 (Moon in Pisces). Strange dark clouds continue to hover over your career or business interests, but, after today, they should clear up for many months to come. That said, it's a good idea today not to make any important job or vocational decisions until conditions are more favorable.

Saturday, October 10 (Moon in Pisces to Aries 12:37 A.M.). Today you enter a fresh cycle of luck in your career aspirations; think back twelve years and you will have a good clue as to what to expect. Whether or not it comes your way on a silver tray, however, you'll have to do your part to derive maximum benefits.

Sunday, October 11 (FULL MOON in Aries). Don't look for peace and quiet around the home front. Quite the reverse, in fact, is likely to dominate the day—especially regarding property interests and family relationships, which are apt to be choppy at best. Realize that you and others are probably overreacting.

Monday, October 12 (Moon in Aries to Taurus 10:49 A.M.). Today will probably add up to a nonevent, which you most likely won't mind in view of yesterday's unsettling developments. A former friend might reenter your life under some provocative circumstances that remind you of the reason you dropped him or her.

Tuesday, October 13 (Moon in Taurus). Getting into an upward swing today may include selling some of your financial ideas, which may be a bit too conservative for some tastes. Though you possibly meet with questions or resistance, you will be able to turn around others' thinking to your own advantage.

Wednesday, October 14 (Moon in Taurus to Gemini 7:09 P.M.). The financial theme continues in ways that will make today seem almost like a replay of yesterday. The timetable is practically the same; the day starts with disagreements, and then after some perambulations, others wind up agreeing with you.

Thursday, October 15 (Moon in Gemini). You are a convincing force today, and can be well on your way toward attaining a special goal; but probably not without some skepticism or opposition here and there. A new money-making venture may have to be put on temporary hold because of a job or health problem.

Friday, October 16 (Moon in Gemini). A new vocational project (perhaps a better paying assignment) appears to have excellent potential and you can gain from the advice of an expert as well. Your efforts in other directions, however, may not add up to much—because either you or others can't focus on essentials.

Saturday, October 17 (Moon in Gemini to Cancer 1:37 A.M.). The day begins on a contentious note and—probably an anxious spillover from recent disputes—you may also reject news or advice you receive concerning an important new venture or decision. If the evening tends to just drift along, flow with it.

Sunday, October 18 (Moon in Cancer). This long and busy day begins with trouble and ends with same, but there is a respite here and there in the middle that will make some sense to your practical nature. This will probably be in the form of news or advice that you've been waiting to hear about a social plan.

Monday, October 19 (Moon in Cancer to Leo 6:02 A.M.). Put your heart in your work today and take pride in the results of your labors. The rewards of this well-invested workday could be generous. It could be particularly fruitful if you seek backing for a business venture or other important career activity.

Tuesday, October 20 (Moon in Leo). In your own mind, you may be revising your views on a couple of major matters but are not quite ready to disclose your new incentives. You will probably first need to iron out a few financial obstacles blocking the path to relationship harmony, but "persevere" is your middle name.

Wednesday, October 21 (Moon in Leo to Virgo 8:28 A.M.). Concentrate on doing your best in a business transaction today rather than worrying over romantic uncertainties. In fact, bypass uncertainties of all kinds, particularly a decision that can affect the future of a relationship currently under wraps.

Thursday, October 22 (Moon in Virgo). Today you could feel larger than life and ready and able to win any and all contests. Or you may wish to work on a personal goal or reassemble next week's scenario with an emphasis on bringing the future in a little ahead of schedule. Friends and close allies are very supportive.

Friday, October 23 (Moon in Virgo to Libra 9:40 A.M.). A lucky opportunity, perhaps privately social in nature, enables you to climb up a few more rungs on the ladder of success. For some, a behind-the-scenes romance may be blossoming in the business or professional milieu. Your lucky period is gaining momentum.

Saturday, October 24 (Moon in Libra). Although you start the day with good intentions, the stellar patterns do not favor putting in any weekend overtime on the job. All you're apt to encounter is trouble if you persist. If any authority figure appears to be in a hostile mood, give that person a wide berth.

Sunday, October 25 (Moon in Libra to Scorpio 11:05 A.M.—NEW MOON in Scorpio). The New Moon may make you feel as though there's a new chapter in your social life waiting to begin—but that's the key word, "waiting." Although there may be some developments today, nothing concrete is likely to occur.

Monday, October 26 (Moon in Scorpio). The early morning bleak outlook (stemming from a financial concern) fades soon enough into the bright promise of an exciting day for your social life and personal affairs in general. Thanks to unexpected meetings or encounters, the odds are now in your favor in the marital sweepstakes.

Tuesday, October 27 (Moon in Scorpio to Sagittarius 2:30 P.M.). Your best work will be done in solitude today, away from distractions, complaints, and dissent. (You need periods of seclusion, anyway, in order to give your nerves and ambitious nature a rest.) Keep your ear to the ground for insider information.

Wednesday, October 28 (Moon in Sagittarius). For whatever motive, this is an ideal day for a secret rendezvous. If romance is the lure, a quiet walk with a loved one brings new depths of meaning to the relationship, made more piquant by the need for secrecy. It's also a good day for insider financial information.

Thursday, October 29 (Moon in Sagittarius to Capricorn 9:19 P.M.). You're able to capitalize on yesterday's good fortune by following through on auspicious relationship developments or some privileged information about a profitable financial opportunity. A blossoming duo may now reach the commitment stage.

Friday, October 30 (Moon in Capricorn). While subsequent developments today may take some of the wind out of your sails regarding the inflated optimism with which you bounce into the day this morning, you know how to trim your expectations to practical guidelines, especially when dealing with a VIP.

Saturday, October 31 (Moon in Capricorn). You could be pretty jittery about a personal matter when the day begins, and although you're able to rationalize the situation (perhaps through the help of an understanding friend) as the day rolls along, you'll probably let off a lot of steam when the workday ends.

November 1992

Sunday, November 1 (Moon in Capricorn to Aquarius 7:44 A.M.). Confidential news you hear this afternoon is almost sure to include welcome financial information. Then, shortly thereafter, more glad tidings come your way that enable you to effortlessly ascend a few more rungs up the ladder of success.

Monday, November 2 (Moon in Aquarius). You're all business this morning when it comes to personal financial matters, but then you may have little choice if you're being pressured for a payment or an accounting. After a day with your shoulder to the wheel, you'll be ready for some pleasant socializing tonight.

Tuesday, November 3 (Moon in Aquarius to Pisces 8:14 P.M.). News you heard from a confidant a few days ago can be put to even better (and more profitable) use than you anticipated—thanks to today's follow-up developments. The matter is still hush-hush, however, so that you have first crack at the benefits.

Wednesday, November 4 (Moon in Pisces). Due to a big headache (financial) or other anxiety during the postmidnight hours, you'll probably start the day not feeling so chipper nor in the best of moods. You might still be in the grips of a fatigue hangover much of the day, but at least the P.M. shapes up better.

Thursday, November 5 (Moon in Pisces). The things that go well today go very well indeed, and whatever doesn't will be due more to sins of omission—such as thoughtlessness about a sensitive confidential matter. On the bright side are sudden good news, favorable publicity, and/or an enjoyable short trip.

Friday, November 6 (Moon in Pisces to Aries 8:20 A.M.). Your confidence and personal magnetism are high today, and you are definitely in the mood to give a solo performance. The innovative and/or individualistic way you now promote a personal goal via social networking prompts an exciting breakthrough.

Saturday, November 7 (Moon in Aries). The morning starts out well enough, but you'll not only be wasting your time if you try to get any more mileage out of yesterday's fortuitous developments, you could also alienate an important career or business associate. It's time to stop a bit while you're ahead.

Sunday, November 8 (Moon in Aries to Taurus 6:20 P.M.). Although you may have planned a day of rest and relaxation to ring down the curtain on the weekend, be prepared for a flare up with your mate or steady date if you bring up a touchy topic (innocently or on purpose). However, "alls well that ends well tonight."

Monday, November 9 (Moon in Taurus). The day seems to add up to a succession of minor aggravations, with one in particular about money that will probably be more pronounced at the end of the workday. Once past that hurdle, however, the evening may be a lot more enjoyable in a way that you will least expect.

Tuesday, November 10 (FULL MOON in Taurus). The Full Moon points to a few leftovers in terms of yesterday's aggravations and the money theme—a situation that may strain an affectional tie or an important friendship. The evening brings a welcome change of pace, however, thanks to a companion's initiatives.

Wednesday, November 11 (Moon in Taurus to Gemini 1:50 A.M.). Just when you're getting plenty of good ideas about job opportunities, methods, or efficiency, you could find it difficult to put them into effect. Nevertheless, there's a chance to make some worthwhile progress with your most cherished career aims.

Thursday, November 12 (Moon in Gemini). Today finds you in the mood to work along steadily, even though there are numerous petty distractions to divert you from your goal. You've no doubt learned by now to take each day as it comes, and this will probably turn out to be one in which progress is slow but sure.

Friday, November 13 (Moon in Gemini to Cancer 7:20 A.M.). It's that day again, and while you're probably too practical to be superstitious, it nevertheless may not be wise to tempt fate and walk under any ladders, or go skydiving. You're a bit careless today, but it's more apt to be in the area of relationships.

Saturday, November 14 (Moon in Cancer). Whether a friend, mate, live-in companion, or a group tie, relationships are the top priority theme today. As the day gets under way, people are provocative and not easy to fathom or deal with. By tonight, however, you'll get a fix on whatever is intriguing you.

Sunday, November 15 (Moon in Cancer to Leo 11:24 A.M.). Something could get your dander up early this morning, but whatever it is that makes you mad is also likely to get you motivated. One thing that you could go to work on is a career- or business-related financial deal that you're keeping under wraps.

Monday, November 16 (Moon in Leo). You and your mate (or perhaps your business partner) start the day one hundred and eighty degrees apart about a financial matter that no doubt concerns partnership or other joint funds. In any case, you're probably insisting on a conservative posture that's going over like a lead balloon.

Tuesday, November 17 (Moon in Leo to Virgo 2:29 P.M.). It may seem that whatever you say or do today will antagonize someone, somewhere! Initially, discord may be linked to money differences, perhaps with a friend. Later, a secret revealed could be the root of trouble. However, the P.M. ends on a happy note.

Wednesday, November 18 (Moon in Virgo). If the day just wends its way languidly through the morning and midday period, it will begin to show exciting signs of life that may put you at center stage by late afternoon. By tonight, social life and togetherness with a favorite person make the evening a winner.

Thursday, November 19 (Moon in Virgo to Libra 5:04 P.M.). This should be a pleasant day that finds you in great shape, physically and mentally (emotionally, too, inasmuch as romance is nicely bolstered). Whether you are entertaining on the run, such as lunch, or out in the social whirl, encounters are delightful.

Friday, November 20 (Moon in Libra). Some of that career or business luck that is around you now and for many months ahead could come your way today. Whether it's a power breakfast or a noontime business lunch, you should be able to close a successful negotiation. Tonight, however, be ready for an upset.

Saturday, November 21 (Moon in Libra to Scorpio 7:53 P.M.). Excellent ideas abound today; the only problem is finding a suitable outlet for them. Meanwhile, you may not appreciate it when your mate, favorite companion, or business partner meddles in a career matter that you think is none of their business.

Sunday, November 22 (Moon in Scorpio). As a pleasantly sociable day winds up the weekend, try to avoid an argument with a friend, especially on the subject of money, expenses, who pays for what, etc. Such a dispute could cast a damper on an otherwise upbeat day. For some, a love-at-first-sight encounter is possible.

Monday, November 23 (Moon in Scorpio). Today brings a dynamic upsurge in social activities and involvements with friends—especially one (or more) who shares your interests and is particularly compatible. If you're still unattached and looking, you're very likely to be the target of one of Cupid's darts.

Tuesday, November 24 (Moon in Scorpio to Sagittarius 12:02 A.M.—NEW MOON in Sagittarius). The New Moon coincides with various vexations that intensify your preference for privacy now and for a few days ahead. Confidential projects and strategies seem to be bogged down but they could be more fruitful tomorrow.

Wednesday, November 25 (Moon in Sagittarius). As noted yesterday, you could hatch a profitable business deal behind closed doors today, or otherwise strike it lucky where your worldly ambitions and other outside activities are concerned. You can't just go on automatic pilot, but things do come your way.

Thursday, November 26 (Moon in Sagittarius to Capricorn 6:29 A.M.). Along with the deserved recognition that brightens your day, there may be more job or career opportunities in store, but don't make the mistake of overestimating the results you can expect from them. Lower your sights; it's not like you to be unrealistic.

Friday, November 27 (Moon in Capricorn). People may not know how to take you today; you might seem to be coming from another planet. It will be hard to pin you down to what you want—not because you don't know, but because you may have trouble putting it into words. However, you're secretly following a personal dream.

Saturday, November 28 (Moon in Capricorn to Aquarius 4:20 P.M.). It's full speed ahead for your personal desires and social aspirations as the weekend gets under way. A coveted invitation may center around people whose upscale lifestyle you'd like to emulate. However, you and your mate might differ on this.

Sunday, November 29 (Moon in Aquarius). There are excellent prospects for a rewarding financial day. Everything you touch seems to turn to gold; you have the Midas touch. Pay particular attention to a VIP who may be the bearer of highly profitable insider information, helpful to both your career and finances.

Monday, November 30 (Moon in Aquarius). The flack you get from a friend today may be tinged with (or motivated by) jealousy for your apparently superior financial status (or recent luck, perhaps due to a more prestigious new job). Well, that's his or her problem as you go about enjoying your success.

December 1992

Tuesday, December 1 (Moon in Aquarius to Pisces 4:24 A.M.). The month gets off to a flying start with a particularly fortunate job, career, or business opportunity, possibly coming about through a VIP who prefers to remain in the background for now. Your good humor and sociability will be contagious tonight.

Wednesday, December 2 (Moon in Pisces). This is a good day to sound off about your intentions, particularly if you're pursuing an important personal goal these days. For many of you, it should be noted, a big change in lifestyle is in the works or has already occurred. People are singing your praises now.

Thursday, December 3 (Moon in Pisces to Aries 4:50 P.M.). Today is an even better day than yesterday for promoting yourself and/or spreading the good word about your current projects. On a more mundane level, you could also be busy running a variety of errands in connection with the upcoming holidays.

Friday, December 4 (Moon in Aries). Somewhat akin to yesterday, today can find you busy around the home front getting ready for the upcoming surge of seasonal entertaining, welcoming holiday visitors from both near and afar, and so on. There may be a family powwow about decorations, readying the guest room.

Saturday, December 5 (Moon in Aries). It might be best to remain discreetly in the background, or spend time with friends, rather than try to get any of your domestic projects accomplished. For one reason or another, there's liable to be a lot of friction around home base, so there's no use fighting the odds.

Sunday, December 6 (Moon in Aries to Taurus 3:17 A.M.). Today is a lot less active than yesterday, but the friction persists. Try as you might, you can't seem to do anything right as far as your mate or live-in companion is concerned (or it may be vice versa). In any case, lie low; tomorrow is a better day.

Monday, December 7 (Moon in Taurus). The morning can bring an exhilarating breakthrough where your quest for personal recognition is concerned. You may be unexpectedly invited to appear somewhere on the strength of your accomplishments. If some friends aren't enthused, there's a bit of envy lurking somewhere.

Tuesday, December 8 (Moon in Taurus to Gemini 10:38 A.M.). A stimulating morning incident marks the beginning of today's fortunate trends that bring romantic aspirations, personal aims, and social activities to a peak—affording you, if still unattached, an opportunity to meet a dazzling new attraction.

Wednesday, December 9 (FULL MOON in Gemini). The Full Moon shows that a marvelous new assignment or a big improvement in your physical fitness will have you floating on air today. Lines of communication are wide open and very productive between you and your closest associates, including work colleagues.

Thursday, December 10 (Moon in Gemini to Cancer 3:06 P.M.). Although certainly not as intense, that's about the only way that today isn't as satisfactory as yesterday, especially where your ties of affection are concerned. If you're creative, that realm could provide a setback. Don't clutch at straws now.

Friday, December 11 (Moon in Cancer). The important relationships in your life are touch and go, partly because of your own doubts and frustrations, and partly because others seem to be painting too rosy a picture—which appear to you to be far wide of the mark of the gut realities of a relationship.

Saturday, December 12 (Moon in Cancer to Leo 5:48 P.M.). You'll be keeping a lot of your thoughts to yourself in the weeks ahead, possibly as one refuge from the stepped-up hustle and bustle of the coming seasonal festivities. Meanwhile, those of you in love may be finalizing plans for a holiday wedding.

Sunday, December 13 (Moon in Leo). The weekend windup may be as good a time as any to get in some of your seasonal shopping—although it may already be too late to escape the thundering herd. Be that as it may, either you're too picky and choosy, or the prices are too high, or the colors and sizes you want are unavailable.

Monday, December 14 (Moon in Leo to Virgo 7:57 P.M.). Expect a vexing day in the job or financial realm; your activities will be blocked at every turn, and nothing will seem to proceed as scheduled. Shopping opportunities are nil, and you could be your own worst enemy when dealing with a friend who wants to argue about money.

Tuesday, December 15 (Moon in Virgo). News from a distance might pertain to holiday travel or visiting plans, which may be canceled or changed. The rest of the day finds you dealing with a variety of minor aggravations that keep you from attending to more important things. Tomorrow is a lot more productive.

Wednesday, December 16 (Moon in Virgo). As noted yesterday, the way is cleared for you to get a lot accomplished, particularly pertaining to a winter vacation or other holiday travel, arrangements with in-laws, or deciding on next term's academic curriculum. Very little interferes with your progress now.

Thursday, December 17 (Moon in Virgo to Libra 10:34 A.M.). The accent is on the job and business realm, which today might be the stimulus for the seasonal office party or other business- or career-related gathering. In any case, a good time will be had by all, along with some luck re your worldly ambitions.

Friday, December 18 (Moon in Libra). Today isn't all smooth sailing like yesterday. You won't get to first base if you try to put over a new idea (probably too far ahead of its time) to your boss or other upper echelon type. Try not to end the workday with an argument. Anyway, the evening is pleasant.

Saturday, December 19 (Moon in Libra to Scorpio 2:21 A.M.). Aside from some postmidnight merriment, weekend social plans get off to a flying stop. Plans for holiday gatherings are likely to fizzle. At least, however, this will give you some extra time to catch up with seasonal chores that slipped by the wayside.

Sunday, December 20 (Moon in Scorpio). After a bumpy start, today shapes up as a lot more fun for the holiday social merry-go-round—which now seems to be going full speed ahead. You might have to step lively to touch all the bases, but as the momentum increases, you'll find it exhilarating to keep up with it.

Monday, December 21 (Moon in Scorpio to Sagittarius 7:43 A.M.). Today's trends show that the recent stepped-up activities might be catching up with your energy and vitality reserves, putting you in the mood to distance yourself for now from the holiday whirl. Someone may have a sad story and request money.

Tuesday, December 22 (Moon in Sagittarius). As you come down to the wire, you might decide this is a good day for a shopping trek with a companion, one who knows those out-of-the-way places for bargains or finding those last-minute items. To top it off, you can enjoy a delightful lunch in some secluded spot.

Wednesday, December 23 (Moon in Sagittarius to Capricorn 3:05 P.M.—NEW MOON in Capricorn). This is definitely your day, although it might not be as full of events as you would prefer. Nevertheless, you can move forward with important personal projects, secure in the knowledge that you're making the right impression.

Thursday, December 24 (Moon in Capricorn). You're so delighted to be in the driver's seat that you might not be too careful about how you are managing things—especially when other people's happiness depends on you. A surprise late tonight might be the kind that you could just as happily live without.

Friday, December 25 (Moon in Capricorn). As the big day dawns, it will repay you to be as traditional and practical as possible with loved ones and friends. Don't follow all your inspirations, especially if they're a bit far-out. It's no time to tease anyone, who may be in a more sensitive mood than you realize.

Saturday, December 26 (Moon in Capricorn to Aquarius 12:44 A.M.). Today could be a letdown after all the recent heightened activity and excitement. However, take advantage of a respite in the seasonal festivities to catch your breath and relax a bit. There are still some active days ahead that will keep you busy.

Sunday, December 27 (Moon in Aquarius). This is probably as good a day as any to head for the stores or boutiques to exchange gifts that aren't right, or to obtain a credit or a refund. Perhaps you'll be lucky and find the very item you're looking for, and might indulge yourself with an extra purchase.

Monday, December 28 (Moon in Aquarius to Pisces 12:29 P.M.). Whether or not it's back to the real world of work, business deals, or daily routine, you won't be much in the mood for it. Either you can't get up any steam in the boiler, or there's a lack of opportunities to manage even a modest accomplishment or two.

Tuesday, December 29 (Moon in Pisces). The day gets off to a lively start, and if you can maintain the brisk momentum, you'll get a lot more done than was possible yesterday. For one thing, you could sell ice to an Eskimo now, so if you have a project to put over, you'll be able to go to town with it.

Wednesday, December 30 (Moon in Pisces). This is another favorable day, only it offers a lot more opportunity, and will be more active and productive than yesterday. Socially it will be delightful, and whether you're spending time with relatives, friends, or neighbors—the hours are going to pass by like minutes.

Thursday, December 31 (Moon in Pisces to Aries 1:08 A.M.). This doesn't seem to be the year for one of those big New Year's Eve extravaganzas. You're likely to have more fun if you bring in 1993 quietly, with a small but select group of your closest friends. If you make big plans, they will probably just fizzle.

WIN A FREE PERSONALIZED STAR CHART FROM DELL

Congratulations! You are a reader of one or more titles featured in Dell's 1992 Day By Day Horoscopes Promotion. Our goal is to provide you with quality reading and entertainment, so we are pleased to extend to you a one-time only, limited sweepstakes offer to receive a personalized STAR CHART — developed just for you. Ten winners will be drawn on or about February 1, 1992. Please read the official rules for details.

Official Star Chart Sweepstakes Rules

1. **No purchase necessary.** Enter by completing the coupon below and returning it to the address provided. No facsimiles or copies of the coupons allowed. To obtain a free entry coupon, write to Dell Star Chart Sweepstakes, Dept. BP, 666 Fifth Avenue, New York, NY 10103. One entry per person.

2. All entries must be postmarked before January 24, 1992 and received before January 31, 1992 to be eligible. Dell is not responsible for late, lost or misdirected entries, and all entries become the property of Dell and will not be returned. Incomplete or illegible entries will not be accepted. Winners will be chosen in a random drawing on or about February 1, 1992 from among all completed entries received. Odds of winning depend upon the number of entries received.

3. Prizes: Ten winners will be awarded a personalized star chart prepared by the editors of *Dell Horoscope* magazines. Winners will be notified by mail and may be asked to provide within 30 days of notification additional personal information to complete the star chart.

4. This sweepstakes is open to the residents of the U.S. and Canada, excluding the Province of Quebec, who are 18 years of age or older at the time of entry. Employees and their immediate family members of Dell Publishing, Bantam Doubleday Dell Publishing Group, Inc. and their subsidiaries and affiliates are not eligible. The winner, if Canadian, will be required to answer correctly a time-limited arithmetical skill-testing question in order to be awarded the prize. All federal, state and local rules apply. Entering the sweepstakes constitutes permission for the use of the winner's name, likeness and biographical data for advertising and promotional purposes with no additional compensation.

5. For a list of winners, send a self-addressed envelope, entirely separate from your entry, to: Dell Personalized Star Chart Sweepstakes Winner, Dell Publishing, 666 Fifth Avenue, New York, NY 10103.

Please print all the information below and mail to:

Dell Star Chart Sweepstakes • Dept. BP
Dell Publishing • 666 Fifth Avenue • New York, NY 10103

Name _____

Address _____

City _____ Phone: ( ) _____

State _____ Zip _____

Books Purchased at (if applicable) _____

_____

I was born on _____ , 19 _____ in _____ ,
           (month, day)   (year)   (city)

_____ , _____ at _____ : _____ a.m./p.m.
(state)   (country)   (hour) (minute) (circle one)

Entries must be received before January 31, 1992.